Valentine's Manual of
Old New York

MUSEUM OF THE CITY OF NEW YORK, FOUNDED 1923.
GRACIE MANSION, IN CARL SCHURZ PARK, FOOT OF EIGHTY-EIGHTH STREET.

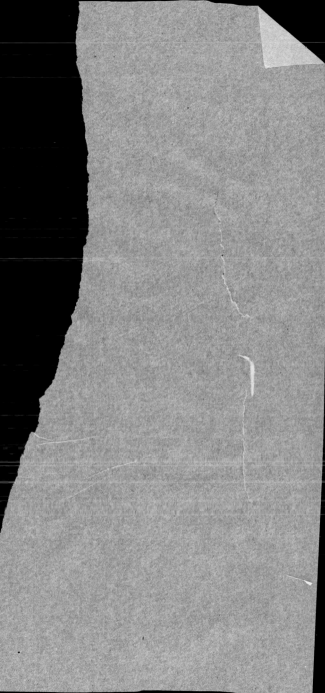

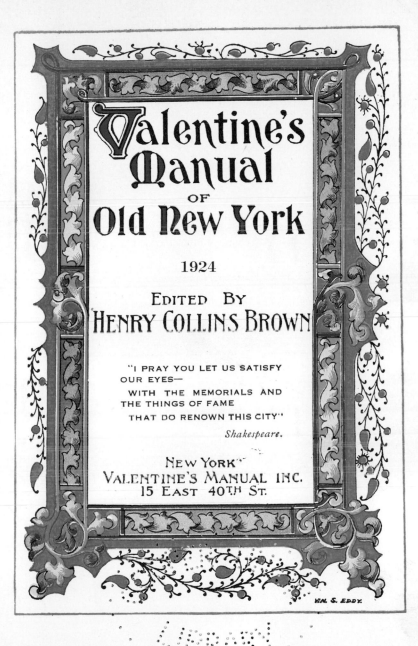

Valentine's Manual of Old New York

1924

EDITED BY
HENRY COLLINS BROWN

"I PRAY YOU LET US SATISFY OUR EYES—

WITH THE MEMORIALS AND THE THINGS OF FAME

THAT DO RENOWN THIS CITY"

Shakespeare.

NEW YORK
VALENTINE'S MANUAL INC.
15 EAST 40TH ST.

WM. S. EDDY.

Press of
The Chauncey Holt Co.
New York City

To the Museum of the City of New York

with best wishes

this volume is cordially dedicated.

New York, 1923.

TABLE OF CONTENTS

[XI]

LIST OF ILLUSTRATIONS

[XIV]

[xv]

[XIX]

(Original owned by the Long Island Historical Society.)

Old No. 1 Engine, Volunteer Fire Department, Borough of Brooklyn, New York City.

NEW YORK OF YESTERDAY

By Henry Collins Brown

The City of New York as I knew it when a boy was a vastly different place from what it is today. When we kids took an Eighth Avenue car, going north of Fifty-ninth Street, the conductor always said: "Keep your nickel, Johnny, it's so good to have a little company up here, it's worth the money." And no wonder! All around us was a wilderness of crags and boulders. Little wooden shanties peeked out here and there from behind occasional level spaces among the rocks. A long step-ladder was needed to reach some of these eerie dwellings.

[1]

Pigs and children abounded, but the chief inhabitants seemed to be goats. They were everywhere and appeared to thrive on a diet of tin cans and waste paper. This was "Shantytown" and its inhabitants were known as "Squatters."

This strange region is now covered by the Grand Central, The Biltmore, Park Avenue and both sides of Central Park. To a very great extent these people were Irish emigrants, with no idea of property rights. It was a picturesque feature of Old New York life, and no city ever showed such a contrast as now exists in the row of splendid mansions facing the east side of Central Park, where were formerly the little shacks of "Shantytown."

In all the world there was no Telephone, no Subway, no Skyscraper, no Electric Light. The Broadway Stages and the Harlem Boats on the East River—the "Sylvan Stream," "Sylvan Glen," etc., were the Rapid Transit of the day. When there was fog on the river half the business population was late. It became a by-word to say to anyone dilatory in reaching the office: "Fog on the river this morning?"

When the Elevated first began to run we carried Time Tables, the same as you do today for the Pennsylvania or the New York Central. All the engines had names and the conductor collected your fare after you were seated in the train. The well-to-do patrons of the Third Avenue horse-cars rode in a "Drawing Room" car, for which they paid ten cents extra. Most of the surface lines had "hill horses" every few blocks. That was a third horse, to help the other two up the steep places that existed all the way to Harlem.

Some of the street cars on Sixth Avenue bore the sign: "For Colored Persons Only." None of them had heat.

"Checkers Up At the Farm."

One of the famous Rogers Group of Statuettes, which stood in the "best room" of every house in the Seventies.

A Harlem "Flyer"—the *Sylvan Dell*.

The floors were covered with straw, which was supposed to provide a certain degree of warmth. On rainy days it certainly supplied a lot of mud, which the feet of incoming passengers sprinkled liberally over those already seated. Many of the cars had no conductor, the driver doing duty for both. He jangled a bell in the fare box whenever he thought it necessary, and usually some passenger would thus be induced to part reluctantly with a belated nickel, to the huge delight of his fellow travelers.

The drivers on the Broadway stages always stopped for boys, who climbed up the front wheel to a seat on the box with him. Incidentally, the driver always got the dime that otherwise would have gone in the box. These old conveyances made a picturesque sight tacking up and down Broadway like a fleet of mackerel boats. Some very pretty landscapes were painted on the panels of

[4]

A contemporary sketch by E. L. Viel.

On the way to the Gracie Mansion, 1860. How Second Avenue looked north from Forty-second Street before it was leveled. It was on these hills that "hill horses" were used a few years later to pull up the street cars.

THE NEW YORK

ELEVATED

Railroad.

TIME TABLE.

Change of Time.

OCTOBER 16TH 1872.

Between Battery and 29th St.

these buses by well-known artists too. The disappear-ance of these old vehicles produced a sudden quietness in old Broadway, much to the consternation of the inhabit-ants who dearly love the boiler-factory-like atmosphere of the main street in our village.

Along with the stages went the awnings. Almost every store clear up to Grace Church sported an awning of some kind. They were of all colors and stripes. Their iron and wooden supports lined the edges of the side-walks, with numerous breaks, caused by trees and front stoops. The awnings have long ago disappeared, the trees have perished, and the front stoops have been shaved off.

"These old stages made a picturesque sight. . . . Almost every store on Broadway clear up to Grace Church sported an awning of some kind."

Everywhere in New York transportation was by horse-drawn vehicles. In the early 70's a mysterious disease suddenly attacked our quadruped friends, and for a few weeks business was practically at a standstill. There was absolutely no transportation for either man or merchandise. Street cars ceased to run. Wheelbarrows and man-drawn carts took the place of trucks and express wagons. Had the epidemic been of a fatal nature, there is no telling what would have been the result. Fortunately, most of the animals were up and about again in about a month, but the situation while it lasted caused tremendous inconvenience and no little excitement. The disease was known as the Epizoötic.

1871				TIME TABLE				1871
Third Ave. R. R. Drawing Room Car.								
DOWN.				STREETS.	UP.			
A.M.	A.M.	P.M.	P.M.	HARLEM BRIDGE.	A.M.	P.M.	P.M.	P.M.
7.30	10.30	1.30	4.30	Leave..130th..Arrive.	10.15	1.15	4.15	7.15
7.52	10.52	1.52	4.52	"......86th..Leave.	9.55	12.55	3.55	6.55
8.02	11.02	2.02	5.02	"......65th......"	9.45	12.45	3.45	6.45
8.13	11.13	2.13	5.13	"......42d......"	9.34	12.34	3.34	6.34
8.17	11.17	2.17	5.17	"......34th......"	9.30	12.30	3.30	6.30
8.23	11.23	2.23	5.23	"......23d......"	9.25	12.25	3.25	6.25
8.27	11.27	2.27	5.27	"......14th......"	9.20	12.20	3.20	6.20
8.32	11.32	2.32	5.32	"......5th......"	9.15	12.15	3.15	6.15
8.37	11.37	2.37	5.37	"......Grand ...."	9.08	12.08	3.08	6.08
8.52	11.52	2.52	5.52	Arr..City Hall..Leave.	9.55	11.55	2.55	5.55

THIS CAR WILL NOT RUN ON SUNDAYS.

This Car is run only for such Passengers as Voluntarily pay the Conductor 10 CENTS for their seat in addition to the fare.

"Style" on the old Third Avenue horse cars—the "Drawing Room."

It was still the days of the Clipper and the California Packet, though the square rigged beauties were falling fast before the advancing power of steam. All along South Street were the spice laden airs of the Orient, the sweet smelling pine shavings and the pungent odor of turpentine and tar. The bowsprits of these fine old ships stretched clear across the street, sometimes poking into the windows of the counting rooms opposite. All these ships carried on the foresail the distinguishing mark of the house flag—a huge round ball painted black for the Black Ball Line; a red Greek cross for the Red Cross Line; etc., etc. The various shipping firms distributed gaudily printed cards in all the colors of the rainbow, announcing that the "RED JACKET" "FLYING CLOUD" or "DREADNOUGHT" was now loading for San Francisco and would leave in about three weeks, etc. Thus

The Ships in South Street, 1875.

was founded the popularity of "Chromo Cards" which raged with unabated fury in the eighties.

The fine old deep sea Yankee Captains of a still earlier day scorned the assistance of tugs to reach their piers, and a more fascinating sight can hardly be imagined than to see Captain Charles Low of Brooklyn bring his ship into the swiftly flowing tide of the East River, and slowly but surely bring her to a full stop within a few feet of the bulkhead. A moment later, studding sails, flying jibs, fore and main sails would be clewed and made fast. It was a marvelous performance. The huge vessel would be under considerable headway and a crash seemed inevitable. In some marvelous manner Captain Low would turn a trick and the wheel, whereby the

whole driving power of the sails was controlled, was suddenly reversed, and the vessel at once came to a full stop.

Drawn by Edwin A. Abbey

"Fog on the River this morning?" The bell ringer who stood at the end of the ferry slips to direct the approach of Ferry Boats. About 1875.

There were no Flats or Apartments in those days. There were monotonous rows of "brownstone fronts" on the more fashionable streets, but most of the houses were two-story red brick affairs with front stoops. On summer evenings we young folks sat around and sang, "Sweet Genevieve," "Grandfather's Clock," "Silver Threads Among the Gold," "You'd Look Sweet Upon the Seat

Time Table of STEAMER EMILY, on Harlem River.

GOING SOUTH.			GOING NORTH.		
Leaves F'dham, touching at Morris' Dock & High Bridge.	Leaves Morris' Dock, Touching at High Bridge.	Leaves High Bridge only.	LEAVES HARLEM		
			For High Brge. Morris' Dock and Fordham.	For High Bridge & Morris' Dock.	For High Bridge only.
A. M.	A. M.	P. M.	A. M.	A. M.	P. M.
7.15			9		
	8.25			7.55	
9.35			10.20		
	12.30		P. M.	11.50	
11	P. M.	4.30	2.15		
P. M.	5.30			P. M.	4
3				5	
			6.15		

Connecting with Steamers SYLVAN GROVE and SYLVAN SHORE, to and from New York.   FORDHAM, August 1859.

of a Bicycle Built for Two," and other popular songs of the day. Strange to relate, although we were all fond of singing together, it was difficult to persuade any of us to sing alone, most of us saying we had a bad cold, or something equally stupid. I was the one exception, and sang whenever requested. After I was through everybody else would say: "What a terrible cold that young man has."

We had no furnaces in those days. The whole family gathered in the front parlor, which was kept warm by a big round stove, called a Base Burner. These stoves had wonderful names: Hiawatha, Armageddan, Joan of Arc, etc. Ours was called the "Clinton Airtight." This made such a hit with the colored lady who did our washing that she bestowed it upon her first born—Clinton Airtight Johnson. We lighted lamps and fires with brimstone matches which nearly choked you with their pungent sulphur fumes.

Another charming domestic memory which also seems to have disappeared with the Base Burner was the young piano player. In my day she always performed in the front parlor, facing the street, so as to give the entire neighborhood the benefit of her skill. Perhaps she exists

THE TELEGRAPH POLES EITHER HAD TO COME DOWN OR FALL DOWN.
The Equitable Block with only three buildings—Metropolitan Bank, Café Savarin, and Equitable. Note the telegraph wires. (1878.)

today just the same, but her performance is lost among the babel of phonographs, telephones and radios. I don't know. I miss very keenly her, "One *and* two *and* three *and* four *and.*"

Our interior furnishings were slightly ornate, compared with the tastes of today. Wax flowers under a round glass case, occupied a prominent place on the mantelpiece. Wreaths made of shells with locks of hair of the dear departed, hung on the walls, flanked with worsted mottoes asking, "What Is Home Without a Mother?" The corner "Whatnot" contained baby's first pair of shoes, neatly preserved in bronze, stereoscopic views, and tintypes of Uncle John and Aunt Mary. A crayon portrait of Dad in a violent red plush frame, stood defiantly on a scroll work easel in the middle of the "best room," surrounded by horsehair furniture. Wide satin sashes adorned piano legs and the handle of the coal scuttle; the shovel and whisk broom were neatly tied with true lovers' knots in baby blue ribbon; hand-painted placques, lambrequins and tidies were everywhere. Favored visitors were entertained with the family album and the kaleidoscope. The whole ended with one of John Roger's famous statuettes—"Weighing the Baby," "Checkers Down at the Farm" or "Neighboring Pews."

We also built bird houses at public expense for the newly imported English sparrow, which we coddled a good deal in those days.

Our pleasures in the social way were also of a rather primitive sort. Among the young people "surprise parties" for a time were very popular. It was customary to send out, written in longhand on a sheet of plain paper, an invitation to "Dear Frank" or "Dear Eddie," to the effect that "You are cordially invited to attend a surprise party,

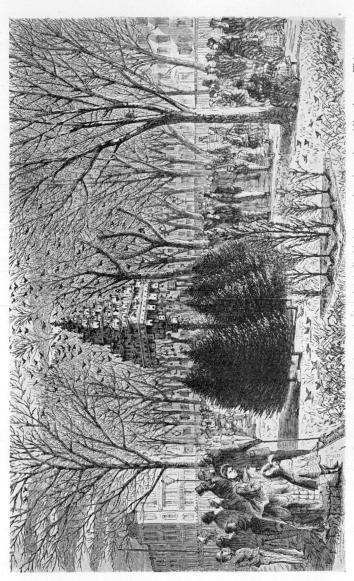

When the English Sparrows were first imported, the city built bird houses for them in public places. This shows the one in Union Square. These bird houses had special names—"City Hall," "Battery," "Central Park," etc. They were certainly a pampered lot (1859).

to meet at the residence of Miss Sallie Patchen, 29 East 28th Street, on Thursday at 8 P. M. Yours truly, The Committee. P. S. Please bring oranges." The last line was changed to provide a variety of edibles, and it might read candy, or cake, or fruit, or lemons, or what not. In due time the young people would assemble at the house designated, carrying their votive offerings in paper bags, and proceed in a body to the home of the young lady who was to be surprised. Occasionally the secret was well preserved, and the young lady was discovered helping mother wash the supper dishes, which was not at all unusual in those lowly and guileless days; but as a rule, advance information robbed us of this particular thrill, but otherwise had no effect on our pleasure.

Another great popular dissipation was the custom of making New Year's calls. This was an old Dutch practice and had descended from generation to generation. A week or two before the first of the year, the young men would receive cards from their various girl friends, giving them the address at which they would receive on New Year's. Some families observed the tradition of keeping it strictly within the family circle, but in a majority of cases, three or four young ladies would combine and receive in one of the houses mutually agreed upon. The young men were supposed to leave a card for each of the young ladies upon whom they called. Quite a good deal of ingenuity was exercised in the manufacture of these New Year's cards, and just before the custom went out, they were a riot. Some were richly decorated in powdered tinsel to represent glistening snow, and others in gorgeously embossed floral designs. A very popular design was one which had a silk fringe all around, in modest reds, greens and blues.

"WEIGHING THE BABY."
Another popular "Rogers Group."

Strange to relate, this custom died out practically over night. It began to be somewhat abused, which, I presume, was the cause of its sudden termination.

All over town there were still evidences of the bucolic existence from which we were just emerging. Tall poplars and sycamores still threw their grateful shade in many of our downtown streets. The women wore tremendous hoop skirts, little dinky hats, and parasols about a foot wide. The Grecian bend, long trailing skirts, bustles, bosom pads of inflated rubber or stuffed with horsehair; and a formidable line of corsets, made up the ensemble of a well dressed woman. White cotton stockings were universally worn. These were later embellished with horizontal stripes, in red, yellow, green, and other pastel colors, producing a refined barber-pole effect, which was considered the acme of artistic achievement. Our worthy forefathers had, of course, nothing like our present-day facilities for observation in this direction; so to correct any misjudging on this point, let me say that my information comes from the catalogs of the day issued by the dry goods people.

The men wore paper collars and cuffs and "dickies." A "dickie" was a white piece that covered the vest opening and hid the blue flannel shirt underneath. They also wore as much hair on their face as they could raise, and the less wool there was on the top of the head, the longer and bushier were the whiskers. His long white night gown, reaching to his heels, was a sight. He wound up his watch every night with a key. He pounded his stylographic pen to bring down the ink. His "spring bottom" pants were "skin tight"; his coat stopped short at the hips; his shoes were elastic or "Congress" gaiters; his shirt buttoned up the back; and he wore a flat, pancake derby.

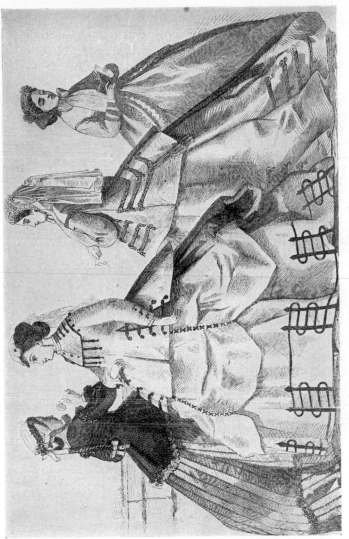

Popular costumes in the late 60's.

But the last word in ultra-fashionableness was undoubtedly the pocket toothpick. This was an indispensable
adjunct to the man who would be well dressed. Recollections of whaling days were still vivid enough to find us

THE SAILORS ADIEU.

"The Sailor's Adieu." One of two very popular chromos framed in
seashells, which were sold by the carload in the old Ship
Chandler's stores and were found in every home.

fairly familiar with the harpoon, and this method of publicly dislodging recalcitrant remnants of food, was considered quite the proper thing. To possess a toothpick that had come to you by inheritance, was considered a mark of ancient lineage.

"The Sailor's Return." The gladsome companion to the other.

Archery and Croquet led the outdoor sports in both Central and Prospects Parks, the latter being played on moonlight nights. "Lawn Tennis," as it was called, suddenly appeared and brought with it the first eruption of sport clothes. Grotesque automobile toggery had also not yet appeared.

The exciting game of Archery. Very popular in Central Park in the 70's.

Bathing suits were wholly different from the one-piece garment of today. We had also just begun to permit the mingling of the sexes in this delightful pastime.

"Is it you?"

Our illustrators, among whom were several who achieved fame in later life—Will H. Low, Winslow Homer, E. A. Abbey, among the number—affected a mollycoddle school of drawing which strikes us today as rather unsophisticated. However, in those days, "Prepared to Conquer" was supposed to very thrilling, while the illustrators who

"Mother, my future wife." The hero was always springing some such glad surprise on his mama—who was always pictured as a haughty, disdainful person, ready to annihilate her prospective daughter-in-law.

portrayed the principal characters in a love story, always had the mother a Lady Vere de Vere sort of type; while Sonny, who was a real lady-killer to look at, always presented a poor but "beyootiful" young thing, as his future wife, in a manner that suggested coming trouble all around.

Baseball was just coming into vogue. Nobody ever thought it would become our national pastime. *Harper's Weekly* said it was "impossible," as the crowds "disputed

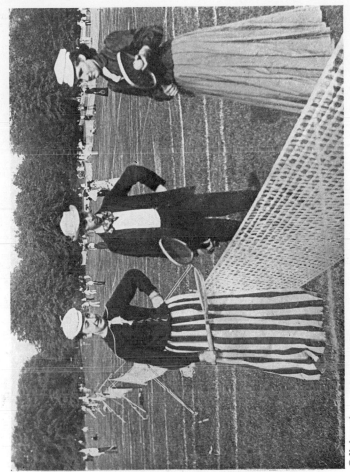

© Underwood   The swagger set of the 80's playing tennis.

the umpire; declined to applaud the visiting teams, even
when they outplayed the home team; and otherwise conducted themselves in a very impolite manner. Cricket was
a gentlemanly sport, while the other was fit only for the
lower classes."

Croquet. "Never too old, never too young to play." That was the
slogan. It raged with great fury in the 80's, and was
even played at night.

The Unions of Morrisania—the first Champion Baseball Nine, 1867.

The Prince of Wales paid us a visit in '61, and of all the toadying that was ever exhibited this occasion capped the climax. At the great ball in the Academy of Music, bulletins were despatched every ten minutes to the *Herald* office, to the effect that: "10:10, the Prince is approaching; 10:20, He arrives; 10:30, He is now dancing, etc., etc." We gave him a wild time. There wasn't a public charity, a lying-in hospital, an orphan asylum, a deaf, dumb or blind institution to which we did not take him. As a relaxation we once allowed him to visit the studio of a famous (?) sculptor, and there to feast his eyes on a colossal figure for some railroad depot or public building.

It was about this time that the sulphur-brimstone match reigned supreme. The head of each match was dipped in sulphur and a small portion of saltpeter formed a head for ignition purposes. The sulphur emitted a pungent odor and gave forth a blue flame that lasted until the wood was reached. When lighting a "segar" the fumes of the sulphur might have injured the aroma of the weed, if that had been humanly possible. Unfortunately, most of the "segars" came from Connecticut and Long Island. Nothing above the earth or in the waters underneath the earth could possibly add anything to the natural suffocating odor of these awful five-centers. Sometimes the "segar" would burn down on one side only, leaving the other side entirely intact, and another time the end would blossom like an ear of cauliflower.

After a while, the "parlor match," as the present match was then called, made its appearance. At first it was an explosive contrivance, going off with a loud report, and sometimes sending a dangerous spark clear across the room. There were occasional fires from this source and

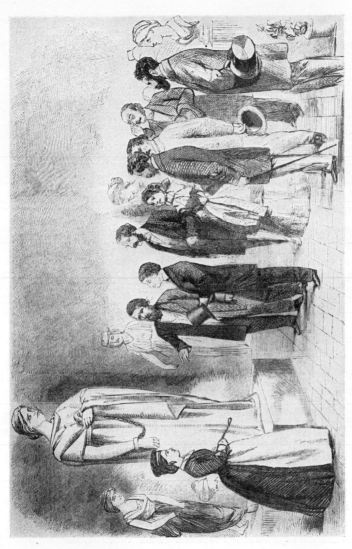

The Prince of Wales having a wild time during his visit to New York in 1860. A visit to Miss Hosmer's studios. The Deaf and Dumb Asylum, the Blind Asylum and other similar diversions kept him carefree and happy.

for a while we were obliged to keep them in tin boxes, set apart from every other article in the closet, and none of the children, under any circumstances, were allowed to use them.

Every "segar" store had a fierce looking Indian holding a tomahawk in one hand and a box of conchas in the other. I am sorry to say also that many of these "segar" stores were used for other purposes, and many of them derived considerable revenue for the privilege of receiving clandestine correspondence. It would be difficult to imagine a greater improvement than the chain store system of today, over the old retail shop of forty or fifty years ago.

Another institution which attained national celebrity, was the "Free Lunch" dispensed at the corner saloon. For the modest sum of five cents, a large "schooner" of really first-class beer could be obtained in addition to which the proprietor set out in some cases what amounted to a first-class meal. Like everything else, competition brought the free lunch to a splendor that threatened the proprietor's ruin; so it finally gave way in time to a bowl of crackers and a piece of cheese, in place of the clam chowder, roast beef, soup, fish and other delectable viands which formerly went with the glass of lager. In the spring, all the saloons blossomed with brilliantly-colored posters of a billy goat jumping over a "kag." This was a certain infallible harbinger of spring. Bock beer had arrived. At one time most of the saloons had white sand on the floor and the floors had a gentle, but nevertheless decided slant to the brass rail. A large mirror usually hung behind the barkeeps' head and on this mirror "soap artists" used to draw with amazing flourishes, highly artistic and ornamental designs, especially around Christmas time. "Chasing the

There was no public Art Gallery in New York till the Metropolitan was established, in 1878. Private galleries owned by men like Mr. Aspinwall, Mr. A. T. Stewart, Mr. Henry G. Marquand, Mr. Wm. H. Vanderbilt, were open to visitors, by writing for a card. This shows the interior of Mr. Aspinwall's Gallery, 1859.

duck," "a pail of suds," "rushing the growler" were favorite nicknames for the purchase of a pint in a tin can for home consumption. A side door called "Family Entrance" catered to this branch of the business. Whatever else may be said of the Volstead Act, none of us regret the disappearance of the corner saloon.

Another curious custom was that of grotesque parades on Thanksgiving. These performances were largely by children dressed up in their parents' clothes and wearing false faces. Usually they made the rounds of their respective neighborhoods and collected a few pennies in a tin cup from the guileless public who responded in a good-natured way to their appeals. This custom, from all I can learn, is of most ancient origin and persists to this day although in a much less conspicuous manner. I have often tried to find out just how it originated and what it signified, but have never yet found a satisfactory explanation. The nearest and most plausible is that in some way it is connected with Guy Fox's day in England, but there is no logical reason assigned to prove the connection.

Another equally mysterious custom was that of having bonfires on Election night. In my time this was an important adjunct of every election and many thousands of barrels were regularly consumed in these celebrations. Some of the fires were rather dangerous—a dozen or more barrels being piled pyramid-shaped before the torch was applied.

In addition to barrels, fences, gates and loose scantling of all kinds were quickly gathered in the neighborhood, and in sections where wooden houses still prevailed, they were badly despoiled of everything movable made of wood.

Tar barrels afforded the most excitement, as they burned fiercely and gave out clouds of dense smoke and somehow

A Forgotten Custom. New Year's Calls. This function died very early in the 80's and has never been revived. It was an old Dutch custom which had been followed for generations.

or other there always seemed plenty of them to be had. Kerosene was also called upon to aid in hastening the work of the flames and each succeeding year increased the danger to surrounding property. The city was fast filling up and the vacant lots where these fires were originally placed soon disappeared and the middle of the street substituted. Most of the fires I saw were thus located. The danger, always great, became greater each year and finally the authorities called a halt. Occasionally, of late years, I have seen an election bonfire, but compared with the old days when every street and almost every block on every street had a huge blaze, these exhibitions were nothing at all. The end had come. And like the mummers' parade, I have never yet found out the origin of the election bonfire or its significance, nor why it happens to enjoy that French descriptive prefix. Perhaps some of my readers can enlighten me on one or both?

Vaudeville theatres in those days were taboo. P. T. Barnum had the only approach to a show of this kind, and in deference to the prejudice then existing, he disguised his acts by giving them in what he called a lecture room. He had a lot of signs leading to his Side Shows— "This Way to the Fat Lady," "This Way to the Happy Family," etc. One read: "This Way to the Egress." It led to the street, and it cost a dime to get back. A Long Island farmer advertised a cherry colored cat for sale, and Barnum bought it. When pussy arrived he found it was *black*. It was then that he made his now famous remark: "There's a sucker born every minute." However, Barnum covered the town with posters, inviting everyone to see his cherry-colored cat, and they came in thousands.

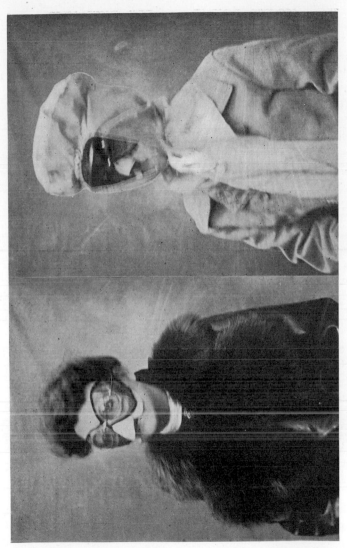

Can you realize that this was the latest agony in motor sport clothes a little more than ten years ago?

It is hard to describe the sensation caused by the appearance of "The Black Crook." I remember my father telling my mother that we could never again as a nation hold up our heads, and I recall my mother's righteous sympathetic indignation. Yet I thought I detected a funny little twinkle in her eye at the time; and from that day to this I have never been quite able to decide whether that gesture was one of holy horror, or of honest admiration, for his colossal nerve in trying to get by with such stuff.

Auction sales were also one of our favorite indoor sports, then as now. I went to one recently and bid on a picture up to six hundred dollars. It was knocked down to another man for eighty-seven thousand dollars. If you think there is no fun at an auction, try it some time.

Target companies used to parade up to Lion Park at 110th Street where the elevated is up in the air, and they shot at a target all day. They always came home half shot. Every year the Scotchman in bare legs had a beautiful time at Jones' Woods—now 66th to 75th Streets, East River. The Irish ruled the town. As soon as they arrived they just naturally joined the force, and at an Irish picnic a good time was had by all—including the surgeons, doctors and innocent bystanders.

And my! what an awful lot of Germans there were! They held their Schutzenfests at Sulzer's Harlem River Park, now 127th Street and 2nd Avenue. One was arrested and the Judge asked him his name, and he said: "Fritz Vanvonderblinkenstoffenheimer-Stoushorn." The Judge sent him up for life.

There were very few Italians. They were generally believed to be Sicilian cutthroats, and they worked mostly for the Irish, building sewers, etc. I can't recall any

A bit of Shantytown. Squatters' houses perched along what is now
"Millionaire's Row" and Central Park West, above
Fifty-ninth Street. 1859.

Poles, Russians or Hungarians in sufficient numbers to be worth remembering. If you remarked casually that you "saw a Jew in the Bronx today," no one would laugh. They would say, "Yes?" and possibly add, "Seems to me, they are getting thicker. I saw one myself yesterday, selling collar buttons on Park Row."

Drawn by Will H. Low

"Prepared to Conquer." This lady killer was supposed to be irresistible in the seventies.

Walking and evening gowns of the vintage of 1857.

The old time gallery gods seem also to have disappeared. In my days we boys never thought of paying more than ten or fifteen cents to see a show and sat under the roof on hard wooden benches. We were liberal in our applause, and when we became too vociferous, it was toned down by the "bouncer," who rapped loudly on the back of one of the benches with a heavy rattan cane.

In the picture theatre that now stands at Third Avenue and Thirtieth Street, originally built by McKee Rankin, there comes to my mind the memory of Frank Jones and Alice Montague, a clever song and dance team. They had a pair of rattling good voices and had practiced harmony until they were perfect. One of their songs that never failed to make a big hit was "Twenty Years Ago." The two sang in unison, and strange to relate, of all my recollections this song seems to come first to my memory. The words, as near as I can remember are about as follows:

> I wandered by the school house, Tom,
> Beneath the same old tree
> The boys were playing some old game—
> You played it oft with me.
>
> 'Twas done with knives upon the grass
> All throwing so and so;
> The leader had a task to do
> Twenty years ago.

There were quite a number of verses, but I have forgotten all but the last, which was a regular "weeper."

> But some are in the churchyard laid
> Some sleep beneath the sea;
> And few are left of our old crowd
> Excepting you and me.
>
> And when at last our time has come
> And we are called to go
> I hope they'll lay us where we played,
> Just twenty years ago.

Along the waterfront in West Street, looking north from about Pier 3.   About 1873.

There was, it seems to me, an altogether different attitude between the vaudeville artists and their admirers, than exists today. We felt personally acquainted and the different teams were well known to us. Each one had an enthusiastic following, but we were very catholic in our tastes and bestowed our favors on a large number of them indiscriminately. There were not more than eight theatres downtown, where these performances were a feature, so we made a round of them pretty regularly; about once every two weeks. Tony Williams and Mike Sullivan, who sang "The Lackawanna Spooners," for a time equalled the popularity of "Gallagher and Shean."

In the late 70's, James A. Bland, a colored man, wrote some very fine songs, among which was "Carry Me Back to Ole Virginny," "In the Morning by the Bright Light," and "In the Evening by the Moonlight," a quartet piece. He sang some of his compositions with Haverly's Mastodon Minstrels at that time.

In 1875, James P. Skelly wrote "I've Only Been Down to the Club," "My Pretty Red Rose," and others. In the 80's, Frank Howard sang his song, "When the Robins Nest Again," with Thatcher, Primrose and West's Minstrels. His other songs were "I'll Await My Love" and "Sweet Heather Bell," sung by him and Chauncey Olcott.

About this time Julian Jordan wrote his famous song, "The Song That Reached My Heart," which was the first song that had an up-to-date air, with an old song introduced; it had "Home, Sweet Home" in its chorus. J. B. Molloy was the author of some very fine songs, two of which were "Love's Old Sweet Song" and "The Kerry Dance." Michael Watson wrote "Anchored" about 1888; a little later Charles Graham introduced his "Two Little

The old Hell Gate Ferry now at Ninety-second Street, a few blocks from the Gracie Mansion.

Girls in Blue." Paul Dresser was made famous by "On the Banks of the Wabash."

About 1892, J. W. Kelly appeared at Tony Pastor's as the "Rolling Mill Man," a very original monologue in Irish dialect. He wrote many songs, some of which were sung by Maggie Cline. He wrote "Throw Him Down, McCloskey," which she popularized. Another of his songs was "The Bowery Grenadiers," also "Slide, Kelly, Slide." Charles K. Harris became well known by his composition, "After the Ball," and Raymon Moore by his "Sweet Marie." George Evans was responsible for "The Good Old Summer Time," which he sang. Joe Flynn's most popular composition was "Down Went McGinty." They all can compare favorably with the present day "Yes, We Have No Bananas," and "Barney Google."

There were quite a number of popular songs which appeared at this time and which were sung for a number of years. Dave Braham probably wrote more than any single composer. He wrote the songs for the Mulligan Guards series at Harrigan and Hart's Theatre, and there was no end to their popularity. Some of the titles follow:

"Paddy Duffy's Cart," "Going Home With Nellie After Five," "My Johanna Lives in Harlem," "Sunday Night When the Parlor's Full," "East Side, West Side, All Around the Town," "The Skidmore Guards," "The Mulligan Guards' Ball."

The old Sideboard Quartette made up of furniture men, used to gather round the bar in the old Grand Union and sing "Paddy Duffy's Cart" and a few others in the style that was delightful and always got a hand from the crowd.

Those who were privileged to hear the late Lillian Russell sing "Come Down My Evening Star," have one of the pleasantest of all memories.

[44]

Reception to Red Cloud and his band at Cooper Union, at which over five thousand were present, 1870. A curious memory of our busy City.

Many wonderful years have passed since the eyes of youth looked upon our city as I knew it when a boy. The golden glow of the sun as it sinks to rest, no longer seems to flood the streets with the blaze of its departing glory. The eternal shadows dwell between the deep canyons of the skyscrapers.

What has become of the Fairies? Where is the magic wand to wave us back to the land of Make Believe—to the little high chair and its bowl of bread and milk? Why can't we feel again the touch of a vanished hand—the sound of a voice that is still? The old song comes back, but that is all.

> Seven ships a-sailing on the Milky Sea,
> Four of them sank, and then there were three.
> One came to Tobey and one came to me—
> And one went a-sailing on the Milky Sea!

CHRONOLOGICAL SKETCH

of the Progress of

THE CITY OF NEW YORK

To the Close
of the Revolutionary War

1609. (Sept. 4.) A crew of five men, from Hudson's vessel), then anchored within Sandy Hook), passed through the Narrows in a small boat, and discovered Manhattan Island.

1611. A vessel dispatched by Amsterdam merchants, to Manhattan Island, to establish a trading depot.

1613. The trading post on this island consisted of four houses, Hendrick Corstraeusen being the chief of the traders.

1614. The first vessel built on this island, to supply the place of an European yacht which was burnt.

—— A fort erected on the south extremity of the island.

1621. The Dutch West India Company chartered.

1624. Peter Miniut arrived at this island as director.

1626. The island of Manhattan estimated then to contain 22,000 acres, purchased from the Indians for $24.

1629. Charter of privileges to the colonists, granted.

1632. Director Miniut returned to Holland.

—— Wouter Van Twiller arrived as Director.

1633. The privilege of "staple right" granted to New Amsterdam, whereby all vessels trading along the coast, were obliged to unload at this port, or pay certain fixed duties in lieu thereof.

—— The first schoolmaster (Adam Roelantsen,) arrived in the town.

—— The first church erected of wood, in the present Bridge Street; the dominie or pastor being the Rev. Everardus Bogardus.

1635. The fort finished at an expense of $1,688.

—— The first English settlers domiciled in New Amsterdam.

1638. Willem Kieft succeeded Van Twiller as Director.

1641. Cattle fairs established in New Amsterdam, two in each year. The first war between the Dutch and Indians commenced.

1642. A stone tavern built in New Amsterdam, at the head of present Coenties Slip.

—— A new stone church commenced within the walls of the fort, estimated to cost $1,000.

—— The first city lots granted to individuals, before that all were "squatters."

1643. The suburbs of New Amsterdam, devastated by the Indians.

—— The houses in the city at this period were mostly one story cabins, with roofs of straw and chimneys of wood.

1647. *Peter Stuyvesant,* succeeds Kieft as Director General.

—— An excise imposed on liquors retailed in the city.

—— Fence viewers appointed to regulate the public streets, and hog-pens and "little houses" ordered to be removed from along the highways.

1648. Every Monday declared a market day.

—— A wooden wharf completed on the East River, on the present line of Moore Street, being a continuation of the first wharf constructed in the city.

1649. An order first established for the regulation of weights and measures.

1650. The first lawyer, (Dirk Van Schellyne,) commenced practice in this city.

1652. A municipal form of government granted to the city.

1653. Palisades erected along the outskirts of the town (along Wall Street), in apprehension of invasion by the English.

—— A City Hall first established, the city tavern at the head of present Coenties Slip having been granted to the city for that purpose.

—— (Feb.) The first magistrates, (burgomasters and schepens) appointed.

1655. The city invaded by a band of savages, who were repulsed with loss.

1656. The city first surveyed, and the streets, (17 in number,) laid down on a map.

—— A market place for stand of country wagons established on the "strand," at present foot of Whitehall Street.

—— A census of the city taken, which exhibited 120 houses, and 1,000 inhabitants.

—— The shore of the city, along the East River, defended from the tides by a wall of planks stuck into the soil, and filled in behind.

—— The first houses built in Wall Street.

1657. The "chest" being empty, the town drummer's salary could not be paid.

—— P. C. Vandervin built the finest house in town, in Pearl Street, near the Battery.

—— The ditch through Broad Street, sided up with boards.

—— First Treasurer of the city appointed, (Van Cortland).

—— Average price of the best city lots, $50.

1658. Men and women not allowed to live together until legally married. (It being the custom to "bundle" after publication of bans.)

—— Several of the streets paved with stone, being the first streets paved in this city.

—— A "rattle watch" organized, of eight men.

—— Rent of an average good house, $14 per annum.

—— A market house for sale of meat, erected on present site of Bowling Green, being the first market house in the city.

—— Many large lots on the best streets being unimproved are taxed until built upon.

—— All thatched roofs and wooden chimneys ordered to be removed.

1658. Fire buckets and hooks and ladders first furnished for the town.

—— Jacob Van Corlaer opened a private school, but was interdicted by the authorities.

—— Slaves only to be whipped upon application to the Burgomasters.

—— A stated price fixed on all unappropriated lots (before given away on condition to build).

—— A water mill constructed at Deutel Bay (Turtle Bay).

—— The first public well dug in Broadway.

1659. Hendrick Van Bommel appointed town crier.

—— A Latin school established in the city. Carolus Curtius (Charles Curt), first Rector; salary, 500 guilders and perquisites.

—— The ditch through Broad Street lined with plank.

—— Bricks and tiles imported from Holland.

—— A foreign trade first allowed to merchants of this city.

—— Carel Beauvais opens a school.

—— A day of prayer set apart in New Amsterdam on account of the progress of Quaker doctrines.

—— Expedition against the Esopus Indians set out from the city.

—— Harmanus Van Hoboocha town schoolmaster.

1660. The wharf (only one) on site of present Moore Street extended four rods.

—— Made the duty of the Sheriff to go around the city in the night; but he complains that the dogs attack him; also, that people occasion frights by halloing "Indian" in the nights; also, that the boys cut "Koeckies."

1661. Governor Winthrop, of Massachusetts colony, visited New Amsterdam.

1664. The city taken by the English and the name changed to New York. Col. Richard Nichols, Governor of the Province.

—— The name of Fort Amsterdam changed to Fort James.

—— Population of the city, 1,500.

1665. Manhattan Island incorporated under the government of a Mayor, Aldermen and Sheriff.

—— Jury trials first established in this city.

—— (June 19th.) A riot occurred between English soldiers and the inhabitants.

—— The city records kept in both Dutch and English.

1668. Col. Francis Lovelace succeeded Nichols as governor.

1669. The Duke of York sends the Mayor and Aldermen civic gowns, a silver mace and a city seal.

1673. The city retaken by the Dutch, and the old order of municipal government re-established. Anthony Colve, Governor.

1674. The city contained 322 houses.

—— The city and province ceded to England by the Dutch, and the name of New York finally restored. Sir Edmund Andros, Governor.

1676. Vacant lots and decayed buildings ordered to be valued and disposed of to those willing to build.

—— Persons permitted to cut wood on any part of this island at the distance of a mile from a habitation.

—— Two stud horses ordered to be let loose on the commons, for the increase of the animals.

—— The slaughter-houses to be erected over the water at the present foot of Wall Street.

—— The tan pits in Broad Street filled up.

—— The open ditch in Broad Street converted into a sewer.

1677. The new dock (for many years the only one in the city) in course of construction.

—— The number of licensed taverns, fourteen.

—— Seven public wells first erected in the streets of the city—"for the publique good of the cytie."

The old North Battery, foot of Hubert Street built as one of the defenses, War of 1812.

1678. An Admiralty Court established.

—— An act passed giving to the inhabitants of the city the exclusive right to export flour and bread out of this province.

—— The shipping belonging to the city was three ships and fifteen smaller vessels (sloops and barques).

1682. Population about 2,000 whites, besides negroes and slaves; number of houses 207, besides barns and sheds.

1683. Col. Thomas Dongan, Governor.

—— Dongan's charter granted.

—— First police regulations established under authority given the new charter.

—— City divided into six wards.

1684. No swine permitted to run in streets.

—— The shipping belonging to this port consisted of three ships, three barques, twenty-three sloops and forty-six small boats.

—— The sole privilege given to this city for packing flour and making bread for exportation.

—— Aldermen and Common Councilmen first chosen by the people.

1685. The city takes upon itself the support of public paupers, and in the first place, Top Knot Betty to have 3s. per week, and Scarbank to have a new suit.

—— Assessors' valuation of property, £75,694.

—— A public chimney sweeper appointed to go through the streets "with such noise or cry" as should discover him to the inhabitants.

1686. "Dongan's charter" granted to the city.

—— Seal of the city, with the inscription "Sigillum Novi Eboraci," presented.

1687. The present Water Street laid out in the East River, from Whitehall to Old Slip.

1688. Wall Street laid out thirty-six feet wide.

1691. Leisler hanged. Col. Slaughter, Governor. The latter died suddenly the same year, and was succeeded by Major Richard Ingoldsby.

—— Water Street projected from Old Slip to present Fulton Street.

—— One butcher's shamble established on the site of the present Bowling Green, where only meat was to be sold.

—— A second meat market established "under the trees by the slip," (Hanover Square).

—— A ducking stool (for punishment of criminals) erected on the wharf in front of the City Hall.

—— Wharf erected on Pearl Street, from Coenties Slip to Broad Street.

—— All "poysonous and stinking weeds before every one's door" to be plucked up.

1692. The present Pine, Cedar and adjoining streets laid out through the old Damen farm.

—— (August.) Col. Benjamin Fletcher arrives as Governor.

1693. A new line of fortifications erected across the island.

—— A bell-man (or town crier) appointed and furnished with a livery dress.

—— The first filling in of the present Battery.

—— The first printing press established in this city by William Bradford.

—— "A platform upon the outmost point of rocks under the fort" designated as a place for a battery, there being at the time actual war existing with the French.

—— A bridge built by the city at "Spikendevil."

1694. Queen Street (now Pearl Street), and formerly Smith's Valley, so named.

1695. A bridge over the Fresh Water made at cost of £1 16s. 0d.

—— The streets cleaned by contract, at £30 per annum.

1696. (July.) Capt. Kidd arrived in New York to recruit for his expedition (in which he turned pirate).

—— Petition for a cartway on the present line of Nassau Street.

—— Maiden Lane regulated.

—— The first Trinity Church erected; also, the first Dutch Church, in Garden Street.

—— Burgers Path (Hanover Square), "made convenient for carts to go to the water side."

—— Erection of Dutch Reformed Church in Garden Street, and Trinity Church, commenced.

—— A sewer constructed in Broad Street.

—— Population of the city about 6,000 souls.

—— Coenties Slip constructed by Jacobus Van Cortland.

1697. The first regular night watch established, consisting of four men.

—— Lamps first hung out from every seventh house, upon a pole, extending from the window.

1698. (April.) Earl Bellamont arrived as Governor.

1699. The old palisades, in Wall Street, demolished.

—— City Hall (in Wall Street), erected; old one disposed of for £920.

—— A brick market-house erected at the foot of Broad Street.

—— A market-house erected at Coenties Slip.

—— Leisler's remains dug up from under the gallows, and interred with public demonstrations, in Garden Street Church-yard.

—— An hospital for the sick poor first established in this city (a house hired for the purpose).

—— Public scavengers first employed to clean the streets.

—— King Street (now William Street), filled up and regulated. Contract for filling £60 and a silver cup of £5.

—— A new City Hall erected in Wall Street, on the present site of the Custom-house.* The old City Hall sold for £920.

* Now U. S. Sub Treasury.

WARNING!

Those persons who have Goats, that keep about the Fort Garden, are desired to take notice, that unless they are taken care of, and prevented from destroying the fruit trees, disagreeable consequences will attend them.- *Common Council minutes 1786.*

THE SONG OF MOSHOLU
By J. J. Meehan

A little brook that tinkles low,
  Beyond the Harlem's tide,
O'er many a rocky, shingled slope
  Adown the green hillside.

Oft have I trod its mossy ways
  In wood of pine and leaf,
Where wound his spear or trimmed his bow
  Some brave Mohican chief.

Here burned the camp-fires long ago
  And rose the bright tepee,
Where now the golfer swings his club,
  Or builds his sanded tee.

Gone are the war-dance and the cry
  That echoed hill and glade;
Long hushed the voice of swarthy sire,
  And lithesome, dusky maid.

But still Van Cortlandt's storied wall
  Looks out on skies of blue;
Still comes at twilight's mystic hour
  The song of Mosholu.

Would that my lot were sometime cast,
  Earth done, where spirits dream;
And smoke their cloudy calumets
  By this old Indian stream!

OBSOLETE NAMES OF LOCALITIES
ON MANHATTAN ISLAND

The Potters Field—In 1794,—The triangular piece of ground at the then junction of the Post and Bloomingdale Roads (now Madison Square), was appropriated to the use of the Alms-house for a burial-ground, and received the name of the Potters Field.

In 1797.—A portion of the Corporation property in that vicinity was granted to the State for arsenal purposes, and about the same time the place was abandoned as a public burial-place, on account of the opposition made to the public exhibition of funerals on the much frequented roads leading to this spot, and it was resolved to purchase a more secluded locality for the Potters Field.

A piece of ground, containing about ninety lots, parcel of the land of William S. Smith, bounded on the road leading from the Bowery lane, at the two mile stone to Greenwich, having been purchased at public auction, and offered to the Corporation as a proper place for a public burial-ground, at the price of £1,800, it was resolved to purchase the same.

Opposition was made to this by the property owners in the vicinity, and the matter being referred to a committee, they reported, "That they had viewed a piece of ground which the petitioners will purchase at their own cost, and convey the same to the Corporation for a public cemetery, and find it well calculated for the purpose, so far as that it is removed a convenient distance from the Greenwich and Albany roads. That the soil is sandy and covered with brush, which will hide the graves and yet not interfere with digging them. But the Committee are obliged to remark, that to get to this ground the hearse (the great subject of complaint) must travel either of the roads above-mentioned."

The Board, however, refused to alter their purpose, and in spite of great opposition, the ground, recently purchased, was established as the new Potters Field. This was the present Washington square.

Crummashie Hill, was an eminence near Governor Stuyvesant's farm. Mr. De Witt, in his compilation of the old farms of New York, has written the name *Krommessie,* and given a derivation of that name to the shape of the farm upon which it was situated, as being that of a shoemaker's knife. The present *Gramercy* park is said to have derived its name from the old Crummashie hill.

Rose Hill was the name of the country seat of John Watts, Esq., prior to the Revolution. The estate covered some twenty-five blocks in the present Eighteenth Ward.

Bosch Bouwery, or Bush farm, was an old estate in the vicinity of the present Seventh Avenue and Twenty-fifth Street.

Horen Hook, a somewhat equivocal Dutch cognomen, given to the point of this island opposite Hell Gate, was in after years changed to Horn's hook.

Brannon's Garden was about the year 1765, established as a place of public resort along the Greenwich road, on the North River shore, about the present foot of Canal Street.

Fitzroy Road formerly led from Greenwich village to the present Forty-second Street. It was originally a part of the *Great Kiln Road,* leading to a rivulet known as the Great Kill brook, near which was a glass furnace, on the northerly boundary of an estate of Sir Peter Warren.

The Parade.—This name was given, at an early period, to the space in front of the old Fort, now known as the Bowling Green.

1770.—Permission was granted that the equestrian statue of King George III, be erected thereon, on its arrival.

1770.—*Ordered,* That a temporary fence be erected round the Bowling Green of posts and rails, not to exceed five rails high.

MANNERS AND CUSTOMS OF THE INDIANS
ON MANHATTAN ISLAND.

"On the right, or eastern bank of the river, from its mouth, dwell the *Manhattæ* or *Manatthanes,* a fierce nation, and hostile to our people, from whom, nevertheless, they purchased the island or point of land which is separated from the main by Helle-gat, and where they laid the foundations of a city, called New Amsterdam. On the left, or western bank of the river, dwell the *Sanhicans,* the deadly enemies of the former nation, and a better and more decent people. They live along the shores of the bay and within the land. Opposite to the Manhattans dwell the Machkentiwonu, and within the first bend of the river, on the same side, the Tappaanes.

"The barbarians are divided into many nations, and the people differ much from one another in language, though very little in manners. Their clothing is composed of the skins of wild animals, especially beavers, foxes and the like, sewed together in the manner of savages, with which they clothe themselves entirely in winter and slightly in summer. Their food, principally, consists of maize, or Indian corn, from which they bake cakes, resembling bread; fish, birds, and wild game. Their weapons are bows and arrows, the latter pointed with sharp flint-stones, or the bones of fishes. Their boats are one piece of wood, hollowed out by fire from the solid trunks of trees. Some of them lead a wandering life in the open air, with no settled habitations, lying stretched upon the ground, or on mats made of bulrushes, they take both their sleep and food, especially in summer, when they go nearer to the sea, for the sake of fishing. Others have fixed places of abode, and dwellings built with rafters, in the form of an oven, covered above with the bark of trees, so large that they are sufficient for several families. Their household furniture is mean and scanty, consisting of mats and wooden dishes, together with hatchets, made of hard flint-stone, by dint of savage labor, and tubes for smoking tobacco, formed, likewise, of flint-stone, ingeniously perforated, so that it is surprising how, in so great a want of iron implements, they are able to carve the stone. They neither know nor desire riches.

"They have no sense of religion—no worship of God; they, indeed, pay homage to the devil, but not so solemnly, nor with such ceremonies as the Africans do. They call him, in their language, *Menutto* or *Menetto,* and whatever is wonderful, and seems to exceed human capacity, they also call Menetto. They have no form of political government, except that they have their chiefs, whom they call *Sackmos* or *Sagamos,* who are almost always the heads of families, for they rarely exceed the limits of one family connection. They are, like most barbarians, suspicious and fearful, though greedy of revenge. They are fickle, but, if humanely treated, hospitable, and ready to perform a service. They ask only a small remuneration for what they do, and will make very long journeys in a short time, with greater fidelity than could be justly expected from such a barbarous people."

"Their houses are usually constructed in the same manner, without any particular costliness or curiosity in or to the same. Sometimes they build their houses above a hundred feet long, but never more than twenty feet wide. When they build a house, they place long slender hickory saplings in the ground, having the bark stripped off as far asunder as they intend the breadth of the house to be, and continuing the rows as far as it is intended the length shall be. These sapling-poles are bent over towards each other in the form of an arch, and secured together, having the appearance of a garden arbour. The sapling-poles are then crossed with split poles, in the form of lathing, which are well fastened to the upright work. The lathings are heaviest near the ground. A space of about a foot wide is left in the crown of the arch. For covering, they use the bark or ash, chestnut, and other trees, which they peel off in pieces of about six feet long, and as broad as they can. They cover their houses, laying the smooth side inward, leaving an open space of about a foot wide in the crown, to let out smoke. They lap the side edges and ends over each other, having regard to the shrinking of the bark, securing the covering with withes to the lathings. A crack or rent they shut up, and in this manner they make their houses proof against wind and rain. They have one door in the centre of the house. When the bark of the ash and chestnut trees is not loose, they have recourse to the timber trees which grow along the brooks, the bark of which can be taken off during the whole summer season. Durability is a primary object in their houses. In short, their houses are tight, and tolerably warm, but they know nothing of chambers, halls, and closetings. They kindle and keep their fires in the middle of their houses, from one end to the other, and the opening in the crown of the roof lets out the smoke. From sixteen to eighteen families frequently dwell in one house, according to its size. The fire being kept in the middle, the people lay on either side thereof, and each family has its own place. If they have a place for a pot or kettle, with a few small articles, with a place to sleep, they have room enough, and in this manner a hundred, and frequently many more, dwell together in one house. Such is the construction of an Indian dwelling in every place, unless they are out on hunting and fishing expeditions, and then they erect temporary huts or shanties.

"All their agriculture is performed by the women; the men give themselves very little trouble about the same, except those who are old; they, with the young children, will do some labor, under the direction of the women. They cultivate no wheat, oats, barley, or rye, and know nothing of ploughing, spading, and spitting up the soil, and are not neat and cleanly in their fields. The grain which they raise for bread and mush, or sapaen, is maize, or turkey-corn, and they raise also various kinds of beans. They also plant tobacco for their own use, which is not so good as ours, and of a different kind, that does not require as much labor and attendance. Of garden vegetables, they raise none, except pumpkins and squashes. They usually leave their fields and garden-spots open, uninclosed and unprotected by fencing, and take very little care of the same, though they raise an abundance of corn and beans, of which we obtain whole cargoes in sloops and galleys in trade. Of manuring and proper tillage they know nothing. All their tillage is done by the hand, and with small adzes, which they purchase from us. Although little can be said in favor of their husbandry, still they prefer their practice to ours, because our methods require too much labor and care to please them.

"The Indians are naturally (with few exceptions) of taciturn, steady, and pensive dispositions and tempers, and of few words, which are well-considered, uttered slowly, and long remembered. They say no more than is necessary to the subject in hand. When they want to buy or sell any article, they say no more than is necessary to the bargain. On other occasions they talk of no subjects, except hunting, fishing, and war. Their young men frequently entertain each other on their gallantry with young female connections. They despise lying, and still they are not very precise in the performance of their engagements. Swearing and scolding are not heard among them, unless it be among those who have learned those habits from us. They do not possess great wisdom or extensive knowledge, but reasonable understanding, resulting from practical experience. They are very revengeful and obstinate, even unto death, and when in trouble they disregard and despise all pain and torture that can be done to them, and will sing with proud contempt until death terminates their sufferings. When abroad, they spend their time in hunting, fishing, or war. At home, they smoke tobacco, and play a game with pieces of reeds, resembling our card-playing. The old men knit nets and make wooden bowls and ladles.

"Whenever an Indian departs this life, all the residents of the place assemble at the funeral. After the body has been watched and wept over several days and nights, they bring it to the grave, wherein they do not lay it down, but place it in a sitting posture upon a stone or a block of wood, as if the body were sitting upon a stool; then they place a pot, kettle, platter, and spoon, with some provisions and money, near the body in the grave; this, they say, is necessary for the journey to the other world. Then they place as much wood around the body as will keep the earth from it. Above the grave they place a large pile of wood, stone, or earth, and around and above the same they place palisades, resembling a small dwelling. The nearest relatives, particularly the women (the men seldom exhibiting much excitement), have their period of lamentation, when they make dreadful wailing. The use and tokens of mourning is common, which usually are black signs upon their bodies. When a woman loses her husband, she shaves off her hair, and paints her whole countenance black as pitch, and men do the same when their wives die. They mourn a year, without marrying until the season of mourning is over.

"The natives generally marry but one wife and no more, unless it be a chief who is great and powerful. Such frequently have two, three or four wives, of the neatest and handsomest women, and no strife, so far as we could ascertain, ever arises in the female household. Marriages with them are not so binding but that either party may altogether dissolve the union, which they frequently do."

DIGEST OF CITY ORDINANCES, PRIOR TO THE REVOLUTION

RELATING TO THE CITY OF NEW AMSTERDAM, DURING THE FIRST PERIOD OF THE DUTCH POSSESSION, WHETHER SAID ORDINANCES WERE ENACTED BY AUTHORITY OF THE COLONIAL OR CITY OFFICERS.

POLICE REGULATIONS (May, 1647).—An ordinance of the Director-General and Council:

All tapsters and inn-keepers are commanded that, on the Sabbath-day, they shall not sell liquors, except to boarders, before two o'clock in the afternoon, in case there is no preaching, or before four o'clock on the days when there is preaching.

They are also enjoined from selling liquors, excepting to boarders, on any day after ringing of the evening bell, at 9 o'clock.

All persons who shall rashly, or in anger, draw a knife or dagger against another, shall be fined one hundred guilders, and, in default of payment, be put to menial labor. In case of wounding another, the fine shall be three hundred guilders.

SELLING LIQUOR TO THE INDIANS (July, 1647).—An ordinance of the Director-General and Council:

All persons are interdicted from selling liquor to the Indians.

TRESPASSING ON ORCHARDS, etc. (July, 1647).—By the Director-General and Council:

All persons are forbidden to trespass on the orchards, fields, and gardens, provided they be inclosed in fence, or planted with fruit-trees, under penalty of one hundred guilders.

FENCES TO BE MADE (July, 1647).—By the Director-General and Council:

All inhabitants are charged to set off and put their plantations in good fence, so that cattle may be kept out.

CATTLE TRESPASSING (July, 1647).—By the Director-General and Council:

Horses, kine, and, in a special manner, goats and hogs, must be taken care of, and kept from trespassing. A pound shall be built to detain such cattle, of which every one must take notice, and look out for costs.

ERECTING HOUSES (July, 1647).—By the Director-General and Council:

Three Surveyors of buildings are appointed, who are empowered to condemn all impropriety and disorder in buildings, fences, palisades, posts, and rails; who may warn all who are preparing to settle in the city of New Amsterdam to observe these orders, and build according to their directions.

All persons who have received grants of house-lots are directed to improve their lots within nine months, or the grant shall be revoked.

BREWERS (January, 1648-9).—By the Director-General and Council:

No brewer in this city shall be permitted to sell beer by the half-pot or small-measure.

ON OCCASION OF THE EXPECTED WAR WITH THE PEOPLE OF NEW ENGLAND (March, 1653).—It is decreed:

That the whole body of citizens keep watch by night.

That the fortress be repaired.

That money be raised.

That the Schipper *Vischer* keep his piece loaded, and have his vessel in readiness at all times.

(SAME DATE).—The Commissioners give notice that they intend to issue proposals for a wall of palisades, 12 to 13 feet in height. Those who desire to estimate, to come to the City Hall.

Proposals issued as follows:

The palisades to be in length 12 feet.
"   "   "   thick in the round, 18 inches.
"   "   "   sharpened at the top, and placed in a line.

At every rod, a post 21 inches thick in the round, to which split-rails shall be nailed, two feet from the top of the palisades.

A breast-work against this 4 feet in height, with a breadth of 4 feet at the bottom, and 3 feet at the top of sod, must be thrown up, with a ditch of 3 feet in breadth, and 2 feet deep, which ditch shall be 2½ feet within the breast-work.

The length that shall be set off is about 180 rods. No more money to be paid than rods completed.

Upon this plan proposals are received, and agreements made.

(This was the city-wall on the present line of Wall Street.)

FINES FOR LATE ATTENDANCE AT MEETINGS OF BURGO-MASTERS AND SCHEPENS (February, 1663):

Who comes half an hour too late, 10 stuyvers.

Who comes an hour too late, 1 guilder.

Who is wholly absent, 2 guilders.

The Boston Post Road, at the Junction of Chatham Square, Pearl Street and the Bowery, as it appeared in the olden time. Rutger's Farm (e) and the Fresh Water Bridge (c) are shown. The new County Court House stands on part of this land.

DIGEST OF THE ORDINANCES DURING THE PERIOD
OF THE FIRST ENGLISH POSSESSION.

CHURCH-YARD (June, 1665).—By the Mayor and Aldermen:

Resolution, that whereas the church-yard* of this city lies very open, so that the hogs root in the same; as there is no money in the chest, a collection must be made for its reparation.

SUPPORT OF THE SOLDIERS (June, 1665).—By the Mayor and Aldermen:

Two hundred guilders in sewant shall be raised weekly from the commonalty of this city, for the support of the soldiers.

COURT RECORDS (June, 1665).—By the Mayor and Aldermen:

The city records to be kept both in English and Dutch.

PORTERS AND CARRIERS (June, 1665).—By the Mayor and Aldermen:

Their fees regulated.

CITY WATCH (August, 1665).—By the Mayor and Aldermen:

Ordered, that six burghers do every night keep watch within this city.

CARTMEN (October, 1665).—By the Mayor and Aldermen:

The cartmen are ordered not to stand on their carts while driving, as much danger arises therefrom.

OVERSEERS OF FENCES (March, 1666).—By the Mayor and Aldermen:

Two overseers of fences and roads appointed.

INSPECTORS OF BREAD (August, 1666).—By the Mayor and Aldermen:

Reciting the disregard of bakers to the ordinances, and appointing two inspectors, to visit the premises of the bakers, and ascertain if the bread have its due quality and quantity.

BAKERS (August, 1666).—By the Mayor and Aldermen:

All persons are forbidden to sell any bread along the houses, but must only retail it on their own premises.

SALE OF BREAD OR CAKES TO INDIANS (August, 1666).—By the Mayor and Aldermen:

All persons are forbidden to take any bread or cakes to the Indian plantations for sale there on commission.

CARTMEN (April, 1667).—By the Mayor and Aldermen:

Eight cartmen commissioned for this city. It being a condition of their license, that on alarm of fire, they render every assistance in its extinguishment.

---

* This was the old church-yard on west side of Broadway, above Morris Street.—[D.T.V.]

CARTMEN (June, 1667).—By the Mayor and Aldermen:
Ordinance, that no one except the licensed cartmen be permitted to cart goods (except his own) within this city.

The fees of the cartmen established.

The cartmen (January, 1668) are permitted to ride on their carts, on condition of driving slowly, and forfeiting their horse and cart in case of injury to any person; and in case any person should be killed, the life of the cartman to be under the lapse of the law; and further, that they shall be bound to keep the streets and highways in order.

BRANDERS OF HORSES AND CATTLE ON MANHATTAN ISLAND (March, 1670).—By the Mayor and Aldermen:
Instructions of those officers established as follows:

1. That they take care no cattle be fed on the commons, but such as are branded with the town-mark. That no stallions be admitted, but such as are approved of. That at least six stallions be continually kept on the commons.

2. That they keep an account of all horses and cattle branded by them, with the color and marks, and the name of the owner.

3. That they appoint two days in the week for branding.

4. The branders of Harlem to give an account of the cattle branded by them.

5. The fees of the branders established.

PACKERS OF BEEF AND PORK (October, 1671).—By the Mayor and Aldermen:
Two packers of beef and pork appointed.

PAVING OF THE STREETS (April, 1672).—By the Mayor and Aldermen:
Ordered, that all persons who have not yet paved the streets, pursuant to the placard, do so without delay. Certain persons appointed to see that the placard be carried out, and to report what other streets require to be paved.

The original cottage and late residence of the Jones Family, foot of Eighty-second Street, East River, almost adjoining Gracie Mansion. Their large holdings were called Jones' Woods, and the site was originally chosen for Central Park, 1866.

THE SHIPS AND VESSELS OF OUR PORT
IN OLDEN TIMES
First, in the Times of the Dutch

In our readings of the chronicles of the past, the names of vessels navigating our waters, when they casually occur, always excite in us a desire to know something more about them. The tastes of our people are essentially maritime, and there is besides a special interest attached to those monarchs of the deep which brought hither our ancestral predecessors, and in their yearly voyages between the old and new worlds, afforded the only means of communication and supply to our citizens.

With what pleasure the arrival of a ship from Holland was hailed in those times! We find it recorded that the national flag was hoisted in the town and the population hastened in boats to meet the vessel. By her they received news from friends and relatives whom, probably, they never expected to see again. They learned the progress of political events, which at that time were of an intensely interesting character in Europe. They received the necessary additions to domestic comfort, or perhaps luxury, in which their increasing prosperity persuaded them to indulge. In short, the periodical arrival of the trading ships, was an event in which every one was interested, and which afforded the most agreeable relief from the routine of a life separated from the active affairs of the great world of civilization, from which our people had recently departed.

Nor, to the reader of the present day, are the craft which navigate our rivers and bays without particular interest. We are apt to picture a wilderness and romance in their wanderings, so different from the scenes of the present day, that our imaginations lend charms to the subject; and the lonely sloop, working her way to the remote settlements, through surrounding solitudes, is invested with far different regard than ordinary scenes of a kindred character, which are now within our observation. The Hudson River, in the times of the Dutch, had but two Christian settlements upon its banks. The meeting of two vessels upon its waters was probably as unusual an event, as the encounter of two ships upon the ocean at the present day. Nor did the river traders confine themselves alone to the Christian settlements. Many guilders were brought into their chest by the Indian trader. For this purpose we find certain traders monopolizing particular districts to themselves. Each became acquainted with the savages in a certain vicinity, and periodically visited them, carrying the coveted articles of civilization, and trading them with the natives for furs and wampum.

Another branch of maritime trade which, after a time, engaged the attention of the New Amsterdam merchants, was that with Virginia and the West Indies. In this, vessels of small size were engaged, and the capital required was within the reach of some of our most prosperous traders, and considerable fortunes were acquired through its means.

It is well known that the vessel in which Hudson discovered the river which bears his name, was called the "Half Moon." She was of small dimensions, being of only eighty tons burthen, and so light in draught that she ascended the river (though with some difficulty at the upper part), as far as the present site of Albany. It is somewhat remarkable that at that early period in the history of ocean navigation, vessels of such small size should have been used to explore unknown seas, and to encounter dangers which would deter the most resolute adventurer of modern times. The "Half Moon" entered the lower bay on the 3rd of September, 1609, finding there, as her journalist says, "a very good land to fall in with, and a pleasant for to see." On the 6th of September, her boats were sent on an excursion of observation, and passed through the narrows. On the 11th of September the ship weighed anchor, and came up into the upper bay, where she lay until the following day, when she commenced her voyage up the river, her commander, hopeful, it is said, that he might be led into the Pacific Ocean, and thus find a short way of passage to the East Indies. Three days were occupied in ascending the river to the Catskill Mountains. On the 21st of September, the vessel reached its furthest point of exploration, which was as far as Albany. On the 23rd of the same month the return passage was commenced, and on the 4th of October the "Half Moon" passed out into the Atlantic Ocean, never to return to our shores. Two years afterwards she was dispatched from Holland on a voyage to the East Indies, but failed to reach her destination; she was wrecked and lost on the island of Mauritius in 1611.

The first trading ships between the North River and Holland, were the "Little Fox" and the "Little Crane," which were brought hither in 1611, upon a speculating trading voyage, and spent a considerable time in bartering the trinkets and other trifles, so much coveted by the Indians, for beaver and peltry, of which the country afforded a bountiful supply. The adventure was successful, and we find the "Little Fox," (or Het Vosje," as she was called in Dutch), repeating her voyages during many subsequent years. She is entitled to a distinguished place in the maritime history of our port, not less as being the pioneer trading ship from the old world, but for her constancy in preserving the connection so happily formed.

In 1614 three vessels were fitted out for the Hudson River, with the design of establishing trading posts in which furs might be collected while the ships were crossing the ocean, and thus save their long detention here. These were called "The Tiger," Schipper Block; "The Fortune," Schipper Corstiaensen; and another vessel, also called "The Fortune," Schipper Mey. By accident, "The Tiger" was burnt shortly after her arrival; an event which occasioned an era in our maritime history, namely, the building of the first vessel on the shores of our harbor. This boat was thirty-eight feet keel, forty-four and a half feet long, and eleven and a half feet wide. She was used for coasting, and made discoveries of most of the bays and rivers on Long Island Sound, and also navigated the Atlantic coast, and penetrated Delaware Bay. She was the first vessel that passed through Hell Gate; and, upon the whole, the little "Onrust," (or Restless), as she was called, may be enrolled upon our record, as peculiarly entitled to be cherished by all New Yorkers, not only as the child of their creation, but as the means of filling many important little blanks in the cosmogony of the world before unknown to civilized people. Schipper Block was her first navigator; but his ambition would not permit him to remain wedded to his little craft, and he returned to his fatherland. Schipper Corstiaensen, captain of "The Fortune" met his fate here, having been murdered by an Indian. Schipper Mey was the first Director of the Colony of New Netherland, ten years later, but did not remain here longer than a year.

A trading company was licensed in Holland, in 1615, with exclusive privilege of trade here for three years. This company was principally composed of those who sent out the vessels previously mentioned. Their squadron was composed of the same vessels before mentioned, with the addition of the "Nochtegael" (The Nightingale); and afterwards "The Scheld" (called after the river of that name) and "De Blyde Boodschap" (The Glad Tidings), were added. These ships traded here during six or seven succeeding years, to the great profit of their owners.

In 1621, the country of New Netherland was granted to the great organization called The West India Company. Among the earliest of the vessels dispatched by this company were the ships "New Netherland," of 260 tons burthen, "The Arms of Amsterdam," Schipper Adrian Joris,

and the bark "Nassau." The "New Netherland" arrived
in the harbor in 1623, and is especially worthy of effection-
ate regard, as being the first ship which brought out
families to found a civilized settlement. She arrived in
1623, having on board thirty families, with cattle, poultry
and farming utensils. This notable vessel continued her
regular passages here during the whole time of the Dutch
possession. She was built expressly for this trade, and
named after the colony which she planted on our shores.
All honor to the venerable vessel! It is said that an
hundred years after her first visit, she was sent here from
Holland upon a casual voyage, and was still in good condition.

At this early period the voyages between Holland and
New Netherland generally occupied about seven or eight
weeks. On clearing the British Channel, they laid their
course for the Canary Islands, whence they stretched across
the Atlantic toward the Guiana and the Carribbees, and
then ran obliquely toward the northwest, between the
Bahamas and the Bermudas, until they made the coast.

In 1629 four vessels were dispatched to the "Manhates,"
as the settlement on this island was called at that period.
In 1630, the "Eendracht" (Union) arrived, and is deserving
of mention as conveying the first colonists of Renselaers-
wyck. On her return voyage, in 1632, having stopped at
Plymouth, she was detained by the English.

The first ship of war that ever entered our port was
"De Troutberg" (The Salt Mountain), of twenty guns,
which arrived in 1633, with a company of soldiers to garri-
son the fort on the south point of Manhattan Island, then
just completed.

One of the trading vessels, which afterwards was regularly employed in this port was "The Hope," Schipper
Jurian Blanck, which first came hither in 1633. This vessel
had been captured from the enemy during the preceding
year. Her Schipper, Blanck, was the first ship captain who
established his residence in this city. The next was Adrian
Blommaert, Schipper of the ship "New Amsterdam," one
of the regular vessels of the company. This gentleman
was at one period a city magistrate.

The second ship of war which arrived in our harbor
was "The Herring," one of the company's ships; she was
of two hundred and eighty tons burthen, carrying two
metal, sixteen iron and two stone guns. This formidable
vessel brought out the new Director, William Kieft.

It is affirmed that even before this early period several
vessels had been built on this island; and the English,
who were inimical to the progress of the Dutch in this
vicinity, asserted that previous to the year 1632 a ship of

considerable burthen had been constructed here, and sent across the ocean. This, however, is a very improbable story.

One of the most notable maritime events, in connection with the early history of this city, was the loss of the ship "Princess," in 1647. She sailed from this city, having on board a valuable cargo, and conveying home the recent Director-General Kieft, together with several principal inhabitants, among whom was Dominie Bogardus, the first clergyman established in this city. The Princess was navigated by mistake into the Bristol channel, struck upon a rock, and was wrecked on the rugged coast of Wales. Towards morning, the ship went to pieces. Kieft, with eighty other passengers, including Dominie Bogardus, were drowned. Of all on board, only twenty were saved. This occurrence shed a deep gloom upon the town, where so many families remained bereft of their dearest relations.

The expedition which was undertaken in 1655 against the interloping Swedes, on the South or Delaware river, was the greatest maritime event in the history of the Dutch in New Amsterdam. This expedition consisted of seven vessels, carrying between six and seven hundred men. The leading vessel was the "Balance," the valiant Captain Frederick De Coninck, commander. There was also a French privateer, called "L'Esperance," engaged for the occasion, three North river yachts and two other vessels. The expedition sailed on the first Sunday in September, 1655, under the command of Governor Stuyvesant, and was entirely successful, having reduced the forts of the enemy without the loss of a man on either side.

The first shipwreck on our coast, of which we have any account, was in 1659. In December of the preceding year three vessels, the "Prince Maurice," the "Bear," and the "Flower of Guelder," sailed for New Netherland, having on board one hundred and sixty-seven colonists. A storm separated the squadron, and the "Prince Maurice," having several principal citizens on board, struck, about midnight, on the south coast of Long Island, at a place called "Sicktewacky," near Fire Island inlet. The next morning the crew and passengers escaped through the ice to a barren shore, "without weeds, grass, or timber of any sort to make a fire." Assistance being dispatched, all were saved, as was also the cargo. The ship, however, was lost.

We may here mention, in brief, the names of other ships engaged in trade between this port and Holland in the times of the Dutch: "Orange Tree," "Sea Mew," "Three Kings," "Houttuyn," (Woodyard), "Blue Cock," the "New

Netherland's Fortune," "Moesmann," the "Whitehorse," (a slaver), "Great Christopher," "Black Eagle," "Pear Tree," "King Solomon," "De Trow," "Hope."

In connection with the subject of the ships trading between Holland and New Amsterdam, it is proper to say that they were mostly owned by Holland merchants. The only exceptions, of which we are aware, were the "New Netherland Indian" and the "Morning Star," which were owned partly by merchants in this city. The coasters, however, were owned by our principal merchants, among whom may be mentioned, Pieter Cornelisen Vanderveen, Cornelius D'Potter, who, with several other gentlemen, built a small ship, called the "New Love," which is the first three-masted vessel positively known to have been built on our shores. Isaac Allerton, an English merchant, resident in this city, owned the "William and John," a ketch, trading with Virginia. Allerton's great tobacco-house stood on the shore of the East River, near the present Maiden Lane; Cornelius Steenwyck, Govert Loockermann, Jacob Leisler, Jacob Backer, Johannes Van Brugh, and other of the leading merchants and traders, were likewise engaged in the coasting trade.

The river trade, as has been mentioned, was carried on in small sloops or yachts, sometimes for itinerant trading purposes, and in other instances these vessels were regular packets between New Amsterdam and the settlements at Esopus (Kingston) and Fort Orange (Albany). The yachts were all provided with a gun, set upon a rest on the deck of the vessel, for the purposes of defense. This was probably the cumbrous matchlock which the soldiers in old times carried, and which they stood upon a rest set on the ground. We find in our old records the complaint of a yacht captain that a ship-carpenter, who had been repairing the vessel, detains his "gun and rest"; and on the occasion of the expected assault upon the city by the English, in 1653, the Burgomasters resolved to privately speak to the skipper of the yacht in the harbor to "keep his match lighted" and his sails bent. We can only give the names of some of the yacht traders in the times of the Dutch.

Isaac Kip, Govert Loockermann, Hendrick Arenzen, Thomas Davidts, Reindert Jansen Hoorn, Arent Leenderzen, Pieter Jacobs Marius, Jan Etsal, Jan Peeck (the settler of Peekskill), Reintje Pietersen, E. D. Vanass, Captain De Boogh.

The anchoring place for vessels in the harbor was regulated by law.

All vessels under fifty tons were obliged to anchor between "Capsey hook" (the present Battery) and a guide-board set up on the shore at the present Coenties Slip.

Larger vessels were permitted to anchor as far as a second guide-board, which was erected at "Smith's Valley," probably near the present Fulton Ferry.

The Grade of Broadway, from the present Duane Street to Canal Street established

1797.—The regulation of Broadway and the intersecting streets, from Barclay Street, to the arched bridge, (across the drain now known as Canal Street). By this regulation, Broadway required digging down at Magazine Street (now Pearl Street), to the depth of four feet nine inches from the natural elevation of the soil. At the intersection of the present Leonard Street, it required digging down to the depth of fifteen feet six inches; thence by the regulation it was to descend by a gradual descent to the arched bridge; but the hill through which it was cut increased in height above Leonard Street, so that at a distance of five hundred and twenty-five feet above Leonard Street, the cutting had increased in depth to twenty-two feet ten inches. This was the highest point, and thence the natural hill descended somewhat steeply to the meadow; the line of Broadway, through the meadow, required raising seven inches. The arched bridge was ten feet seven inches above the surface of the meadow. The digging was commenced within a year or two subsequent to the above date.

Standing Water in the Meadows

1798.—A letter from the Health Commissioners was read, representing that the swamp or meadow between the Fresh Water Pond and Hudson River is overflowed with standing water, and requires immediate measures for draining it. Ordered that it be attended to.

This was afterwards known as Lispenard's Meadow, and extended from about the present new County Court House to the North River, between Lispenard and Canal Streets.

VERREZANO'S VOYAGE

NOTE.—It has been a question considerably discussed whether
Hudson is entitled the place in our history, commonly accredited to
him, of having been the first European discoverer of the mouth of
the Hudson River. By some it is supposed (and we confess ourself
among the number), that Verrezano was the actual discoverer,
nearly an hundred years previous to the visit of Hudson. That our
readers may form an opinion on this subject from the original report
of the voyage, as well as peruse an interesting account of one of the
earliest European expeditions to the American coast, we furnish in
part, a copy (in which the ancient English orthography is preserved)
of Verrezano's letter to his Royal Master, the King of France, under
whose auspices the expedition sailed.

To the Most Christian King of France, Francis the
First:

*The Relation of John De Verrezano, a Florentine, of the
the Land by him discovered in the name of his Ma-
iestie. Written at Diepe the eight of July, 1524.*

I wrote not to your Maiesty, most Christian King, since
the time we suffered the tempest in the north partes, of
the successe of the four shippes which your Maiesty sent
forth to discover new lands by the ocean, thinking your
Maiesty had bene already duely enformed thereof. Now
by these presents I will giue your Maiesty to understand
how by the violence of the windes, we were forced with the
two shippes, the Norman and the Dolphin, (in such evil
case as they were,) to land in Britaine, where, after wee
had repayred them in all poynts as was needful, and armed
them very well, we took our course along by the coast of
Spaine, which your Maiesty shall understand by the profite
that we received thereby. Afterwards with the Dolphin
alone we determined to make discouerie of new countries,
to prosecute the nauigation we had already begun, which
I purpose at this present to recount unto your Maiesty, to
make manifest the whole proceeding of the matter.

The 17th of January, the yeere 1524, by the grace of
God, we departed from the dishabited rocke by the isle of
Madeira, apperteining to the King of Portugal, with 50
men, with victuals, weapons and other ship-munition, very
well prouided and furnished for eight months: and sailing
westward with a faire easterly winde, in 25 dayes we ran
500 leagues, and the 20 of Februarie, we were ouertaken
with as sharpe and terrible a tempest as euer any saylors
suffered, whereof with the diuine helpe and mercifull assistance of almighty God, and the goodnesse of our shippe,
accompanied with the good happe of her fortunate name,
we were deliuered, and with a prosperous winde followed

our course west and by north. And in other 25 dayes we made aboue 400 leagues more, where we discouered a new land, neuer before seene of any man either ancient or moderne, and at the first sight it seemed somewhat low, but being within a quarter of it, we perceiued by the great fires that we saw by the sea coast, that it was inhabited; and saw that the lande stretched to the southwards. In seeking some convenient harborough, wherein to anchor and to have knowledge of the place, we sayled fiftie leagues in vaine, and seeing the lande to runne still to the southwards, we resolved to returne backe againe towards the north where we found ourselues troubled with the like difficultie. At length, being in despaire to find any porte, wee cast anchor upon the coast, and sent our boate to shore, where we saw great store of people which came to the sea side; and seeing us approach they fled away, and sometimes would stand still and looke backe, beholding us with great admiration; but afterwards being animated and assured with signes that we made them, some of them came hard to the sea side, seeming to rejoyce very much at the sight of us, and marvelling greatly at our apparel, shape and whitenesse, shewed us by sundry signes, where we might most commodiously come alande with our boate, offering us also of their victuals to eat. Now I will briefly declare to your Maiesty their life and manners, as farre as we could have notice thereof: These people goe altogether naked, except only that they cover their privie parts with certain skins of beasts, like unto martens, wnich they fasten unto a narrow girdle made of grasse very artificially wrought, hanged about with tayles of divers other beastes, which, round about their bodies, hang dangling down to their knees. Some of them weare garlands of byrdes feathers. The people are of colour russet, and not much unlike the Saracens: their hayre blacke thicke, and not very long, which they tye together in a knot behind, and weare it like a little taile. They are well featured in their limbes, of middling stature, and commonly somewhat bigger than wee, broad breasted, strong armed, their legs and other parts of their bodies well fashioned, and they are disfigured in nothing, saving that they have somewhat broade visages, and yet not all of them, for we saw many of them well favoured, having blacke and greate eyes, with a cheereful and steady looke, not strong of body, yet sharpe witted, nimble and exceeding great runners, as farre as we could learn by experience, and in those two last qualities they are like to the people of the east partes of the world, and especially to them of the uttermost partes of China.

The first picture of the Fifth Avenue Hotel as completed (1858), and then known as "Eno's Folly." Erected on the site of Corporal Thompson's Road House. Present location of the Garfield National Bank.

FORTY YEARS ON TWENTY-THIRD STREET
By Henry Irving Dodge

Just what does forty years on Twenty-third Street
mean? It means something quite different from what
forty years on Vesey Street, or what forty years on
Grand Street would mean. Why? Because every prominent section of the City has a history all its own—dis-
tinct—Bowling Green, Wall Street, The Swamp—old
leather district near Brooklyn Bridge; Cherry Hill, fragrant from a snowstorm of blossoms, where the old ship
owners used to sit on their front piazzas and watch their
matchless clippers, just home from India, swinging at
anchor in the East River—Cherry Hill, since passed into
the hands of the Italians and Greeks; the Bowery, formerly the "Bouwerie," a long line of rose bowers, gentlemen's gardens, since turned into a long line of saloons
and dives, and again into a line of cheap lodging houses,
each a history of shifting human sands, each a demonstration of the inevitable, the inscrutable operation of the
economic law.

Twenty-third Street is the Middle Ages of New York
history, neither very old nor very new, destined for a time
to be the hub of the wheel of historic activities.

Social life bloomed, bloomed gorgeously, on Twenty
third Street, and departed. Great concerns, prompted
by the exigencies of trade, came and went. In Twenty-
third Street the sands of social and business life shifted,
shifted, shifted. But whether its metier be social, intellectual, or commercial, the words "Twenty-third Street"
always carry the conviction of importance.

Twenty years before the Garfield National Bank was established on Twenty-third Street, Fifth Avenue and Broadway at their intersection were little better than country roads and Madison Square, although a park, was contemptuously and quite graphically alluded to as a rocky cow pasture. Where the bank now stands was Madison Cottage, a road house, famous for hot toddy and other forms of hospitality, and run by one Corporal Thompson. It bore a printed notice to the effect that stages left every four minutes, presumably for the south, the Battery, since there was nowhere to go to the north. Things were crude and desolate at that point, relieved mostly by Corporal Thompson's good cheer. But, hold! There was also Franconi's Hippodrome in those days that stood on another corner, across the way, covered two whole acres of land and had a frontage of a couple of hundred feet on Broadway. That was in 1853. Patrons of the Astor House, Broadway and Vesey Street, used to come all the way out there to see Franconi's wonder place. No visit to town was complete without the experience.

The day after the Hippodrome was established the following writeup, in style characteristic of the period, appeared:

> "But if the exterior at once surprises, attracts, and elicits admiration, what must be the effect of the internal arrangements? Classic lore, ancient history, Walter Scott's pictures of the tournament, the songs of chivalry, all are competent to give an idea of what is to be seen at Franconi's Hippodrome."

Such was Twenty-third Street when Amos R. Eno had a vision of a great hotel to be located there, to draw the fashionable from all parts of the world. There were many so-called "wise ones" of those days who, having

The Masonic Temple, 1876, at Sixth Avenue and Twenty-third Street, where the Garfield Bank started. The Schermerhorn residence, the fourth house above, was the site of the Eden Musee.

eyes, yet did not perceive. Franconi's place and the Corporal's road house to their way of thinking, nailed fast the extreme northern limit of the city. When Eno let it be known that he was going to put up a vast hotel on the site of the Corporal's tavern his enemies secretly laughed the project to scorn and watched and waited to see him fall down. And his wiseacre friends lugubriously warned: "Amos, you're committing financial suicide. You'd better throw your money into the river and have done with it." And, being ignored quite humanly they longed for the day when they could twit him with: "I told you so." All manner of wiseacres shook heads over the Corporal's toddy. Ridiculous scheme! Nobody would ever live above Twenty-third Street. And as for any persons moving from the Astor House to live up there among the goats with Eno. Absurd! And so the project got to be known as "Eno's Folly." But Eno knew in his heart he had a better scheme than chucking his money into the river, as his friends had suggested.

He realized that the apprehension of his friends and the scorn of his enemies in regard to his project was not without some reason. The spot selected for the hotel in which he planned to entertain the most fashionable persons of the whole world was practically on the outskirts of civilization. But he was sustained by the example of Commodore Vanderbilt who rebuked his advisors, when warned not to build the Hudson River railroad along a sparsely inhabited stretch of country, with the words: "Put the road there and people'll go there to live."

With his own proper eyes, Eno had seen the filthy waters of the canal, the present Canal Street, disappear under paving stones, trucks instead of barges hauling freight through the great thoroughfare. He had seen

Statue of Edwin Booth as Hamlet erected in Gramercy Park 1918
opposite the Players' Club which he founded.

Spring Street pass from an outpost to a downtown street. He had watched the edge of the city proceed northward with the inevitableness of an advancing tide while the reactionary Canutes sought to halt it by shaking restraining but impotent fists.

Then why should New York stop at Twenty-third Street, Eno asked himself.

Mr. Eno started work on the structure that was to make the crossing of Twenty-third Street, Broadway and Fifth Avenue the social and diplomatic centre of the Western hemisphere. Where six years before had stood the Corporal's road house, with stages leaving every four minutes for the south, the north being practically a blank— now came a life new to New York, a cosmopolitan life.

Once the great hotel was completed, the very spot on which the Garfield National Bank now stands became the hub of the history-making activities of the day. Twenty-third Street was now permanently on the map. The hotel was almost born famous, so quickly did it become famous. And royalty played no small part in its meteoric ascent. Here came the Prince of Wales in 1860, full of youthful joys and escapades. Here he lodged under the hospitable roof of Messrs. Hitchcock, Darling & Company. Paran Stevens, of Boston, was the silent partner. Certainly it was a *coup* to get the Prince to come to the hotel. And what an advertisement! All New York was talking about it. It was estimated that more fashionable persons passed that corner in a day—while the royal youngster was there—than had passed in any week. For Twenty-third Street was then away uptown, mind you. Washington Square was the sacrosanct. Delmonico's was at Fourteenth Street. It was almost unethical for the elect to go above the Union Club at Twentieth Street,

THE OLD SCHERMERHORN MANSION AT THE FOOT OF SEVENTY-THIRD STREET AND EAST RIVER—A NEIGHBOR OF ARCHIBALD GRACIE. NOW PART OF THE ROCKEFELLER INSTITUTE OF RESEARCH.

But the royal magnet drew them across the line in flocks, ethics or no ethics, belles and dandies alike. And Amos R. Eno sat back and watched them throng "Eno's Folly," he chuckled, and wondered where were the I-told-you-so boys today.

Legend has it that on this historic spot the royal youth, Wales, did elude the watchful eyes of his train, the train selected and charged with the conservation of his royal morals by the austere and decorous Victoria, climbed down a ladder from his window to the street, and under the guidance of certain, *very certain,* New Yorkers "saw the town" after midnight.

The Crown Prince's endorsement spread the fame of the Fifth Avenue hotel to the four quarters of the earth. And so surely as the night follows the day, so does one royal visit beget another royal visit. Later, Dom Pedro, the last of the Brazilian emperors, held court in the great parlors of the hotel and in the magnificent suite assigned to him. Here also the Crown Prince Nareo of Siam was entertained with splendor that made the fashionable of lower Fifth Avenue blink. In '81 Prince Napoleon, son of Plon Plon, was a guest. And in the very parlors where Dom Pedro had held forth the Arcadian Club gave a reception to Charlotte Cushman on the occasion of that queen's retirement from the stage. And it was here the movement for the nomination of Grant for the Presidency was started, two years after Appomattox.

With the advent of the Fifth Avenue hotel, the social centre of the city began to move uptown. The Astor House had held it fast for many years, then it was pegged at Washington Square. And presently Delmonico set Fourteenth Street as the limit, with the Union Club a few blocks to the north.

The Fifth Avenue hotel was born right into the dark clouds of the Civil War. In fact, to write the history of the present site of the Garfield National Bank would mean practically to write the inside history of the Rebellion. The hotel became almost at once the gathering place for Republicans and remained so until its demolition a few years back, 1908. Here the stout defenders of the Union foregathered, here some of the most momentous conferences of the day took place. It is said that Lincoln used to come and go, and always at night in order to escape attention. As tragic events followed in our nation's life the attention of the whole world was more and more focused on this spot. It was a rendezvous for the great, if we may judge men by their bearing upon public affairs.

And others than the great gathered here. For no sooner did war assail the nation that the vultures attacked its backbone. Gamblers began operating in gold. The old Gold Board downtown was not big enough for the voracious activities. Members would trade there till three o'clock, the official closing hour, trade in the life blood of the nation, then adjourn to the "curb" and trade till six. After supper they would reconvene in the lobby of the hotel and gamble in gold till midnight. And they kept that uptown Gold Board going from the early 60's away up to '79.

The men who had helped to pull the nation through the Rebellion now helped to reconstruct it. They continued to foregather her in the old Fifth Avenue, for the hotel never lost caste from the day it was built until it was pulled down.

One might dwell on the old Y. M. C. A. building at the corner of Fourth Avenue and Twenty-third Street,

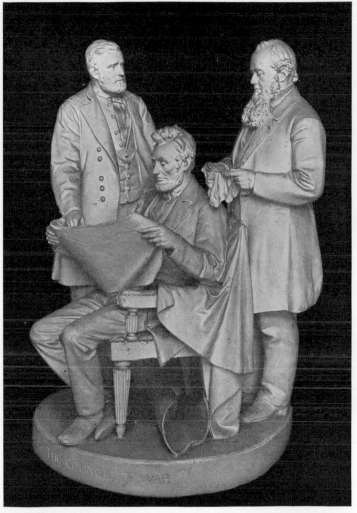

"The Fifth Avenue Hotel was born right into the dark clouds of the Civil War."

Grant, Lincoln and Stanton, from the famous group by John Rogers.

deemed by many the best architectural structure of the time, or the City College at Lexington Avenue or the Academy of Design or the old Masonic building at Sixth Avenue, or other buildings, public and private. But it is not the brick and mortar, the brown stone fronts that make a street conspicuous, for a street practically unheard of has these. It's the men who live and move and have their being in it that give it character. It was the men who made Twenty-third Street a place of rendezvous, a place of constructive activity that gave it significance. Many of these men lived on other streets, but this was the section of the city they belonged to. Theodore Roosevelt, for instance, was more identified with this immediate neighborhood than with any other part of New York. And one could walk from the Fifth Avenue hotel to his birthplace in two minutes. Many of the aforesaid Twenty-third Street group, who had homes in other parts of the country, still retained permanent quarters in that section. Conkling, a Utica man, lived principally at the Hoffman House, and Senator Platt, also hailing from up-state, lived at the Fifth Avenue. Ben Butler had apartments there by the year, it is said. Legend hath it that this doughty warrior lunched midnightly on doughnuts and whiskey.

Such instances serve to show that Twenty-third Street was for years the cosmopolitan colony of the city. And the cosmopolitan colony of any city, because of its fresh, compelling blood, is what makes that city great. New York never before had just such a community of interests, intellects, and forces as the Twenty-third Street colony. It was because of just such men that Twenty-third Street was for years the uptown Wall Street. Great operations in securities were technically transacted on the Exchange. But the master minds were uptown, colloquially known as the Fifth Avenue crowd and the Hoffman House crowd.

Swing a two hundred foot radius around the paying teller's window of the Garfield National Bank today and you will describe an area sacred to American History— a charmed circle. Within this circle fashionable life bubbled and boiled and scattered its froth abroad. One might shut his eyes and conjure the shades of those who strode within that charmed circle or who took part in the tragedies and comedies enacted therein, only a few short years ago.

At the head of the procession of shades is the huge figure of General Winfield Scott. Scott lived for many years at the Fifth Avenue and died there. And here comes with scornful stride Cornelius Vanderbilt, the Commodore, tall, thin, erect almost to bending backwards, He had curly, white hair and short side-whiskers. Dignity was his long suit. It was said that no man could be so much a king as the Commodore looked. And those wonderful blue eyes. They could cut holes right through you.

It is not on record that anyone ever volunteered advice to the Commodore more than once. Once when the Commodore was "bulling" Harlem, one of his brokers was a Mr. C., a peculiarly conservative individual, who used to boast that he never offered advice, even to his humblest customer. From time to time, and in the most casual way, the Commodore would order C. to buy a five thousand share lot. But Harlem did not advance. It occurred to Mr. C. that his patron was trying to put the stock up and was having hard sledding. So one day he said: "Commodore, it occurred to me that you are trying to put Harlem to par. I know a very rich man who'd like to join forces with you, I——" he stopped short, fixed by those penetrating eyes. Then came the stern words, uttered with unmistakable finality:

"Mr. C., I want you to understand, sir, that it doesn't take two men to put Harlem to par when Cornelius Vanderbilt is one of them."

The Commodore was one of the most familiar figures in the old Fifth Avenue until he died in '77, then in his eighty-third year, spirited, and erect and quite as great as he looked, up to his very last hour.

Here daily strolled Thurlow Weed, modern Warwick, king-maker, Lincoln's unofficial ambassador to England, on the arm of his daughter, Harriet, his constant companion and support, and always thinking, thinking, thinking. For Weed was a man who rarely talked, and when he did, the world hung on his words. We see him, pause to chat with Gilbert Cummings Davidson, Treasurer of the State Republican Committee, and closest friend and advisor to the old king-maker. Davidson lived just down the street. And here come Secretary Seward and his son Fred. Seward's statue is in Madison Square. Fred was always with his father, watching over him. It was owing to the same solicitous vigilance that the Secretary escaped assassination in Washington, Fred taking in his head the dagger thrust that was meant for his father, and as a consequence, carrying a gold plate in his skull to the end of his days. Among the shades are Salmon P. Chase and his daughter Kate, the handsomest man and the most beautiful woman of the Lincoln administration.

And here is the aristocratic McClellan. Men of long range memory will tell you how the General saved the hotel from destruction at the hands of the mob during the draft riots. And the appearance of McClellan sug-

The house where Theodore Roosevelt was born—No. 28 East
Twentieth Street.   Restored and kept as a memorial
of the Great American.

gests the famous friendship between him and Charley Delmonico, the best beloved man of his day, and the tragedy years later. The General was living out in the Orange mountains and Delmonico sought to visit him there. It was night and a blizzard. Delmonico could get no vehicle to take him from the station, so he tried to make it on foot. But he was not strong enough. Days later his body was found in a snow bank. One sees the shade of Benjamin Nathan, the venerable Jewish banker and philanthropist, with his latch key letting himself into his house, 12 West Twenty-third Street, just across the way, at midnight. He mounts the stairs, enters his bedroom and shuts the door. And, then occurs the most mysterious murder in the annals of the New York Police Department. In the morning the aged philanthropist was found strangled before an open private safe. Papers scattered about the floor and upset furniture indicated a struggle. There was a theory that the murderer had entered through a skylight. The affair created more than a nine day's sensation. Because of the great prominence of the victim and the weird conditions under which the crime was committed, criminologists from all parts of the world sought to ravel out the mystery. But it was never done.

In the charmed circle one observes Cyrus Field, bent with care over Atlantic cable problems, and his friend and patron, Peter Cooper, of whom it might have been said: "No one could be as benevolent as Peter looked, no one but Peter Cooper." Here was a man whose constructive influence, through the agency of the Cooper Institute, reached out into the four corners of the earth. Arm in arm, come George Jones, owner of the *Times,*

Franconi's Hippodrome which preceded the Fifth Avenue Hotel, corner Fifth Avenue and Twenty-third Street. (1854.)

and Honorable Russell Sage, then a member of Congress, as few remember.

And among the throng moves with marvelous grace Edwin Booth—Edwin, the Beloved, he might have been called, for he was the idol of the hour. There wasn't a great man of that section who didn't brag of the personal friendship of Booth.

Now saunters along Samuel J. Tilden in frock coat and famous plug hat, hands clasped behind. In Tilden's wake come the Damon and Pythias of the day, John Kelly and Augustus Schell. Kelly was the Boss of Tammany, said to be the most dignified chieftain that body ever had, and Schell, Schell, was simply a gentleman, crony of Kelly's, a man of vicarious fame, but one of the sweetest natures of the day. These men were not simply passers-by. This particular section was the centre of their activities. For the Fifth Avenue hotel, Republican headquarters, and the Hoffman House, Democratic headquarters, stood practically cheek by jowl, with only a thin slice of a hotel, the Albemarle, in between to keep them from coming to blows. And in the charmed circle we see another Damon and Pythias, Henry W. Raymond, the most brilliant editor of the day, and James G. Blaine.

Among the shades of Twenty-third Street section is Roscoe Conklin, the magnificent, Blaine's most determined enemy, walking arm in arm with Chester Allan Arthur, the President and the man who made him President. Their statues are in the park. The scene shifts to the first night of the blizzard of '88. Right across the edge of the charmed circle one can see the mighty form of the Senator, alone, at midnight, breasting his way through the storm to his rooms in the Hoffman House,

Madison Cottage, present site of Garfield Bank, Twenty-third Street, Fifth Avenue and Broadway.

contracting a cold which caused his death little more than a month later. In the charmed circle one also sees the incomparable Beecher who rocked the Republican party in its cradle on this very spot.

It was only a minute's walk from the bank to the Union Club on the Avenue where Larry Jerome, Bill Travers, and other good and hospitable souls held forth. Here Travers used to stammer out his scintillations, and lucky were they who caught said sparks and re-issued them at a future date as their own. One H., a prominent banker, was in the habit of airing his views in letters to the *Times*. On one occasion H., unperceived, was standing near a group of which Travers was the centre. "Say Bill," said Larry Jerome, "have you seen H.'s last letter in the *Times?*" "No such luck," replied Travers.

Just across the Square lived Catherine Lorillard Wolfe, the great philanthropist and art collector, who gave away four millions. Miss Wolfe founded the Newsboys' Lodging House at East Broadway and Gouverneur Street, and many is the rich man today who calls her blessed because of the sheltering arms her mercy cast about him when he was a child.

A stone's throw from the bank, George Francis Train, the oracle of Madison Square, held forth. Train was the most brilliantly erratic and erratically brilliant man of his day. In his earlier days he had been identified with the Credit Mobillier, and gossip, probably well founded, had it that at one time he had owned half the city of Omaha. He was very fond of children and always had a pocketful of candy and peanuts for the little ones who played about his bench in the park. He had small use for grown-ups, however. For months at a stretch he would speak to no person above ten or a dozen years old.

To repel intruders, he always had at his side a great yellow umbrella. Should a man or a woman persist in asking him questions, as such a one often did, that is, during one of his periods of affected dumbness, the oracle would put up the umbrella, draw it close down over his head, and keep it there until the would-be invader had departed. I've seen him do that many times.

A bit west of the charmed circle lived the Schermerhorns and the Dows and the Butterfields and other notables, all conspicuous in the activities of Twenty-third Street.

Across the edge of the charmed circle strolled Mark Twain every fair day, that is, in summer, his mustache tawny and his hair as white as the flannels he affected, stopping to chat with Chauncey Depew, the coolest-looking and best natured man in the whole broad metropolis.

Within the charmed circle was the Amen Corner with "Easy Boss Platt" presiding. It was known as "Amen" because Platt would opine and the satellites would say: "So be it." One paper describes the "Corner" as "not far from the Clerk's desk and exceedingly convenient to the Cafe."

Art and amusement are concomitants of social life. In the days when Twenty-third Street was the fashionable centre of the city we find Booth's theatre at Twenty-third Street and Sixth Avenue; a step further west Koster & Bials, the first legitimate music hall in New York, and two blocks beyond the Grand Opera House, official headquarters of Messrs. Gould and Fiske, where Henry Adams' "Chapter in Erie" was for the most part enacted. Right up against the Fifth Avenue hotel on Twenty-fourth Street was the Madison Square theatre, for a long time one of the principal playhouses of the city.

It was about forty years ago that Twenty-third Street society lifted its hands aghast at the idea of the invasion of its precincts by trade. But you can't help the onrush of the inevitable by superciliously staring at it through lorgnettes. A line of retail concerns stretched along a mile to the south on Broadway and beyond that whole- sale houses and jobbers trade had crept up to and crossed Twenty-third Street, casting covetous eyes to the east and to the west, but had not ventured either way. But here was a thoroughfare abounding with the most fash- ionable life of the day. At the crossing of Fifth Avenue was a perfect maelstrom of cosmopolitan humanity—peo- ple with money in their pockets. Why shouldn't mer- chants plant their show windows there? For is not trade the handmaiden to society? At least, that's what Isaac Stern reckoned.

Messrs. Stern Brothers—Isaac, Louis, Bernhard and Benjamin, were then running a modest store on Sixth Avenue next door to Moirs' jewelry shop. That was in 1878. When Isaac Stern let it be known that he was going to pull up stakes from Sixth Avenue and establish himself on Twenty-third Street, opposite the Fifth Ave- nue hotel, he was called a lunatic by the wiseacres. But Stern, like Eno, was a man of courage. He, too, was familiar with the unrealized, cynical prognostications of the timorous, the weak-kneed. Even the shrewd William H. Vanderbilt had erred on the side of caution, he knew. It was said that when the projectors of the elevated road had asked Mr. Vanderbilt to loan them money he had refused on the ground that no one would walk upstairs to take a train. Also Stern had dreamed dreams of long lines of the carriages of the fashionable drawn up be- fore his store, so he planted his banner right in the heart of the most aristocratic section of the city. Nor did the social blue-noses turn him down. In fact, the long line of carriages—Stern's realized dream—was the talk of the day. And Stern Brothers stayed right there and prospered for thirty-five years.

The eyes commercial of New York were on the Isaac Stern venture. The ice being broken, Best and Company followed Stern Brothers, 1880, and during its thirty year sojourn expanded from 60 to 62 West its first quarters, way through the block and took in 47, 49 and 51 West Twenty-second Street. Then came Bonwit Teller, the pioneer in women's specialties, the one price store, settling at 48, 50 and 52.

Trade was now in full swing. Twenty-third Street was regarded the highest-toned retail street in New York. None but fashionable concerns obtained there. And now downtown concerns determined to try for a share of the gold of the new centre. James McCutcheon and Company, who had moved in the wake of advancing trade from Tenth Street and Broadway to Fourteenth Street and halted there, now moved on to 64 West Twenty-third. The uptown progress of Le Boutillier Brothers marked probably more definitely than that of any other concern the steps of advancing trade. From '40 to '45 they were on Canal Street; from '45 to '72 on Spring Street; from '72 to '81 on Fourteenth Street; from '81 to 1911 on Twenty-third Street.

In 1895 James McCreery and Company opened their Twenty-third Street branch. In two years so great was the business here that this branch was made the main store and continued so for ten years, sharing the great retail trade with Stern Brothers, each vieing with the other as to the line of carriages leading to its front door.

There is irony in the fact that a bas-relief of Shakespeare, the same that was over the entrance of the Booth playhouse, is now over Number 70 West Twenty-third Street, which was once the entrance to the dry goods store, a symbol of the interrelations of art and trade.

Just west of the bank was the great publishing house of G. P. Putnam's Sons. Putnam's following the trend of trade, moved to Twenty-third Street from Fifth Avenue in the early 80's and halted there for thirty years before resuming its onward march.

The life of G. P. Putnam's Sons is peculiarly fraught with historic interest. Its present head, George Haven Putnam, is probably the only man alive today, 1923, who had personal relations with Washington Irving. Mr. Putnam, when a boy, and a keenly appreciative boy at that, used to carry manuscripts and proof to Irving up at Sunnyside. And Mr. Irving took a fancy to the little chap and would tell him stories.

It was at a desk in Mr. Putnam's office that Theodore Roosevelt wrote *The Winning of the West*. This manuscript had a remarkable experience. It was written, proof read, set up, printed and bound, and eventually sent down stairs to the book store and retailed, all in the same building. Later on, young Roosevelt was a special partner in the house. It was Mr. Putnam who suggested to the nominating committee of the assembly district that it name his young partner for the legislature. This was done and probably started the Colonel on his political career.

Eventually, the upward swing of the residential district carried many of the retail stores up Fifth Avenue, and their places in and about Twenty-third Street were

Booth's Theater, corner Sixth Avenue and
Twenty-third Street. (1879.)

taken by leaders in other lines, notably the great silk and cotton and woolen commission houses, so that today Twenty-third Street is the centre of a great commercial and industrial life.

Delmonico's in Fourteenth Street.

A FINE VEW OF HELL GATE, FROM THE GRACIE MANSION, ABOUT 1830. THE SUNKEN SHIPS
TESTIFY TO THE DANGER OF NAVIGATION IN THOSE DAYS.

THE GRAVE OF JACOB LEISLER

This spot indicates the scene of one of the most doleful
events in the history of New York. It is only within recent
years that the particulars of the affair in which Mr. Leisler
was engaged, have attracted public attention; but the interest taken in our historic annals has served as an incen-
tive to the antiquary to bring before the public many documents which have illustrated that portion of our annals,
and the subject is no longer a novelty. A brief narrative,
however, it is supposed will not be out of place, in connection with the exhibition of his place of execution as
shown on old maps.

Jacob Leisler was a native of Holland, and emigrated to
this country in the time of the Dutch possession; his first
employment was as an officer in the troops of the government, but he married soon after his arrival in New Amsterdam, and then engaged in commercial pursuits. He became
allied, by his marriage, to some of the principal families
in this province, and acquired a large estate, being ranked
among the wealthiest citizens. His commercial operations
were principally in foreign trade, and he is found to
have been one of the leading shipping merchants in this
city at that period.

The religious controversies of that time were violent,
and pervaded all classes. They were more particularly
animated after the surrender of the city to the English,
for although the Dutch had stipulated for their own mode
of worship, yet little reliance could be placed on the guar-
anty that it should be allowed; for the government of
England was itself on the point of civil war, arising out of
the rivalries of the various sects of Catholics, Episcopalians
and Dissenters, which were contending for the place of
power, and the countenance of the government. The reflex
of opinions from the European shores found their way
here, and occasioned, if possible, more individual excitement among the various sects than was shown at the foun-
tain-head of the government. Thus matters stood during
twenty or thirty years, embracing the time from the death
of Cromwell, and the overthrow of Presbyterianism in
England, through the succeeding reigns of Charles and
James, witnessing the restoration of Episcopalianism under
the former, and as it was supposed with the latter mon-
arch, the precursing signs of the rebuilding of the Roman
Catholic authority in Great Britain. The Dissenters, as
this state of things was in progress, began to murmur

openly, and to speak of forcible means of preventing the advance of their ancient enemy. The rebellious feeling prevailed throughout Great Britain and in all her colonies. Here the people watched for the blow to be struck at home (as the parent country was called), and when, what is called the rebellion of 1688, took place, and King James was deposed, the news here occasioned a general outburst of sympathy, and the people laid violent hands upon the strongholds of the government in this province. The people acted in the first instance by a committee of safety, but owing to the long delays of receiving orders from the government over the water, they finally appointed Mr. Leisler, who was one of their leaders, as the temporary executive of the government.

The leading defect in Leisler's character appears to have been an impulsiveness and headstrong force of will which led him beyond the limits of prudence in carrying out the measures of his party. At the present day his position does not seem to have been a difficult one. The leading principles contended for by those with whom he acted, were such as commanded almost universal support; but the turning-point upon which his administration centred, was brought down to a personal contest for the places of government between two factions who professed to work for the same end. It was altogether (as it would seem) trivial in comparison with the extraordinary results produced in this country; brothers, parent and child, indeed all social ties were forgotten in the strife between neighbors for the foot-hold of power. The contest waged between one and two years; some of Leisler's opponents were banished, others imprisoned, and in short he exercised his power with severity, and without regard to consequences. His defence is to be found in the popular excitement, of which he was the exponent; in the pent up feelings of a whole community, during a score of years, now brought into active display. He finally was deposed by the government in England. His enemies being reinstated in the government turned upon him with a blood-thirsty desire for vengeance. He was tried upon insufficient charges, and his condemnation being a foregone conclusion, his conviction followed, and he was sentenced, with his son-in-law, to be hanged. The great majority of the people regarded him as a martyr; fire-eyed fury fairly burnt within the households of the people of New York; but the *law,* that great principle of government, backed, as it was by power, restrained any positive demonstration toward the relief of the popular leader.

It was said that he was allowed to choose the place of his execution, and that he selected his own grounds for the site of the scaffold (he owned a seat near Tammany Hall), designated his garden as his burial place; the spot is pointed out upon the map. The day of his execution was drizzling and disagreeable; the ceremony was equally sad and miserable; the people felt that their own lives were struck at through this sacrifice. The tears of thousands silently flowed as the ceremony progressed, and forty or fifty years failed to eradicate the tremendous tide of popular feeling which flowed on that day.

On the scaffold Leisler made a speech, in which he frankly admitted that he might have been guilty of excesses and, in his religious penitence, he prayed forgiveness of those who pursued him to this extremity.

Some years after his remains were taken up, and removed with great solemnity, by a popular assemblage, to the common burial-place of his religious sect, the Dutch Reformed Church in Garden Street (now Exchange Place).

PROFESSOR LOWE'S MAMMOTH BALLOON, CITY OF NEW YORK, AS SHE WILL APPEAR WHEN FULLY INFLATED. *Nov. 1859.*

Balloon Ascension in Bryant Park in 1859, showing Forty-second Street and rear Reservoir, where Public Library now stands.

RECOLLECTIONS OF POSTMASTER JAMES
By John H. McDevitt

On Saint Patrick's Day in 1873 President Grant signed
the commission of Thomas Lemuel James as Postmaster
of New York. Two months later he appointed the nar-
rator, then a lad of thirteen, as messenger. Seeing for
the first time the Post Office on Nassau, between Cedar
and Liberty Streets, I thought that people who entered
it were attending divine service. It was the Middle Dutch
Church, erected in 1714 and occupied by the Government
in 1845. While it was pathetic to read of the farewell
service on the Sunday evening before it became the "home
of letters," I remember the jubilation of the employees
when vacating the place on the last Saturday in September, 1875, recalling the mail courier, Paul Revere, in
the Old South Church on the 19th of April in '75, with
Longfellow's lament: "and hardly a man is now alive
who remembers" that auspicious day when Postmaster
James and nearly three hundred employees gaily marched
up Broadway to the mammoth "Bird Cage" in granite
at Park Row. As Edmund Burke would exclaim, "O
what a change!" It is gratifying to urge now the destruction of this pile and effect the restoration of the
historic park.

Mr. James served as postmaster under Grant and
Hayes, and became Postmaster General when President
Garfield assumed office on March 4, 1881. He was truly
a genial soul with love for his fellows. In fact, he made
it his business here to personally know fraternally everyone of his clerks and carriers. Their troubles, sorrows,

and joys were his, and he always manifested a desire to improve the conditions of his subordinates, who keenly appreciated his more than paternal solicitude. He seemed to possess the traits of the first Postmaster General, Samuel Osgood, and the initial Federal postmaster Sebastian Bauman. He loved New York and her institutions and constantly proclaimed our city's glory and grandeur. He also introduced the first women in office work, having a room with all comforts and facilities for their performance in those embryo days of merely nominal duties. He was fond of the opera and I often saw him and Mrs. James and their son and two daughters in their box at the Academy of Music during the season of Her Majestys' Opera Company, Henry Mapleson being the impressario. Gladly do I think of them now at the first production in America of "Carmen" with Campanini and Minnie Hauk, Galassi, Del Puente, and others. When the famous tenor came to the office an elaborate luncheon would be sent from the Astor Home to Mr. James' private office. I almost hear again the bouncing corks of Mumms's inspiring nectar.

Many prominent men were among the postmaster's visitors, including Thurlow Weed, ex-Governors Dix and Morgan, Postmaster Generals, Creswell, Tyner, and the imperial Marshall Jewell (peace to his soul), Senators Evarts, Conklin, Platt, General Arthur, then Collector, Carl Schurz, George William Curtis, Dorman B. Eaton, Theodore Roosevelt, father of Civil Service, Joe Howard, Thomas Murphy, Amos Cummings, Whitelaw Reid, Hugh Hastings, Melville Stone, Patrick Ford and the patriarchal James McMaster, editor of the *Freeman's Journal*. Many well known clergymen were his intimate friends, especially Father Mooney, pastor of Saint Brigid's, Tompkins

Square, chaplain of the Sixty-ninth Regiment in the Civil War, and the late Monsignor Brann, Rector of Saint Agnes, where Mr. James occasionally appeared, though a communicant of the Church of the Heavenly Rest, from which he was buried a few years ago.

There are two niches in the Post Office on Eighth Avenue, one of which we ardently pray will some day be adorned with the imperishable figure of this good and faithful servant of the Government, of whom it can be recorded:

> "None knew him but to love him,
> Nor named him but to praise."

North side of Warren Street, showing site of Stewart's old cafe, of beloved memory.
From a rare Stephenson print. 1853.

The Governor addressing the audience in City Hall Park.

THE SONS OF THE REVOLUTION CELEBRATE FLAG DAY

Third Anniversary

Three years have already passed since the Sons of the Revolution restored the ancient Liberty Pole to City Hall Park. As is now the custom of the Society, the Flag Day celebration was held at the Liberty Pole, under the supervision of Director-General James Mortimer Montgomery, assisted by President Robert Olyphant, Mr. Geo. A. Zabriskie, and other officers of the Sons.

The guest of the day was Gov. Lee Trinkle of Virginia, who came to lay the first of the stones which are to form the base of the pole. The stone chosen for this interesting ceremony was taken from the house of General Henry

The Veteran Artillery Corps in the procession.

and was a door step leading to the headquarters of General Cornwallis during the Battle of Yorktown.

The plan of the base of the Liberty Pole is to have around it as an inner circle one stone from each of the thirteen original states, and for an outer circle, one stone from each of the states that have been formed since the Revolution. So for many years to come we shall see a distinguished gathering at this historic spot. In 1924 we will probably see the Governors of North Carolina and South Carolina as guests of the Society for this purpose.

The Gloria Trumpeters rendered an excellent program. A thousand school children sang "Carry Me Back to Ole Virginia" and other patriotic songs. The orator of the day was the Governor of Virginia, and his eloquent remarks were listened to with great interest and greeted with applause.

This yearly celebration is now attracting widespread attention throughout the country, and the Sons have rendered a singularly important service, by this annual observance. The ceremonies were preceded by a colorful parade headed by the Police Band, from Fraunces Tavern, the headquarters of the Sons. Delegations from St. Nicholas Society, Tammany Society, Society of Colonial Wars, Sons of the American Revolution, Daughters of the American Revolution, and many other patriotic organizations participated. This annual parade has become one of the most interesting sights that New York provides, and when the strains of the Police Band are heard, it is a signal for the gathering of many citizens to view it going by.

The Liberty Pole stands exactly on the site of the poles which were cut down during the Revolution. It has the same iron bands which were finally placed around the original to prevent further destruction by British soldiers, who had already cut down no less than six on the same site.

The procession passing Wall Street toward Broadway.

The restoration of this pole is an achievement of which this Society may well feel proud, and its influence is felt throughout the whole country. The celebration receives notice in the press in every section of the Union.

Governor Trinkle made a fine impression and our citizens were pleased to greet so distinguished a son of the Old Dominion.

The Governor of Virginia at left; Director-General Montgomery, S.O.R., centre; Mr. George A. Zabriskie, middle-right.

The beautiful Audubon Quadrangle, the home of the Hispanic Society, the Indian Museum, Heye Foundation, the American Geographical, the American Society of Arts and Letters and the Numismatic Society, Broadway between One Hundred and Fifty-fifth and One Hundred and Fifty-sixth Streets.

Washington arriving at New York for his Inauguration,
April, 1789.

WASHINGTON IN NEW YORK

By Willis Holly
Sec'y to the Society of Tammany

You have all heard that the object of the formation of
the Society of Tammany was to uphold and support General Washington and President Washington against
aristocrats and aristocratic tendencies. I remember that
the lamented Sachem Lynn, who was so long our mentor,
guide and friend, as well as our inspiration, in matters
of patriotic moment, read such a meaning into the chronicles of the evolution of the Society of Tammany. He
held that it grew out of the activities of the Liberty Boys
and their popular demonstrations of anti-British sentiment.

So accurate and painstaking a historian as Moncure D. Conway accepts this theory in one of the chapters he contributed to James Grant Wilson's *Memorial History of New York*. I find that in considering the personnel of those connected with those earlier deeds of defiance and those concerned in the establishment of the Society of Tammany we come upon the same names. They must have referred to the identical individuals and thus we may take pride in a related and connected part in the stirring events of our City's history while those events were dominated by the presence here of the Great Washington.

This enables us to support the claim that the Society of Tammany was established so that our predecessors in its membership could hold up the hands of Washington as the hands of Moses were held up by the Children of Israel. In further support, we find that Washington, in the formative days of the Nation, put all of his strength and influence with his fellow-men behind the contention that the declaration of the equality of all men, meant just exactly that and he welcomed the assistance and support of every element in the great body of our citizenship. We enjoy, therefore, the honor that substantially the whole of our earlier membership was with and of the people whose fidelity and loyalty were Washington's reliance, under the Divine Providence to which he ascribed the power and the glory of his every achievement. They were thoroughly identified with all Revolutionary and pre-Revolutionary patriotic activities.

An illuminating instance of the historical fact that the membership of the Society of Tammany was recruited from among the militant patriots of those strenuous days is revealed in the list of the signers of the address to

Washington adopted by the citizens at a public meeting in New York in 1783. There were thirteen names signed to the address "at the request of the meeting." Of these thirteen, we find that four men, William Gilbert, Ephraim Brashier, Samuel Broome and Pat Dennis were afterward conspicuous in the organization of the Society of Tammany. The two first named were Sachems at a later period. The same proportion of four to thirteen in the body at the meeting would go far to shape its pur-

Where Washington was inaugurated, 1789. Federal Hall, corner Wall and Nassau Streets, present site Sub-Treasury Building

pose and control its sentiment. The men named all joined the Society in 1789, the year of its incorporation, the year that Washington became President of the United States. There are records of the organization in 1787 and traces even earlier, of the association of the men who organized it. This is only one of the many indications which support the claim that our institution was a force with a worth-while meaning to Washington in those days of trial and doubt.

The occasion of the address referred to was a meeting to celebrate the return of New York to the New Yorkers, the City having been given up so long and so largely to British and Tory occupancy and the accompaniment of Refugee tenancy from all the Colonies. In that period, however, a leaven of loyal American citizenship had remained in the city and had constituted a continual thorn in the sides of the Red Coats and their commanders. Among them, also, the spirit and the persons of the founders of the Society of Tammany appeared prominently. The address is not too long to be quoted here and it is an interesting exemplification of the thought and sentiment of the times.

> To His Excellency, George Washington, Esquire, General and Commander-in-Chief of the Armies of the United States of America.
>
> The address of the Citizens of New York, who have returned from Exile, in behalf of themselves and their Suffering Brethren:
>
> SIR:
>
> At a moment when the arm of Tyranny is yielding up its fondest Usurpations, we hope the salutations of long suffering Exiles, but now Happy Freemen, will not be deemed an unworthy tribute. In this place and at this moment of exultation and triumph, while the ensigns of slavery still linger in our sight, we look to you, our deliverer, with unusual transports of Gratitude and Joy. Permit us to welcome you to this City, long torn from us by the hand of Oppression, but now, by your wisdom and energy, under the guidance of Providence, once more the seat of Peace and Freedom. We forbear to speak our gratitude or your praise; we should but echo the voice of applauding millions. But the citizens of New York are eminently indebted to your virtues and we who now have the honour to address your Excellency, have often been the witnesses of your exertions and the companions of your sufferings. Permit us, therefore, to approach your Excellency with the dignity and sincerity of Freemen, and to assure you that we shall preserve with our latest breath our Gratitude for your services and veneration for your character. And accept of our sincere

and earnest wishes that you may long enjoy that calm domestic felicity which you have so generously sacrificed; that the cries of Injured Liberty may never more interrupt your repose and that your happiness may be equal to your virtues.

New York, November 26, 1783.

The enemy had evacuated the city on the previous day, but its army was still this side of Sandy Hook aboard of the British war ships and transports.

Washington's acknowledgment of and response to this address is not less interesting and characteristic.

GENTLEMEN:

I thank you sincerely for your affectionate address and entreat you to be persuaded that nothing could be more agreeable to me than your polite congratulations. Permit me, in turn, to felicitate you on the happy repossession of your City. Great as your Joy must be on this pleasing occasion, it can scarcely exceed that which I feel at seeing you Gentlemen, who from the noblest motives have suffered a voluntary exile of many years, return again in Peace and Triumph to enjoy the fruits of your virtuous conduct.

The fortitude and perseverance which you and your suffering brethren have exhibited in the course of the War, have not only endeared you to your Countrymen, but will be remembered with admiration and applause to the latest posterity.

May the tranquility of your City be perpetual—may its ruins soon be repaired—Commerce flourish, Science be fostered, and all the civil and social virtues be cherished in the same illustrious manner which formerly reflected so much credit on the inhabitants of New York. In fine Gentlemen, may every species of felicity attend you, and your worthy fellow citizens.

These letters remind me that there can be nothing of greater value in fixing upon an accurate estimate of the character, personality and high minded patriotism of Washington than to follow closely the papers which contain in his own handwriting the views he conveyed in private correspondence and public documents. In that conception I shall read another one of his letters to the people of New York. It is all the more of interest to us because it is taken by some historians to have been the origin of the designation of New York as the Empire State. I think that this is a rather strained construction. Washington's reference seems to be very plainly to a temporary condition and one which proved to be quite brief. New York State's title to the designation of the Empire State seems to me to rest more securely upon its broad domain, its wealth of products of nature and of manufacture and its position in art, science and education. This letter of Washington's was written in response to the presentation of the freedom of the City which was one of the many public honors showered on him between the time of the close of the war and his election to the Presidency of the United States of America.

To the Honorable, the Mayor, the Recorder, Aldermen and Commonalty of the City of New York.

GENTLEMEN:

I received your address and the freedom of the City with which you have been pleased to present me in a golden box, with the sensibility and gratitude which such distinguished honors have a claim to. The flattering expressions of both, stamps value upon the acts and call for stronger language than I am master of to convey my sense of the obligation in adequate terms.

To have had the good fortune amid the vicissitudes of a long and arduous contest "never to have known a moment when I did not possess the confidence and esteem of my Country" and that my conduct should have met the approbation and obtained the affectionate regard of the State of New York (where difficulties were numerous and complicated) may be ascribed more to the effect of Divine Wisdom, which had disposed the minds of the people, harassed on all sides, to make allowances for the embarrassments of my situation, whilst with fortitude and patience they sustained the loss of their Capital and a valuable part of their territory, and to the liberal sentiments and great exertions of her virtuous citizens, than to any merit of mine.

I pray that Heaven may bestow its choicest blessing upon your City—that the devastations of war, in which you found it, may soon be without a trace—that a well regulated and beneficial commerce may enrich your citizens and that your State (at present the seat of the Empire) may set such examples of wisdom and liberality as shall have a tendency to give permanency to the Union at home and credit and respectability to it abroad, the accomplishment of which is a remaining wish and the primary object of all my desires.

With Washington as President and New York as the seat of the government of the Nation we come upon a chapter full of interest from the standpoint of our City and of our Society of Tammany. Here he confirmed and added to the great impression he had already made upon the Country as a Statesman and a Patriot, undimmed even by the glory of the record he had made as a soldier. Here he continued to display his remarkable qualities, his high dignity without austerity, his pure piety without narrowness and his strong leadership.

Fraunces' Tavern, Broad and Pearl Streets, where Washington took farewell of his officers, 1784

THE FIRST ATTEMPT TO INTRODUCE RUNNING WATER INTO THE HOUSES OF NEW YORK

1774.—The proposal of Christopher Colles, heretofore preferred to this Board respecting the building of a Reservoir and the conveyance of fresh water through the city, being under consideration, it was resolved that it be carried into execution.

Messrs. Augustus and Frederick Van Cortland offered to convey to the Corporation sufficient ground, fronting Great Gorge Street, (now Broadway, above Chambers Street,) as might be necessary for the Reservoir, at the rate of £600 per acre, which being thought reasonable, it was resolved to purchase the same, provided that upon sinking a well there, the water should be found of good quality.

Having subsequently tried the experiment of digging a well, and judging the water to be of a very good quality, the Corporation resolved to carry out the plan, and to issue notes to the amount of £2,500, to be drawn up in the following sums, 4,000 of sixpense, (£100,) 4,000 of one shilling each, (£200,) 4,000 of two shillings (£400,) 4,000 of four shilling, (£800,) and 2,500 of eight shillings, (£1,000;) and Mr. Colles was directed to enlarge the well and go on with the work.

The Board soon after entered into a contract with parties at Albany for 60,000 feet of pitch-pine timber, for the making of pipes for the water works, for the sum of £1,250. The land purchased for the purpose, (about two acres,) was paid for. The sum of £1,000 was advanced to Colles in 1774, and in 1775 £600. In January, 1776, the Board allowed Mr. Colles £10 per month toward his support. In March, 1776, new notes, to the amount of £2,000, were issued toward defraying the expense of the water works. The works were completed about April, 1776, and Mr. Colles was appointed to take charge of them, at £6 per month. This Reservoir stood on the present east side of Broadway, between Pearl and White Streets.

LAST OF THE KISSING BRIDGE ON THE OLD BOSTON POST ROAD,
NOW FIFTIETH STREET AND SECOND AVENUE.

MANNERS AND CUSTOMS IN
DUTCH NEW YORK

About the only Dutch custom aside from Christmas, which was continued till the end of the last century, was that of New Years Calls, described at length elsewhere in these pages. The following account of other social pastimes in Dutch New York are worth recalling.

The Dutch kept five festivals, of peculiar notoriety, in the year, say Kerstrydt, (Christmas;) Nieuw jar, (New year,) a great day of cake; Paas, (the Passover;) Pinxter, (*i. e.* Whitsuntide;) and San Claas, (*i. e.* Saint Nicholas, or Christ-kinkle day.) The negroes on Long Island, on some of those days, came in great crowds to Brooklyn, and held their field frolics. The observances of New Year day (Nieuw jar) is an occasion of much good feeling and hospitality, come down to the present generation from their Dutch forefathers. No other city in the Union ever aims at the like general interchange of visits. Cakes, wines and punch abound in every house; and, from morning till night, houses are open to receive the calls of acquaintances, and to pass the mutual salutations of a "happy new year," &c. It was the general practice of families in middle life to spin and make much of their domestic wear at home. Short gowns and petticoats were the general in-door dresses. Young women who dressed gay, to go abroad to visit, or to church, never failed to take off that dress, and put on their home-made, as soon as they got home; even on Sunday evenings, when they expected company, or even their beaux, it was their best recommendation to seem thus frugal, and ready for any domestic avocation. The boys and young men of a family always changed their dress for a common dress in the same way. There was no custom of offering drink to their guests; when punch was offered, it was in great bowls.

Dutch dances were very common; the supper on such occasions was a pot of chocolate and bread. The Rev. Dr. Laidlie, who arrived in 1764, did much to preach them into disuse. He was very exact in his piety, and was the first minister of the Dutch Reformed Church who was called to preach in the English language. The negroes used to dance in the markets, where they used tomtoms, horns, &c., for music. They used often to sell negro slaves at the coffee-house. All marriages had to be published beforehand, three weeks at the churches, or else, to avoid that, they had to purchase a license of the governor—a seemingly singular surveillance for a great military chief. We may presume he cared little for the fact, beyond his fee.

Before the Revolution, tradesmen of good repute worked hard; there were none, as masters, mere lookers-on; they hardly expected to be rich; their chief concern, in summer, was to make enough ahead to lay up carefully for a living in severe winter. Wood was even a serious concern to such, when only 2s. 6d. to 3s. a load. None of the stores or tradesmen's shops then aimed at any rivalry, as now. There were no glaring allurements at windows, no over-reaching sign, no big bulk windows; they were content to sell things at honest profits, and to trust to an earned reputation for their share of business. It was the English-men from Britain who brought in the painted glass and display. They also brought in the use of open shops at night, an expensive and needless service, for who sells more in day and night, where all are competitors, than they would in one day, if all were closed at night? In former days, the same class who applied diligently in business hours, were accustomed to close their shops and stores at an early hour, and to go abroad for exercise and recrea-tion, or to gardens, &c. All was done on foot, for chaises and horses were few.

The candidates for the Assembly, usually from the city, kept open houses in each ward for one week, producing much excitement among those who thought more of the regale than the public weal.

Physicians in that day were moderate in their charges, although their personal labor was great. They had to make all their calls on foot—none thought of riding. Drs. Baylie and McKnight, when old, were the first who are remembered as riding to their patients. Dr. Attwood is remembered as the physician who had the hardihood to proclaim himself as a man midwife; it was deemed a scandal to some delicate ears, and Mrs. Grany Brown, with her fees of two or three dollars, was still deemed the choice of all who thought women should be modest.

Moving-day was, as now, the first of May from time immemorial. They held no fairs, but they often went to the Philadelphia fairs, once celebrated. At the New Year and Christmas festivals, it was the custom to go out to the ice on Beekman's and such like swamps, to shoot at

Broadway, the Main Street in

From a contemporary sketch. Looking south from St. Paul's (at right)

ge as it appeared in 1835.

awnings and the apparent width of the street due to the low buildings.

turkeys; every one paid a price for his shot, as at a mark, and if he hit it so as to draw blood, it was his for a New Year or Christmas dinner. A fine subject this for Dr. Laidlie's preaching and reformation. At funerals, the Dutch gave hot wine in winter, and in summer they gave wine sangaree. I have noticed a singular custom among Dutch families—a father gives a bundle of goose quills to a son, telling him to give one to each of his male posterity.

I saw one in the possession of Mr. James Bogert, which had a scroll appended, saying: "This quill, given by Petrus Byranck to James Bogert, in 1789, was a present, in 1689, from his grandfather, from Holland."

It is now deemed a rule of high life in New York, that ladies should not attend funerals; it was not always so. Having been surprised at the change, and not being aware of any sufficient reason why females should have an exemption from personal attention to departed friends, from which their male relatives could not, I have been curious to inquire into the facts in the case. I find that females among the Friends attend funerals, and also among some other religious communities. I have been well assured that, before the Revolution, the genteelest families had ladies to their funerals, and especially if it was a female's. On such occasions, "burnt wine" was handed about in tankards, often of silver. On one occasion—the case of the wife of Daniel Phœnix, the City Treasurer—all the pallbearers were ladies, and this fact occurred since the Revolution.

Many aged persons have spoken to me of the former delightful practice of families sitting out on their "stoops," in the shades of the evening, and there saluting the passing friends, or talking across the narrow streets with neighbors. It was one of the grand links of union in the Knickerbocker social compact. It endeared and made social neighbors made intercourse on easy terms. It was only to say come, sit down. It helped the young to easy introductions, and made courtships of readier attainment. I give some facts to illustrate the above remarks, deduced from the family of B——, with which I am personally acquainted. It shows primitive Dutch manners. His grandfather died at the age of sixty-three, in 1782, holding the office of alderman eleven years, and once chosen mayor and declined. Such a man, in easy circumstances in life, following the true Dutch custom, had all his family to breakfast, all the year round, at day-light. Before the breakfast, he universally smoked his pipe. His family always dined at twelve exactly. At that time, the kettle was invariably set on the fire for tea, of Bohea, which was always as punctually furnished at three o'clock. Then the old people went abroad, on purpose to visit relatives, changing the families each night in succession, over and over again, all the year round. The regale at every such house was expected, as matter of course, to be chocolate supper and soft waffles. Afterward, when green tea came in as a new luxury, loaf-sugar also came with it; this was broken in large lumps, and laid severally by each cup, and was nibbled or bitten, as needed. The family before referred to actually continued the practice till as late as seventeen years ago, with a steady determination in the patriarch to resist the modern innovation of dissolved sugar while he lived.

Besides the foregoing facts, I have had them abundantly confirmed by others. While they occupied the stoops in the evening, you could see, every here and there, an old Knickerbocker, with his long pipe, fuming away his cares, and ready, on any occasion, to offer another for the use of any passing friend who would sit down and join him. The ideal picture has every lineament of contented comfort and cheerful repose—something much more composed and happy than the bustling anxiety of over-business "in the moderns."

The cleanliness of Dutch housewifery was always extreme; everything had to submit to scrubbing and scouring; dirt in no form could be endured by them, and, as water was in the city, where it was generally sold, still it was in perpetual requisition. It was their honest pride to see a well-furnished dresser, showing copper and pewter in shining splendor, as if for ornament, rather than for use. In all this they widely differed from the Germans—a people with whom they have been erroneously and often confounded. Roost-fowls and ducks are not more different; as water draws one, it repels the other. It was common in families then to cleanse their own chimneys, without the aid of hired sweeps, and all tradesmen, &c., were accustomed to saw their own fuel. No man in middle circumstances of life ever scrupled to carry home his one hundred weight of meal from the market; it would have been his shame to have avoided it. A greater change in the state of society cannot be named than that of hired persons.

Hired women, from being formerly lowly in dress, wearing short gowns of green baize, and petticoats of linsey-woolsey, and receiving but half a dollar a week, have, since they have trebled that wages, got to all the pride and vanity of showing out to strangers as well-dressed ladies. The cheapness of foreign finery gives them the ready means of wasting all their wages in decorations. So true it is, that the Quarterly Review has preserved one fact of menial impudence, in the case of the New York girl, telling her mis-

On the way to Gracie Mansion. The elegant residence and garden of N. W. Stuyvesant, between First and Second Avenues. All the upper East Side in Eighth Street, between First and Second Avenues. All the upper East Side in these days had beautiful country homes, 1857.

tress, before her guest, "the more you ring, the more I won't come."

General La Fayette, too, left us a compliment of dubious import, on his late formal entree at New York, when, seeing such crowds of well-dressed people, and no remains of such as he had seen in the period of the Revolution—a people whose dress was adapted to their condition—he exclaimed, "But where is the people "—emphatically meaning, where is the useful class of citizens, the hewers of wood and drawers of water. Before the Revolution, all men who worked in any employ, always wore his leathern apron before him, never took it off to go in the street, and never had on a long coat.

COLLECT OR FRESH WATER POND

Site of the New County Court House.
A Sketch of Its Early History.

The beautiful lake, at various periods of our history, known by the appellations above named, has been at different times mentioned in the previous editions of the *Manual*, and some accounts of its early history have been casually given. The object of the present article is to show the manner and the time when it was obliterated from the topography of the city by the inevitable process of "filling in and improving;" certainly, the least interesting memento of its existence, except in the practical light, which enables us to appreciate the changes from ancient to modern times.

The Collect is presented in old maps, on which its outlines are laid down, but its peculiar topographical features —the noble hills rising abruptly from its sides, the groves upon its borders, the blackberry wilds, which covered the surrounding hills, in many parts, the depth and purity of its waters—these are not brought to mind by maps, and their illustration must be by description or pictorial views.

It will not be regarded as a "twice told tale," if we review its earlier condition, and before recounting its destruction, we show its antecedent history, from the primitive time when it rested in placid beauty, surrounded by the wilderness alone, or the rude fields of Indian culture, to the time when the march of civilization progressed towards its borders, and they became the seat of mechanical industry, and finally to the time when its depths received the earth of the surrounding eminences, and its former site was embraced within the populated parts of the city.

There is little doubt that on the western borders of this lake was situated an Indian village, probably a favorite home of the fierce "Manhattans," described by Hudson, in his itinerary of the discovery of the river called after his name. They appear to have been a nomadic tribe, depending less upon the cultivation of the soil than upon the more precarious methods of subsistence by hunting and fishing. In all the early history of the Christian settlers, no indication is made of the locality of Indian settlements on this island, except from inference. Deposits of shells, which invariably indicate a native settlement, were abundantly strewn over the hill, on the western side of the lake, and gave to that promontory, in early times, the Dutch

The Hudson River at Hoboken, when the Elysian fields stretched to the shore front. About 1850.

name of the "Katchhook," or, as translated, "Lime-Shell Point."

The waters of this little lake were of great depth, and of unusual purity. One of its principal fountains, afterwards well known as "the tea water spring," supplied a population of ten or twelve thousand inhabitants with water for their favorite beverage. Other, but smaller brooks, trended from different valleys between the surrounding hills, and preserved its pellucid depths. A sparkling brook carried off its waters into the East River while, towards the North River, stretched a marsh, covering several score of acres, through which streamlets from this pond percolated.

For more than a hundred years after the Christian settlement of the island, fish were abundant in the "Fresh-Water Pond," and were even caught by nets during all that period. By an ordinance of the Common Council, in 1734, it was ordered "that if any person or persons whatsoever do from henceforth presume to put, place or cast into the pond, commonly called Fresh-Water Pond, belonging to this Corporation, any hoop-net, draw-net, purse-net, casting-net, cod-net, bley-net, or any other net or nets whatsoever, and shall take and catch any of the fish within the said pond therewith, or by any other engine, machine, arts, ways or means whatsoever, other than by angling with angle rod, hook and line only, every person so offending against the tenor of this law shall, for every offence, forfeit and pay the sum of twenty shillings current money."

The ownership of this pond was for some time a matter of dispute. It was claimed by the city, as a part of the "unpatented" lands, granted to them by the Dongan Charter, in 1686. About the year 1694, however, Governor Fletcher granted the pond, together with the adjacent meadows, embracing in all about seventy acres, to one John Evans. This grant was, however, annulled in 1698, by act of assembly.

In 1730, Anthony Rutgers, who owned the greater part of the Katchhook, on the western borders of the pond, petitioned the King in Council for a grant of the swamp and pond, which was granted in 1733.

The conflicting claims between the Corporation and Rutgers' representatives were settled in the year 1791, by the latter executing a release of the pond for the consideration of one hundred and fifty pounds, paid by the Corporation.

After the Revolutionary War, the question as to what should be the permanent regulation of the pond, occasioned discussion. The progress of the city had already formed a considerable settlement around the borders of the pond, and considerable encroachments were made upon its boundaries. The Corporation, therefore, caused a survey of its ancient lines to be made, which was completed in 1790. For the purpose of quieting any question as to the title to the ground under water, it was thought advisable, before adopting any policy in relation to its permanent regulation, to purchase the interest of the Rutgers' heirs. This was effected in the year 1791, the sum before mentioned being paid for a release of their interest. The title thus becoming indisputably in the Corporation, they had the boundaries of the pond staked off to prevent encroachments, and surveys were ordered, with a view to laying out streets, when the pond should be filled in.

Several plans were presented for the permanent regulation of the locality; among others was one, presented in 1766, by Monsieur Mangin, a French engineer, who was then one of the leading men in his profession in the city. His proposition was to make a dock or basin, in the deep water of the Collect, as a harbor for shipping, and to communicate with both the North and East Rivers by means of a canal of some forty feet in width.

It was concluded, however, in the following year, not to construct a basin, but to fill in the Collect, the question of a canal being still left open. About the year 1800, the work of filling in the Collect was commenced, and was continued about ten years. The general plan adopted in this work, was to pay five cents per load for earth, delivered and dumped into the pond.

The long time occupied in this labor, occasioned a serious inconvenience to the neighborhood, and the pond, in place of its original beautiful appearance, became a nuisance and an eye-sore; dead animals and every species of rubbish and offal were thrown into it, and occasioned an insufferable stench. In connection with this subject, it was thought advisable not only to fill up the pond with the cleanest and best earth which could be obtained, but to dig out the bottom, or sediment soil of the pond, which was found to extend to a great depth, and to be composed of decomposed vegetable matter, similar to peat or turf. A great quantity of this soil having been dug out, the question of making it remunerative, by converting it into fuel, was suggested, and during the summer of 1808, many laborers were employed upon this labor, but from some reason it was discontinued after a month or two.

To recur to the project of a canal, which, as before intimated, was proposed to be constructed from the North to the East Rivers, passing through the Collect Pond. This subject was elaborately discussed during several years. In 1805, a committee, to whom the subject had been referred, reported that they had maturely considered the subject of extending a canal or tunnel from the North to the East Rivers, through the fresh-water pond and the meadows adjacent, for the purpose of carrying off the water from the streets that descend thereto, and that they considered that "the only practicable method that can be adopted to produce the desired effect, without injuring the health of the city." The distance between the two rivers is one hundred and four chains and forty links, or 6,830 feet, and the greatest elevation of ground above low water is twelve feet nine inches. The difference of the time of high water in the two rivers, will give a head of water of about sixteen inches every tide, to carry off such filth as might have entered the tunnel. The committee estimated the cost of construction at an average of eight dollars per foot, or about fifty-four thousand dollars in all. They recommended an ordinance, "for the construction of a tunnel to extend on a level from the East to the North River, one foot above low-water mark, and the internal diameter of which should be six feet in the clear."

It remains to say, on the subject of the canal or tunnel, that after some further consideration, it was decided not to communicate in that manner between the rivers. Various projects of open ditches, etc., were next proposed, and for a temporary period were adopted. For some time an open ditch ran through the street then filled up, and called Collect Street (now Centre Street). The springs around the pond rendered some regulation of this kind necessary. Even as late as 1811, the subject was considered, "how far it would be proper to fill up the Collect, and whether it would not be expedient to leave some of the springs or fountains of it open." But in 1816, we find an ordinance for the regulating and paving of Collect Street; some years before that, the lots had been to some extent improved, and an humble class of buildings were erected on the site of the Collect Pond.

The old springs were uncovered during the excavation for the present Court House and caused considerable trouble before their origin was traced and finally capped. The water was distinctly different in taste and much harder. It was probably this quality which rendered it popular for tea drinking. We follow with some other valuable items concerning this famous Pond and the neighborhood immediately adjoining.

1792.—*Ordered,* That Mr. Carmer be added to the committee appointed to treat with the executors of Mrs. Barclay, deceased, as to the purchasing of the meadow lying between the Corporation lot and the Fresh Water Pond; and that the said committee purchase so much of the said meadow as they shall deem expedient; and that they direct the Fresh Water Pond to be staked off so as to prevent encroachments thereon.

1793.—*Ordered,* That a survey be made of the land and meadows at and about the Fresh Water Pond, with the streets which may be necessary marked thereon.

1791.—The Committee on the subject of the Fresh Water Pond made a verbal report, whereupon it was resolved to be expedient to purchase the right of the representatives of Anthony Rutgers, deceased, to the said pond for the sum of £150, at which price it might be obtained; and the same Committee were authorized to treat for the purchase of the slip of meadow on the north-west side of the pond, which the Board also thought it expedient to purchase. The purchase of the soil under water was soon after consummated.

1796.—*Ordered,* That the Committee on the subject of a canal from the Fresh Water Pond to the Hudson river, be instructed to confer with the proprietors of the Swamp for the obtaining such parts thereof as may be required to make the said canal of the breadth of forty feet, and a street on each side of the breadth of thirty feet.

A great Dock for Shipping proposed to be made in the Fresh Water Pond

1796.—A project or proposal of Mons. Mangin and Brother, engineers, for making a dock or basin in the low grounds at the Fresh Water Pond, as a safe harbor for shipping, and to drain and carry off the water from that quarter into the river, was read and ordered to be taken into consideration, with the subject of the contemplated canal from the Fresh Water Pond into Hudson River.

The Island in the Pond surveyed

1797.—*Ordered,* That the ground belonging to the Corporation in the vicinity of the old Powder Magazine be surveyed and staked out, and that the same be filled up to a proper height.

Encroachments on the Fresh Water Pond, or Collect

1787.—It being represented to the Board that encroachments were daily made on the Fresh Water Pond, and that filth and dirt were thrown into it by persons residing there. Ordered that a Committee examine into the matter and report to the Board.

The Condition of the "Old Tea Water Pump"

1797.—A petition against the inconvenience arising from the spout of the tea water pump projecting over the street, was presented, and referred.

The Committee subsequently reported as follows: "The Committee on the subject of the petition complaining of the obstruction in Chatham Street, caused by the tea water pump delivering its water in the street, and by the water carts being drawn up across the street, when about to receive water; report, that they have viewed the premises, and find the matters and things set forth in the petition to be true. That the Committee have maturely considered the premises, and are of opinion that the said obstruction may be removed at no great expense to Mr. Thompson, the present occupant, and part proprietor of the premises, by causing the spout of the said pump to be raised about two feet, and by lengthening it so as to deliver the water at the outer part of the paved walk, which would permit foot passengers to pass under without inconvenience; and if the water carts were ordered to draw up abreast of the spout, near the gutter, and receive the water in rotation, it would remove the obstruction in the street. The Committee recommend, also, that the sidewalks in that vicinity be paved." Their recommendations were adopted except the paving, which was postponed for the time being.

SOME EARLY HOUSES OF LUXURY
IN NEW YORK

The great style in which William Walton (of the Walton House, Pearl Street), lived, has often been mentioned in connection with our domestic history. It was said, that when, in answer to the petition of grievances of some of our people to Parliament, a member stated that the complaints were of an imaginary character, that he had traveled and been entertained in New York, and had seen in the houses of some citizens a display of plate and a style of life that would have been respectable in the establishment of an English nobleman; and it was supposed that in this he had reference to the family of William Walton, whose mansion, erected about the year 1760, was removed to make room for the Brooklyn Bridge. Mr. Walton was one of those merchants who, during the French War, suddenly acquired great wealth by fortunate maritime ventures. Several other private residences, upon a similar scale, were erected about the same period, in different parts of the city, but only one or two approached in style that of Mr. Walton. Some indications of the furniture of this establishment have come down to us, though our account has reference to a later period than that at which it exhibited its early magnificence.

The principal rooms were furnished with silk damask and green worsted curtains, mahogany card-tables and stands, mahogany dining-tables, mahogany chairs, with damask seats; ditto, with hair seats; green Windsor chairs, three large walnut gilt-framed looking-glasses, a large number of prints, framed and glazed, besides a large quantity of the ordinary articles of domestic furniture, which need not be enumerated.

The silver-plate of the family was composed of the following articles:

Two pair of silver candlesticks..weight, 81¼ ounces		
One silver snuffers-stand	"	11¼	"
One large silver waiter................	"	32	"
Two small silver waiters............	"	15½	"
Two pint-mugs	"	21¾	"
Two pint-bowls	"	12½	"
Two sauce-boats	"	29	"
Four salts, and four shovels......	"	12½	"
Twenty tea-spoons		

One sugar-tongs ....weight,	1	ounce
One small chafing-dish................	"	1	"
One small punch-ladle.................	"	½	"
One wine-cock	"	5	ounces
Two table-spoons	"	4½	"
One tankard	"	31¾	"
One punch-strainer	"	1¼	"
One coffee-pot	"	28	"
One large soup-spoon................	"	8	"
One large tankard	"	44	"
Two large cases of knives, forks, and spoons.....................			

Peter Jacobs Marius may be said to be the surviving representative of the Dutch merchants of New Amsterdam. He carried on business at the same place and pretty much in the same style in which he had been wont to do in the palmy days of the Dutch city, fifty years before the period now spoken of. He outlived his companions in the Board of Schepens, and saw another generation of natives of his adopted city grow old, and adopt new tastes and habits under the countenance of a foreign nation. Mynheer Marius was a magistrate of New Amsterdam for several years. At that time he was a merchant on the south side of Pearl Street, between the present Whitehall and State streets, and there he continued to reside, and carry on business for fifty years subsequently. He neither altered his habits of life, nor the character or extent of his business, but vegetated to maturity in a respectable manner, unmindful of the changes which successive years exhibited on all sides around him. Peace be to the memory of the last of the Knickerbockers!

The premises occupied by Mr. Marius were, in the year 1700, a one-story house, the same originally built upon the lot on which it stood, with an extension kitchen, which had been added on the side of the house at a subsequent period. The little shop of merchandise occupied the front room of the house. It was composed of small groceries and a few dry goods, the whole not exceeding in value three or four hundred dollars. In the chief room in the rear of the shop the following articles were enumerated: Eight muslin sheets, twenty-three linen sheets, thirty-two pillow cases, two linen table-cloths, seven diaper table-cloths, sixty-one diaper napkins, three Ozenberg napkins, sixteen small linen cupboard-cloths, one silver tankard, three silver salt-cellars, two silver beakers, silver mustard-pot and spoons, twenty-seven silver sweetmeat spoons, four silver tumblers, nine silver cups with two ears, one old-fashioned salver, a silver mug and cover, a baby's silver chafing-dish and cradle, a silver fork and cup, a parcel of buttons and other broken silver; three gold chains, six gold rings, three gold buckles, four pairs of gold buttons, a gold bodkin and gold ear-wire, two pairs gold pendants, two gold and diamond rings, one amber necklace, two silver-handled knives, one pair of silver-handled scissors, a small Dutch Bible, tipped with silver and a chain. The standing furniture in the same room consisted of a black-framed looking-glass, sixteen small pictures, a black-walnut table with its rug or carpet, six Turkey-leather chairs, one blue elbow chair, thirteen old matted chairs, a red cedar chest, an old-fashioned clock, a brass warming-pan, stool cushions, old and new; a bedstead, bed and bedding; three blue curtains for the windows, a money scale and weights, a large Dutch Bible, tipped with brass, and two pairs of bellows.

In the great kitchen, were a chest, four books, a table, a cupboard, a trammel, a lantern, a porringer, and a mortar and pestle.

In the upper chamber, above the great kitchen, were eight black-walnut chairs, covered with blue; a black-walnut table, with its carpet; a large cedar chest, a red cedar cupboard, an old-fashioned linen press, a bedstead, with blue curtains and valance, with bed and bed clothes; eight pictures, a calico valance for the chimney, a green and flowered table-cloth, a blue chest-cloth, two green curtains, and the family table ware and cooking utensils.

There were, besides these rooms, one or two others made under the roof, which could be used as sleeping rooms, and this composed the whole establishment, except the slave-house and kitchen in the yard.

Mr. Marius was in comfortable circumstances, being considered worth fifteen or twenty thousand dollars.

THE PROVOOST'S

The Provoost family was one of the oldest of the resident inhabitants of the city, and among the male members the most conspicuous during a century were of the Christian name of David, which was that of the original emigrant. This individual came to this city at an early period of the Dutch era, and pursued the occupation of a notary and attorney in the Court of Burgomasters and Schepens.

The memorial of the Provoost family, has been demolished in the course of the street improvements now in progress in that section of the city. It stood in what has in late years been generally known as Jones' Woods, a tract of near an hundred acres, which has been permitted until recently, to exist in its natural condition. This was part of the original Provoost estate; a view of the mansion of the family being also given on another page in this volume. The precise locality of this tomb was on the block inclosed between Avenue A and the East River, and Seventy-first and Seventy-second Streets. We have understood that Mrs. Provoost, one of the tenants of this family tomb, procured the promise of her husband, in anticipation of her decease, that she should be interred upon the estate, and that her husband, in fulfillment of her wishes, erected this substantial sepulchre to her memory. He was himself laid at her side, upon his death, as were several others of the family. The tomb has remained unopened for half a century, until its recent final demolition. Upon effecting an entrance, the vault was found to contain the remains of three or four coffins. The lid of one of these measured over seven feet in length. Among the bones were those of a child, and those of an adult female. There were also found one or two vertebrae, which, from their size, must have belonged to a man much above the ordinary size, and probably were those of the occupant of the large coffin.

His son David was a conspicuous merchant, and an active politician, in those troublesome times which characterized the *Leisler* administration, to which side Mr. Provoost bestowed his adherence. He was subsequently Mayor of the city in the year 1699. The son of this latter gentleman was also a merchant conspicuous for intelligence and enterprise. He was an Alderman for several years, and enjoyed the soubriquet of "Ready-money Provoost." His widow married James Alexander, a lawyer of this city, and became the mother of Lord Stirling, of Revolutionary celebrity.

Captain Kidd, the Pirate.—We have, in some former editions of the Manual, given some account of this famous individual, in which we have stated our conclusions to be, that he was, in great measure, the victim of circumstances, and that, instead of meriting the opprobrious celebrity which is attached to his memory, he was neither possessed of the sanguinary propensities of a blood-thirsty pirate, nor the reckless characteristics of the professional rover, but was, on the whole, rather a gentlemanly and clever man. Certain it is, that as a citizen of New York, he occupied a respectable position, and neither in his domestic relations nor in his personal history previous to the unfortunate voyage of the "Adventure Galley," could aught be said against him. It is not our business here, however, to discuss the moral character of Captain Kidd. We propose to refer to his domestic concerns as a citizen of New York, and to contrast his style of life, while still in the respectable position of captain of the Antigua packet ship,

Portrait of Samuel Fraunces, proprietor of
Fraunces Tavern, Broad and Pearl Streets,
now owned by the Sons of the Revolution.

trading between this port and London, with those of Dutch citizens of equal respectability: such, for instance, as Mayor Rombouts. Captain Kidd married in this city, in 1692, Sarah, the widow of John Oort, a ship captain in regular trade, as was Captain Kidd at that period. Captain Kidd, immediately after his marriage, resided in Hanover Square, then one of the best portions of the town. The domestic furniture of the house occupied by Captain Oort had been purchased in bulk from the representatives of the estate of William Cox, one of the leading flour merchants of the city; and upon the marriage of the widow Oort with Captain Kidd, the style assumed by the happy couple could favorably compare with that of any household establishment in the city. The following description will show in what style he lived: he possessed one dozen Turkey-work chairs, one dozen double-nailed leather chairs, two dozen single-nailed leather chairs, one Turkey-worked carpet, one oval table, three chests of drawers, four looking-glasses, four feather beds, bolsters and pillows; three suits of curtains and valance, four bedsteads, ten blankets, one glass case, one dozen drinking-glasses, four tables, five carpets or rugs, one screen frame, two stands, one desk, two dressing-boxes, three chamber-pots, one close stool, one warming-pan, two bed-pans, three pewter tankards, four kettles, two iron pots, one skillet, three pairs of fire-irons, one pair of andirons, one pair of small andirons, three pairs of tongs, two fire-shovels, two fenders, one spit, one jack, one clock, one coat of arms, three quilts, three rugs, three chafing-dishes, one gridiron, one flesh fork, one brass skimmer, four brass candlesticks, two pewter candlesticks, four tin candlesticks, one brass pestle and iron mortar, two and a half dozen of pewter plates, five pewter basins, thirteen pewter dishes, five leather buckets, one pipe Madeira wine, one half-pipe Madeira wine, two pewter salt-cellars, three box smoothing-irons and six heaters, a parcel of linen sheets, table-cloths and napkins of the value of thirty dollars; one hundred and four ounces of silver plate, of the value of three hundred dollars; a negro woman, valued at seventy-five dollars, and three barrels of pricked cider.

The old Brunswick Hotel. Twenty-sixth Street and Madison Avenue.

FAMOUS NEW YORK HOTELS
OF THE "SEVENTIES"

By James L. Ford

As we grow older we are apt to realize that the most deeply etched and warmly treasured of the memories that have survived the passing years are those connected with places of merriment of good cheer, such as theatres, hotels and restaurants, and I will venture to say that few old New Yorkers do not look back with affectionate regret to the hotels that flourished when they were young and the town was a better place to live in than it is now.

Most of those houses of entertainment have long since made way for the steel and cement skyscrapers, for which the city is famous, but neither they nor the land-lords have been altogether forgotten. There are scores of those hotels that I remember well, far better than I do the counting rooms of the firms with which my employers did business. In no respect has the town undergone more radical change during the past half century than in its manner of entertaining strangers, and as the old customs passed away the old time landlords made way for the corporations and men of large affairs who operate modern caravanseries in businesslike fashion and are, as a general thing, personally unknown to the men and women to whom they give shelter. The old order survives in the word "guest" which has lost its original significance and should have been changed to "customer."

The landlord of the Seventies was a personality, not a corporation. There were families of landlords, too, for hotel-keeping ran in the blood as acting does in the veins

The old St. Germain, on present site of Flatiron Building.

of players. The Stetsons, the Lelands, the Kerrs were of the race that gave "entertainment for man and beast," a term designed to set the biped apart from the quadruped. On the shoulders of each member of those families had fallen the mantle of the old-fashioned country tavern-keeper who knew his guests by sight and greeted the arriving traveler by name and with what well-fed reporters have frequently called a "grasp of the hand with his heart in it." This branch of the business has long since been relegated to the clerk behind the marble counter who is usually a member of the social club appropriately termed "The Greeters."

The hotels of the Seventies were for the most part on Broadway below Twenty-third Street, and were as a rule, more home-like than the modern caravanseries and each one had its special and distinctive clientele. The rooms were larger, and many of them were heated by open fireplaces, but bathrooms were few and far between. The hotel-keepers prided themselves on their food, aiming at the high standard set by Delmonico whose uptown restaurant was then at the northeast corner of Fifth Avenue and Fourteenth Street. I remember that as I walked downtown in the morning I always met Ciro Delmonico returning in a cab from his morning's marketing, a duty that he never entrusted to a subordinate. Another reminder of this famous house awaited me at Bowling Green in the shape of the Stevens House, one of the earliest of the Delmonico ventures and an object of wonder not only because of its good fare but also because of the great size and number of its bathtubs. My father lived there, I think in the Forties, paying four-fifty a week for his room and board, and in later years he considered that the Delmonico kitchen had slightly deteriorated since then. It was in this hostelry that Frank Forrester, one of the earliest writers on American sport, killed himself, and it was here that Midy Morgan, the pioneer newspaper reporter of her sex, worked as a chambermaid.

The Astor House, considered a marvelous edifice at the time of its erection, was the New York abiding place of Daniel Webster, and many of the most distinguished statesmen of his day. It had an open fireplace in every

The old Gilsey House.

one of its rooms and was built around a court with a fountain in the middle; the entire space was afterward utilized for the lunch room. The St. Nicholas Hotel was a distinctively American House and the St. Charles on the other side of the street was patronized almost exclusively by circus people. A little further uptown was the Metropolitan, where Tweed had entertained his friends of the Albany legislature. It was famous for its crystal chandeliers and at the time of its demolition these were purchased by Oscar Hammerstein and placed in the huge amusement building that he erected at Broadway and Forty-fourth Street. What is now the Broadway Central and was then, I believe, called the Grand Central, was regarded as a veritable palace when it was first opened to the public. It was here that Fisk was killed by Stokes and it stands today not only as a reminder of that tragedy but as an interesting relic of hotel-keeping of by-gone days. I believe it is still conducted on the American plan and that throngs of colored waiters roam as of yore, through its vast dining room, bearing trays on the palms of their uplifted hands, an art now extinct elsewhere.

The New York Hotel, also built around an open court, had enjoyed, even during the Civil War, for internment was unknown then, a large Southern patronage and was conducted by Hildreth of later Long Branch renown. The Sinclair House, at the corner of Eighth Street, was famous for its American cookery, sharing honors with the Ashland on Fourth Avenue. Mr. Ashman of the Sinclair and Mr. Brockway of the Ashland were about the last of New York's landlords of the old school. Artemus Ward lived at the Sinclair during his stay in New York as editor of *Vanity Fair*. The St. Denis at the corner of Eleventh Street was popular with citizens and out of town patrons of the better class until the Sullivan clan moved over from their fitting habitat, the Occidental, on the Bowery. What was in later years the Morton House was then the Union Place, the favorite abiding place of players and journalists, a patronage that it enjoyed until the Rialto moved away from Union

Square. Many actors were also to be found at the Union Square Hotel, kept by Andrew J. Dam and his son. The last named dabbled in theatricals and was said to have advanced money to Henry E. Abbey for a small interest in the first Bernhardt season.

On the northern side of Union Square was the Everett House, for years the favorite stopping place of opera singers and musicians, many of whom, Clara Louise Kellogg among the number patronized it until its demolition not many years ago, although grand opera had long since migrated from the Academy of Music to the Metropolitan Opera House. A block further uptown on Fourth Avenue was the Clarendon, which boasted, and not without reason of its aristocratic clientele. It was conducted on the American plan and there was a long table in its dining room where whole families ate together in har-

Famous Windsor Hotel, Fifth Avenue and Forty-seventh Street,

mony. If it possessed a bar I never discovered it, but I doubt if its patrons, many of whom were of the opulent British class, were permitted to go dry. Further north on Fourth Avenue was the Ashland, already mentioned, as the home of excellent American cookery, and beyond that one came upon the Putnam House, kept by Lawrence Kerr, and as popular as the Clarendon though catering to a very different class, among whom were many circus folk from the Madison Square Garden across the way. Following an ancient country custom Mr. Kerr kept a basket of apples on his bar for free munching. At Forty-second Street was the Grand Union, always renowned for its excellent bar and restaurant and in later years for its picture gallery.

Taking up once more the route up Broadway interrupted at Fourteenth Street, we find the Spingler House, built by the family of that name on the west side of Union Square, and a little further north the Continental, where Chester A. Arthur lived in his bachelor days. The St. Germain stood on the site now occupied by the Flatiron Building, and on the west side of the block between Twenty-third and Twenty-fourth Streets was the Fifth Avenue, perhaps the most famous of the city's many hotels. Built on ground once occupied by a country tavern it served during the Civil War as a night exchange for brokers engaged in the frantic speculations in gold that marked that period. Its spacious lobby was to the last a public thoroughfare, thronged at all times by well-to-do citizens and strangers of every profession. It was the New York headquarters of the Republican party who held important conferences and conventions within its walls. When President Grant visited the city, and in those simple days he came from Washington alone

EVERETT HOUSE,

UNION SQUARE.

Dinner at Two and Half-past Five o'clock.

NEW YORK, WEDNESDAY, OCTOBER 5, 1859.

SOUP.
Vermicelli.

FISH.
Baked Bluefish, wine sauce.

BOILED

Leg of Mutton, caper sauce.	Chickens, with Pork.
Corned Beef, with cabbage.	Calf's Head, brain sauce.
Turkey, celery sauce.	Corned Pork with greens.

ROAST

Ribs of Beef.	Spring Chickens.
Lamb, mint sauce.	Capons, stuffed.
Ham, champagne sauce.	Spring Ducks, currant sauce.
Spareribs of Pork.	Beef, a la mode.

Relishes.

Assorted Pickles.   Horseradish.   Lettuce.   Pickled Beets.

ENTREES.

Escalope of Beef, jardinière sauce, à la Sicilienne.
Sweetbreads, larded, green pea sauce, à l'Anglaise.
Blanquette of Veal, lemon sauce, à la Portugaise.
Soft shell Crabs, fried, à l'Americaine.
Fricassée of Chicken, à l'Espagnole.
Apple Fritters, garnished with sugar, à la Romaine.
Broiled Squabs, piquant sauce, à l'Emperatrice.
Mutton Cutlets, breaded, tomato sauce, à la Cavanagh.
Oyster Pies, with fine herbs, à la Belgeoise.
Macaroni, with cheese, à la Napolitaine.

COLD DISHES.

Lobsters.   Ham   Tongue.   Boned Turkeys.   Pressed Corned Beef.

VEGETABLES.

Mashed Potatoes.	Sweet Potatoes.	Beets.	Cauliflower.
Irish Potatoes.	Boiled Onions.	Tomatoes.	Egg Plant.
Lima Beans.	Boiled Rice.	Squash.	Corn.

PASTRY.

French Pudding.	Whortleberry Pies.
Tapioca Pudding.	Lemon Pies.
Custard Pudding.	Pumpkin Pies.
Almond Cakes.	Cinnamon Cakes.

DESSERT,

Walnuts.   Almonds.   Pecan Nuts.   Cheese.
Vergaloo, Bartlett, Princess Royal and Duchess D'Angletaire Pears.   Apples.   Grapes.
Bavarian Cream.   Madeira Jelly.   Coffee.   Vanilla Ice Cream

Parties dining at 2 o'clock, cannot have seats reserved at 5½ o'clock, except by application at the office.

MEALS.

Breakfast, from 7 to 11 o'clock.	Tea, at 8 o'clock.
Lunch, from 12 to 1 o'clock.	Supper, from 9 to 12 o'clock.
Dinner, at 2 and 5½ o'clock.	

☞ Guests inviting friends to the Table, will please give notice at the Office, that seats may be reserved.

DINNER SENT TO ROOMS ONE DOLLAR EXTRA.
Meals, Fruits and Luncheons sent to rooms will in all cases be charged extra.

Wynkoop, Hallenbenbeck & Thomas, Printers, 113 Fulton St.

A three-dollar-a-day American Plan Bill of Fare, 1859.

Everett House Wine List.

SHERRY.

IMPORTED BY GILBERT DAVIS.

Pale, in glass,	$2 00
Pale, in glass—pts.	1 00
Haurie,	2 00
Amontillado,	2 50
Peter Domecq,	2 50
Vino de Pasto,	2 00
Gordon,	5 00
Pemartin, sup'r,	5 00
Brown, old and fine,	3 00
Topaz, Pale Sherry, N. Bloodgood,	2 00
Light Mountain, N. Bloodgood,	2 00

MADEIRA.

On draft, Old London Particular,	3 00
In glass, Old London Particular,	4 00
In glass, March & Benson,	4 00
In glass, Old Reserve,	5 00
In glass, Green Seal,	5 00
In glass, Green Seal—pts	2 50

PORT.

IMPORTED BY GILBERT DAVIS.

Old Round Port,	2 00
Geo. Sandeman & Co.	2 50
Geo. Sandeman & Co., sup'r,	3 00
London Dock,	3 00
White Port,	2 50

HOCK.

IMPORTED BY ADOLPHUS OECHS, FROM THE HOUSE OF HENKELL & CO., IN MAYENCE.

Deidesheimer,	1 25
Deidesheimer—pts.	75
Steinwein,	2 00
Rudesheimer, Berg,	2 50
Marcobrunner,	2 50
Hochheimer,	2 50
Hochheimer Pints,	1 25
Johannisberger,	5 00
Steinberg Cabinet,	4 00
Sparkling Moselle,	2 50
Sparkling Moselle, Pints,	1 00
Johannisberger Cabinet,	7 00
Sparkling Hochheimer,	2 50
Sparkling Hochheimer, Pints,	1 25

BURGUNDY.

R. Bruninghaus's Nuits,	2 50
" Volnay,	2 50
" Chambertin,	2 50
" Clos de Vougeot,	5 00

BRANDIES.

Pinet & Co.'s S. O. P.,	4 00
Pale Hennessey, old,	2 00
Dark Hennessey,	3 00
Otard, Dupuy & Co., Pale,	2 50

CHAMPAGNE.

Moet & Chandon, Verzenay,	$2 00
Moet & Chandon, do. pts.	1 00
Moet & Chandon, grand Vin Imperial, Green Seal,	2 50
Moet & Chandon, do. Pints,	1 25
Jacques Goerg & Co.'s La Perle,	2 00
Jacques Goerg & Co.'s La Perle, pts.	1 00
Jacques Goerg & Co.'s Rubis Cabinet,	3 00
Sillery Soleil, (imported expressly for the Everett House) Sun Champ.	2 50
Heidsieck, Piper & Co.	2 00
Heidsieck, Pints,	1 00
Mumm's Verzenay,	2 00
Mumm's Verzenay—pts.	1 00
Mumm's Cabinet,	2 50
Mumm's Cabinet, Pints,	1 25
Mumm's Imperial,	3 00
Schrieder,	2 00
Schrieder—pts.	1 00

AMERICAN WINES.

Cincinnati Sparkling Catawba,	2 00
Cincinnati Sparkling Catawba—pts.	1 25
Cincinnati Catawba, Still Wine,	1 50

CLARET.

St. Julien,	1 00
St. Julien—pts.	50
Margaux,	1 00
St. Estephe,	1 00
La Rose,	1 50
Chateau Leoville,	2 00
Chateau Leoville—pts.	1 00
Chateau La Rose,	2 00
Chateau La Rose, Pints,	1 00
Chateau Mouton,	2 50
Chateau Montrose,	3 00
Chateau Montrose, Pints,	1 50
Chateau Margaux, grand Vin 1851,	3 00
Chateau Lafitte, grand Vin 1844,	3 00

WHITE WINES.

IMPORTED BY ADOLPHUS OECHS, FROM FOCKE & BRANDENBURG.

Chateau Sauterne,	1 50
Chateau Sauterne—pts.	75
Chateau Latour Blanche,	2 00
Chateau Yquem	3 00

ALES & PORTERS.

Scotch Ale, pints	37c
India Pale Ale, pints	37c
London Porter, pints	37c

LIQUEURS.

Maraschino,	2 00
White Curaçoa,	2 50
Red Curaçoa,	2 00
Annisette, Hulshkamp & Zoon, and Molyn, Rotterdam,	2 00

Each Waiter is provided with a Pencil and Wine Card.

Look at the prices, and also the goods! The Everett House stood at Union Square and Seventeenth Street. Now a silk house.

and without a guard of Secret Service men, he stopped at the Fifth Avenue and was to be seen strolling about the lobby. The famous "Amen" Corner had its origin in the group of politicians and newspaper men who frequented the Fifth Avenue lobby.

To the north of the Fifth Avenue was the Albemarle, a quiet house with an excellent bar on the Broadway side, much frequented by strollers who wished to drink and talk at small tables instead of standing. It was from one of the windows of this hostelry that Mrs. Langtry watched the burning of the Park Theatre on the date of her intended American debut. On the same block was the Hoffman House, conducted by Edward S. Stokes after his release from Sing Sing. It was renowned for the excellence of its kitchen and in later years for the pictures that adorned the walls of its huge bar room and

The Grand Hotel, Broadway and Thirty-first Street.

included one by Bougereau. The lobby of the Hoffman was always crowded with politicians, actors, wine agents, promoters and other bits of flotsam and jetsam from the pavement of Broadway. During a political campaign it was a betting ring for politicians who made huge wagers for the purpose of influencing public opinion and there was also much genuine betting with John Morrissey as stake-holder. After the Returning Board had declared Hayes President, Morrissey announced that all bets were off and returned the money entrusted to him, less his commission of three per cent. Next in order came the St. James, with a cozy bar in the rear of a little room in which cigars were sold by a Russian of high degree. The windows of the restaurant looked out on Broadway and the front tables were always in demand. Across the street was the building to which Delmonico moved from Fourteenth Street in the Seventies and which later became the Cafe Martin. The history of Delmonico's marches side by side with that of social and financial New York. At the time of which I write it stood absolutely alone as the eating-house of the polite world, the Maison Doree having gone out of existence after setting itself up as a rival. It was said, and with no small degree of truth, that no man ever attained eminence in the town without passing through the cafe and restaurant of this world-famous establishment. Its ball-room and private dining-rooms were the scene of countless gatherings of wealth and fashion; its public dining room on the Fifth Avenue side of the building was filled nightly with beautifully dressed women and men of distinction; in its cafe one could always find many of the leading representatives of finance, commerce and the learned professions. There is no one place in New York at the present time of which all this can be said. Although not a hotel in the usual sense of the word there were on its upper floors rooms in which wealthy bachelors were domiciled.

To the north of Delmonico's was the Coleman House on the west side of the street, a hotel that was said to offer to the entomologist an abundant field for scientific research. Nearby was the Brower House of fragrant memory because of the excellence of the food served at its lunch counter. It was liberally patronized by the better class of gamblers and sporting men whose fondness for good eating is notorious. It was also the favorite resort of such well-known exponents of Negro minstrelsy as Billy Birch, Charley Backus and other members of the San Francisco Minstrel Company, on whom we young fellows were wont to gaze with respectful awe as the source of all current humor. Over the way was the Gilsey House at the northeast corner of Twenty-ninth Street and converted in quite recent years into an office building. I am uncertain as to its earliest landlord, but I well remember its popularity under the direction of James Breslin, prior to the opening of the hotel bearing his name on the opposite corner. The Sturtevant, occupying the greater part of the block between Twenty-ninth Street and Thirtieth Street, was a brown stone structure of what would now be regarded as of moderate height, and I recall it as the stopping place of many mine promoters from the far West and a few actors, though it doubtless had other patrons. The Grand Hotel at Thirty-first Street left but a slight dent on my memory, possibly because it was so quiet and respectable.

If there were any hotels at this time between Thirty-fourth and Forty-second Streets I do not recall them, but I do remember the Broadway at the last named corner,

Delmonico's, at Fifth Avenue and Twenty-sixth Street, later known as Martin's, a famous resort in the 90's.

then a peaceful spot and quite unlike the present heart of the Great White Way. In later years the building was divided and part of it became the Metropole under the management of the Considines. It was in another house of the same name that the Rosenthal murder took place. There was a hotel at the northeast corner of Forty-second Street and Broadway, but I am not sure in regard to the date of its erection. The Royal, at the corner of Fortieth Street and Sixth Avenue, I recall distinctly. It was destroyed afterwards by fire with a disastrous death roll, followed by much scandalous gossip concerning the victims.

Fifth Avenue had its hotels as well as Broadway in the Seventies, ranging geographically from the Brevoort at Eighth Street to the newly erected Buckingham on the southeast corner of Fiftieth. The Brevoort was distinctly an aristocratic house, sharing with the Clarendon the honor of sheltering most of the titled and well-connected Englishmen who did not find free lodgings in the homes of socially ambitious citizens. Its register was marked with the names of captains of the ocean liners and I always suspected that they were entertained without cost to themselves because of the passengers whom they steered in that direction. A great banquet was given there in honor of the Prince of Wales, afterwards Edward VII, a fact attested by a framed copy of the menu card that hangs in the hall to this day. Curiously enough the date on the card is some years removed from that of the Prince's visit to this country. The Berkeley and Grosvenor, which, together with the Brevoort, are among the very few old hotels still standing, were quiet family houses entertaining no transient guests and depending entirely on a wealthy and refined clientele. The policy

On the site of the old Windsor Hotel. The Windsor Arcade now the site of Sloane and Strauss buildings.

of both houses has not changed with the passing years. A few blocks further north was the Glenham in one of whose chambers the eccentric son of Commodore Vanderbilt took his own life.

The Brunswick just above Madison Square was an exceedingly fine hotel, kept by Mitchell and Kinsler, who catered successfully to the fashionable element for several years and made it the favorite stopping place for wealthy Yale and Harvard undergraduates. The peculiar happening that brought ruin to this excellent hostelry is well worth relating, for it shows that hotel-keeping must face other dangers than fire and burglary. On a certain bright winter morning, in the late Eighties, unless my memory be at fault, a tall, well dressed gentleman whose manner of speaking rather confirmed his claim to the title, entered the Brunswick and arranged with the clerk for the entertainment of a specified number of friends at supper that night. The feast was to put the finishing touch on a sleighing party. Taking from his pocket a large roll of bills he offered payment in advance, but the clerk had been deceived by his appearance and politely declined the offer. Late that night a huge four-horse sleigh drew up in front of the hotel and from it descended a swarm of men and women of a class never seen in the Brunswick. With the polite stranger leading they entered the dining room and seated themselves at the long table that awaited their coming. There was nothing to do but serve the party and this the astounded waiters proceeded to do. The stranger was none other than the notorious Billy McGlory, proprietor of a low east side resort, called Armory Hall, and his guests were the hangers-on of that delectable establishment. The story

The Pabst Hotel, which formerly stood on
site now occupied by *Times* Building,
Forty-second Street and Seventh Avenue.
The residences at left are rarely seen in
photographs. 1890.

of his sleighing was printed in the newspapers and ruined the fair name of the hotel.

We young fellows of the Seventies regarded the Grand Central as the very acme of splendor and luxury, but it faded from our imagination when the Windsor threw open its doors to a wondering public. The ground on which it was built was below the level of the adjacent sidewalks and had been flooded with water every winter and used as a fashionable skating pond. The Windsor seemed to us the very last word in gorgeous decoration and modern convenience, and visitors from all parts of the country hastened to ensconce themselves in its large, beautifully furnished rooms. Conducted on the American plan it set before its guests a bewildering variety of dishes served in a manner of elegance to which many of those who ate them had previously been strangers. Andrew Carnegie made it his home during his frequent visits to New York and other commercial and financial magnates from the West, and what is now termed the mid-West, were quick to follow in his footsteps. The presence of these visitors attracted New Yorkers of their class together with Wall Street brokers and speculators so that the nightly throng in its corridors had the flavor of the stock market. Thus were visitors from afar frequently enabled to behold Jay Gould in the flesh. The Ultima Thule in the northward march of hotel building was reached in the erection of the Windsor and Buckingham, so far as the history of the Seventies is concerned, and it was many years before anything on a greater scale of magnificence was attempted, for there was a lean era of economy after the panic of '73. The Buckingham has only recently been torn down, but the Windsor was destroyed by a fire that burned with such incredible swift-

The old Stevens House, original site of Delmonico's, lower Broadway.

ness and cost so many lives that the fact that it took place in daytime instead of at night seemed like a special intervention of Providence.

In addition to the hotels on Fifth Avenue and Broadway there were scattered about the city many others deserving of mention. Those on Fourth Avenue I have already named and east of that thoroughfare there was the Gramercy on the east side of the park of that name. A quiet family house with a refined unostentatious patronage, it enjoyed brief notoriety as the scene of the elaborate practical joke played on the simple English husband of Adelaide Neilson by Ed Sothern and a few of his fellow actors. By means of a pretended fight with bowie knives after the fashion of the southwest they gave the young and unsophisticated Briton the fright of his life. On Third Avenue and Twenty-fourth Street was the Bull's Head, a house of quite a different sort, for it was frequented by horse dealers and cattle drovers and bore a rustic aspect unlike anything else in the town. Daniel Drew, an illiterate speculator, had been its landlord in earlier years and it is possible that to him it owed the aroma of the cow-yard that clung to it until the last.

The most conspicuous of the houses catering to visitors abroad were the Cafe Martin, at Ninth Street and University Place, to which all newly arrived French voyagers bent their steps, and the Belvidere at which the German travelers stopped. The last named was successively in Fourteenth, Eighteenth Streets and Fourth Avenue. The Cafe Martin, with its fine kitchen and well stocked cellar, had a Parisian atmosphere that New Yorkers found to their taste and it soon gained a vogue that it retains to the present day. There were also smaller and less famous hotels in which other foreigners sought shelter on reaching our shores. A typical American hotel which never sought alien guests was the Westminster on East Sixteenth Street, the winter home of many literary men. French's Hotel on Park Row lives in the legendry of the town as the place from which Joseph Pulitzer, then a very poor young immigrant, was once excluded because of the shabbiness of his attire. It was because of this affront that years later he bought the property and erected the World building on its site.

I have written these notes on the hotels of an elder day entirely from memory and without notes and have set down only those places of entertainment of which I retain a vivid recollection. There were many less conspicuous houses that I recall only by name and have left unmentioned. The period of which I have written antedated the apartment hotel and I am uncertain as to the date at which the first of the bachelor apartments was built. There is more luxury in the modern steam-heated house of gaudy furnishing, but no more comfort than was afforded by the larger rooms with their cheery open fires. Moreover, the great abundance and variety of game and the low price at which it was served in even the more modest restaurants more than atoned, in my opinion, for the lack of the French chefs now in control of every kitchen.

The Gracie Mansion, now home of the Museum of the City of New York, foot of Eighty-eighth Street, East River, as seen from the river looking south.

MUSEUM OF THE
CITY OF NEW YORK

Prominent Citizens Behind the Movement.
The City Gives the Historic Gracie Mansion in
East River Park for Its Home.

Following in the footsteps of London and Paris, the
City of New York is going to have a Museum of its own
devoted entirely to collections and material relating to
the rise and progress of this great metropolis, now the
chief city of the western world. The existence of New
York as an American city dates only from 1783, and its
population in that year (which saw the end of the Revolution) was only about twelve thousand. At the same
date London and Paris were already important cities with
huge populations and many centuries of growth behind
them. Today New York is over the six million mark
and its growth continues with undiminished vigor. It is
entirely proper therefore that its citizens should provide
a specific institution for the preservation of its annals; and
in the selection of the Gracie Mansion, the city has provided an excellent starting point.

It may not quite compare in quaintness with the curious
medieval building occupied by *The Carnavalet* in the
French capital, as their institution is called; nor in gor-
geousness with the splendor of Stafford House, home of
the London Museum. Yet it must be remembered that the
latter first occupied very modest quarters in a wing of the
Kensington Museum. It was due to the generosity of a

public-spirited citizen of London, Lord Leverhulme, that the Museum now owns and occupies one of the finest buildings in all of London.

*   *   *   *

The Gracie Mansion, by reason of its delightful and peculiarly fitting antecedents is exactly the place in which to establish an enterprise of this kind. It is closely identified with many of New York's old merchants, and in the early part of the last century was one of the prominent social centres on the island. Hither came all the eminent personages of the day. The names of men distinguished in important fields—statesmen, financiers, travelers and poets—were frequent visitors to the genial occupant of this famous mansion. The locality was then the finest in all New York, and was eagerly seized upon for the establishment of country estates by the opulent merchant and the socially important.

It is also closely identified with the very beginning of American literature. Washington Irving was a frequent guest at the old mansion. He had not yet journeyed to England, there to be hailed by Sir Walter Scott as the first to gain European recognition for American letters.

One book in particular, which appeals most strongly to the affections of New Yorkers was "A Tour Around New York," by Felix Oldboy (Capt. Flavell Scott Mines), a charming writer and of remarkable knowledge of his subject. Part of this delightful volume was written one summer in the sixties, during the occupancy of the old Mansion by Capt. Mines. It is pleasant to note that in his article, Felix strongly urged the purchase by the city of the mansion and the surrounding grounds for just such a purpose as has now come to pass. It was not, however, till nearly half a century later that the

THE OLD PEAR TREE PLANTED BY GOV. STUYVESANT, WHICH FLOUR-
ISHED FOR NEARLY TWO HUNDRED YEARS, CORNER THIRD AVENUE
AND THIRTEENTH STREET.

suggestion then made became a realization. It is a very pleasant consummation of Capt. Mines' day dream, and we should all feel highly pleased that such a fortunate thing has come to pass.

The Museum is in a region seldom visited by the average citizen. It is at the foot of 88th Street, East River, in a park of about twelve acres. The waters of the Sound lave its shores. It commands superb views of the Marine life of the river and its situation, in many respects, could not be improved. It is easily reached from all parts of the city. Visitors to the Metropolitan Museum will find the 86th Street crosstown car at the corner of Fifth Avenue, and there is a Bus line crossing from Riverside Drive through the park to the 92nd Street ferry via 86th Street and Avenue A, which takes you within one short block of the new Museum. Both the East and West Side Subways have stations at 86th Street which connect with the 86th Street car line, and the Fifth Avenue Buses pass 86th Street, so it is not half so inaccessible as it seems. Some day the Museum will have its own building directly on the Avenue, but in the meantime don't let its apparent remoteness deter you from a visit.

*   *   *   *

The City of New York furnishes the building, keeps it in repair and maintains the grounds in the same way as other public parks are cared for. The officers, trustees and members of the Museum provide the collections and the funds for the upkeep of its working staff. In a general way, the constitution, by-laws, rules and regulations and contract with the city are identical with those adopted by the Natural Museum and the Metropolitan, with such changes as are needed to fit the charter to the purposes of a Museum of the City of New York.

The unmistakable public interest aroused by the first announcement of a Museum devoted exclusively to Old New York indicates that the moment was propitious for the launching of the project. The plan was carefully thought out and the experience of persons familiar with the management of such a Museum was freely placed at our disposal. In one important particular we are peculiarly fortunate. There is no other institution covering the field which we intend to occupy. Ours is wholly and exclusively devoted to the greater City of New York and its Boroughs. Nothing that does not pertain to this particular metropolis is solicited by our Museum, and under our by-laws nothing can be received that does not directly pertain to our old city.

There is not the slightest doubt in our minds concerning our ultimate success. Within two years New York will celebrate the 300th Anniversary of the Founding of the city by the purchase of Manhattan Island by the Dutch. Historians, alleged and otherwise, may split hairs concerning the exact moment when the city was actually settled, but the purchase of the Island is the one fact we all remember from classroom days, and that is the date which will be celebrated.

* * * *

We are very proud of the conspicuous part played by VALENTINE'S MANUAL in the creation of this interesting Museum. As our readers are aware, we have for sometime been engaged in the work of photographing all that remains of Old New York. This task rapidly assumed unlooked-for proportions and as the project developed, its value became more and more apparent to an ever-increasing audience. We are especially fortunate in having the aid and counsel of Mr. Archer M. Huntington, who from the first insisted that a Museum would be necessary to carry on the work. From that suggestion, constantly repeated, it was a natural step from a Museum of *Photography* to a Museum of *New York,* which brought it directly within the purview of the work with which we were familiar, and which we had pursued enthusiastically for the past ten years. Mr. A. C. Barrow, secretary to Mrs. Andrew Carnegie, made this happy suggestion. The Hon. Francis D. Gallatin, who had long cherished identically the same idea, proved an immensely valuable recruit and called our attention to a bill introduced by the Hon. Maurice Bloch at Albany, designating the Gracie Mansion for just such a purpose.

When the bill finally reached the Mayor and was approved, we duly appeared before the Park Commissioner and set forth our claims for the possession of the Gracie Mansion. After duly considering the merits of all other organizations, the Commissioner finally awarded the lease to our organization, which by this time had been incorporated.

*   *   *   *

Part of the original group to start the project were the following. For complete list see back of book.

Mr. ARCHER M. HUNTINGTON
Mr. ARTHUR CURTISS JAMES
Mr. GEORGE A. ZABRISKIE
Mrs. SCHUYLER VAN RENSSELAER
Mr. JAMES SPEYER
Mr. WILLIAM RHINELANDER STEWART
BISHOP WM. T. MANNING
Mr. THEODORE ROOSEVELT
Mr. HARRY B. THAYER
Mrs. H. F. DIMOCK
Mrs. ADOLF LADENBURG
Mr. GEORGE WEST GAIR
Mr. SIDNEY W. FISH
Mr. CHARLES DANA GIBSON
Mr. SAMUEL VERPLANCK HOFFMAN
Mrs. LEWIS GOUVERNEUR MORRIS
Mrs. J. B. DUKE
Mr. AUGUST BELMONT
Mr. STURGIS S. DUNHAM

Mr. J. S. AUERBACH
Mr. MELVILLE STONE
Mr. JOHN McE. BOWMAN
Mr. JOHN JAY CHAPMAN
Mr. COLEMAN DU PONT
Mr. SAMUEL T. HUBBARD
Mr. CHAS. C. BULL
Mr. M. D. C. CRAWFORD
Mr. LEWIS L. CLARKE
Mr. JAMES POLK
Dr. GEO. F. KUNZ
Mr. CHARLES E. F. McCANN
Hon. FRANKLIN D. ROOSEVELT
COL. JACOB RUPPERT
MAJ. GEN. JOHN F. O'RYAN
Mrs. J. HENRY WATSON
Mr. WILLIAM HAMLIN CHILDS
Mr. GEORGE GORDON BATTLE
Mr. GUY LOWELL

The period of organization consumed by the Metropolitan Museum might be said to cover three years, and the same is practically true of the Museum of Natural History. It may be presumptuous on our part to mention our modest little affair in connection with these world famous institutions, but it must be remembered that the beginnings of these two organizations were also on a very limited scale. Before the Metropolitan was projected, people went to private homes, such as Mr. Aspinwall's— a view of whose gallery is shown elsewhere in these pages— Mr. A. T. Stewart, Mr. Marshall O. Roberts, Mr. Henry G. Marquand and others and the first exhibition gallery of the Metropolitan was in the Cuyler Mansion on 14th Street, a few doors from Sixth Avenue. The Natural History went through a similar experience. So our own unpretentious start is no indication of what the ultimate end may be. Representing the richest and largest city in the Western Hemisphere and possibly the wealthiest in all the whole world, we are certainly entitled to indulge in all the wildest dreams an optimistic spirit may suggest. Of one thing we are sure. We have the heart of the Old New Yorker behind us. And as we have written time and time again, the New Yorker *does* care for his city and the con-

stant growth of the Museum will be our answer to all
who gainsay our position.

* * * *

The following is a copy of the Certificate of Incorporation filed by our counsel, Messrs. Cadwalader, Wickersham
and Taft, with the Secretary of State of New York, July
21, 1923, upon approval thereof by Mr. Justice John
Ford of the Supreme Court of the State of New York:

WE, the undersigned, all being of full age and all
citizens of the United States and at least one a resident of
the State of New York, desiring to form a membership
corporation pursuant to Article III of the Membership
Corporations Law do hereby certify as follows:

FIRST: The name of the proposed corporation is
MUSEUM OF THE CITY OF NEW YORK, INC.

SECOND: The particular objects for which the corporation is formed are:

(a) To collect and preserve all documents, prints, books,
photographs, portraits, engravings, costumes, furniture, objects and materials pertaining or relating to
the culture and history of the City of New York.

(b) To lease, acquire, preserve and maintain buildings
and sites in the City of New York of historical or
cultural interest.

(c) To make and preserve a complete collection of every
object that has had a place in the rise, progress and
development of the City of New York.

(d) To issue year books, books, pamphlets and publica-
tions concerning the work and purposes of the corporation.

(e) To have prepared and delivered lectures on the culture
and history of the City of New York and related
subjects.

(f) To do all things necessary, fit or suitable to create a
love for and interest in all things pertaining to the
City of New York.

(g) To do everything necessary or suitable to effectuate
the foregoing powers; provided that the corporation
shall not have any power not permitted to be exercised by a membership corporation by the laws of the
State of New York or by a corporation not formed
under the Banking, Insurance or Transportation Law.

THIRD: The territory in which the operations of the
corporation will be principally exercised is all the territory in the City of New York.

FOURTH: The principal office of the corporation is to be located in the Gracie Mansion, Borough of Manhattan, City of New York.

An arrangement has been effected by the Board of Trustees whereby VALENTINE'S MANUAL has been adopted as the Official Year Book of the Museum. As provided by law, each institution of this character is obliged to print a yearly report of its proceedings. By this arrangement, this annual report will now appear as part of the MANUAL and members of the Museum will thus get a Year Book of historic and general interest instead of the usual and time-honored, deadly-dull production. A copy bound in cloth—the regular edition as sold in the bookshops at five dollars—goes to each member of the Museum.

* * * *

As the official organ of the new Museum, it will enjoy a character and influence far beyond its possibility as a private enterprise. Its publication has always been more or less in the nature of a public service, and in its new relation it more nearly approaches its manifest destiny. Its future is assured. Corporations, unlike individuals, have a perpetual existence. The group who originally ventured upon this self-imposed task, are rejoiced at what seems now to be an ideal field for the MANUAL.

* * * *

The *Manual* was always a city publication. It ceased to exist as an official enterprise in 1870. By that time, its cost had approached nearly half a million dollars annually. New York had grown tremendously and could no longer wait a year to read the Aldermanic records of the Board's transactions. A change was imperative, so the present *City Record,* published daily was substituted. Thus ended the *"Manual of the Corporation of the City of New York, by D. T. Valentine,"* as its formal title reads.

* * * *

Under the editorship of David T. Valentine, then Clerk of the Common Council, the *Manual* became a veritable respository of antiquarian lore concerning our city and its fame spread to all parts of the world. It is on its historical records and its pictures that its great reputation is solely founded, and it is these features alone that were preserved in the revived series. Many of the pictures which adorned its pages are all that remains to us of how certain streets and public buildings appeared in the 40's and 50's. No other record exists. The day of commercial illustrations had not yet come. Steel engravings were the only form of art available to the early publisher and their great cost placed them beyond the reach of the ordinary firm.

No such limitations prevailed, however, in the case of an opulent city like New York and Mr. Valentine was thus enabled to prepare a book that was not only unique in its day, but has remained so ever since. Most of the edition was distributed gratis through members of the Common Council. A few copies were sold, but not many. At that time, apparently it had little or no commercial value. Time has, however, changed all this and it is now eagerly purchased at many times its original price. It is now seen as the intelligent chronicler of the early years of one of the mightiest cities the world has ever known. The longer its pages are scanned, the greater our admiration for the scholarly, intelligent and enterprising spirits which guided the work.

* * * *

Of Mr. Valentine but little is known outside of his

connection with the *Manual*. After almost thirty years of service, the old Clerk was dismissed. The loss of his position and especially his connection with the *Manual*, his biographer tells us, proved too much for "the faithful old servant" and he soon after died. The *Manual* appeared twice more and was then finally discontinued.

Right here is a very good time and place to render credit to one whose name is seldom, if ever, mentioned in connection with the just fame of the *Manual*. And that was William Kelby, Librarian of the New York Historical Society, and probably the most learned savant on Old New York that has yet appeared. His love and enthusiasm for this old city was boundless. He received no compensation for his labors beyond the modest stipend allowed him by the Society, yet his work was prodigious and enduring. Without in any way disparaging the splendid performances of Mr. Valentine, a belated sense of justice founded on personal knowledge leads the writer to say that to William Kelby belongs the credit for whatever may be of scholarly repute or historical importance in the pages of the *Manual*. And in like measure should the credit go to Mr. Valentine for the statistical facts and the orderly array of municipal records. It was an ideal combination.

* * * *

Mr. Kelby made his home in the old building on Second Avenue, then occupied by the Historical Society. His recreation was to delve into the old records of the city and make notes for future numbers of the *Manual* and for the preservation of rare and unusual items that passed under his notice from time to time. There exists to this day, whole boxes filled with little cards carefully compiled, each one bearing an item of value touching upon some aspect of the city's history, and a reference stating where full details can be found. Among this mass of material is the manuscript for what would make the most interesting biography of New York's leading families ever compiled. It is to be hoped that some day the Society will publish this volume which would make a wonderful addition to their collections.

* * * *

The discontinuance of the *Manual* was ever a source of deep regret to many old New Yorkers and it was the great good fortune of the writer to be the medium through which its revival was finally accomplished just half a century after its disappearance. And as the original *Manual* had a wonderful secret co-worker in the person of Mr. Kelby, so had the new *Manual* in a practical way of Commodore Arthur Curtiss James. There was something infectious about his courage and it is quite impossible to estimate that indefinable quality of his support or what it meant in those early days.

Other friends soon followed the lead of Mr. James. We recall with particular pleasure Mr. George A. Zabriskie.

The late Mr. John Sanford Saltus, Mr. J. P. Morgan, Mr. Archer M. Huntington, Mr. John D. Rockefeller, Jr., Mrs. Richard T. Auchmuty, Mrs. Andrew Carnegie, Mr. Stuyvesant Fish, Mr. William Hamlin Childs, Mr. Samuel T. Hubbard, Mr. Arthur P. Williams, Mrs. Charles E. Sherman, Mr. William F. Peters, Mr. Walter C. Reid, M. J. Sanford Pegram are also affectionately remembered.

It is pleasant to know that by their help we are at last able to say that this valuable publication which means so much to the city, is now on a solid foundation.

The following is the bill as passed by the Legislature creating the Museum and which is now Chapter 220 of the Laws of 1923. The measure was guided through the Assembly and Senate by the Hon. Maurice Bloch, member from the Assembly District in which the Museum is located.

AN ACT

To authorize the City of New York, acting by its commissioner of parks for the Borough of Manhattan, to enter into an agreement or lease for the preservation, use and maintenance of the old historic building known as the Gracie Mansion, and authorizing an appropriation by the Board of Estimate and Apportionment for the support thereof.

The People of the State of New York, represented in Senate and Assembly, do enact as follows:

Section 1. The City of New York, acting by its commissioner of parks for the Borough of Manhattan, is hereby authorized and empowered to make an agreement or lease upon such terms and conditions as may be agreed upon for the adequate restoration, keeping, maintenance, extension, preservation and exhibition of the building and the contents thereof known as the Gracie Mansion, situated in Carl Schurz Park, in the Borough of Manhattan, and such necessary amount of grounds immediately adjacent to such building as may be agreed upon between the parties to the said agreement or lease sufficient to permit of the erection of a fence, railing, guard or other similar structure around such building for the purpose of adequately protecting it. The said agreement or lease is authorized for the purpose of placing and maintaining the said building, in so far as it was in its original condition at the time of its erection and its use during the early part of the nineteenth century and of placing in it appropriate old furniture, objects of art, decorations, fixtures, mementos, relics, records and other objects and collections of historic and patriotic interest, of preserving the said building for the benefit of the people of the City of and State of New York as an historic landmark and for educational and patriotic purposes, and of affording to the public opportunities for pleasure, recreation, amusement and education by means of the exhibition of the said building and its contents; and the said agreement or lease shall also provide how the duty of the commissioner of parks

[188]

for the Borough of Manhattan in respect to maintaining the said Gracie Mansion now imposed upon him by law shall be performed. In the event that the said agreement or lease is entered into between the City of New York, acting by its park commissioner for the Borough of Manhattan, the Board of Estimate and Apportionment may, in its discretion, appropriate to the use of said Gracie Mansion, such sum or sums as it may deem adequate for the purpose of restoring and repairing said Gracie Mansion and of maintaining it, in so far as possible, in its original condition, and may annually, in its discretion, include in its budget for the then next ensuing financial year a sum or sums to the use of and for the adequate support, maintenance and protection of the said Gracie Mansion.

§2. This act shall take effect immediately.

Perhaps the new Museum will be something of a scandal in the Museum line. Already our Director wants Blackwell's Island and Ward's Island cleared of its present inmates and restored to the city as public playgrounds. As the Museum is located directly opposite the Island, he can see the vast benefit that would accrue to the city by the adoption of his suggestion and can see no possible argument in favor of their present use.

STUYVESANT FISH

Our genial, lovable, delightful, old friend is now no more. What a loss he is to antiquarian New York! His deep and abiding interest in all things historical made him a fascinating raconteur and his store of anecdotes was endless.

The old Hudson River has lost a powerful and picturesque figure; his admirers, a companion whose loss can never be replaced, and the Museum a staunch supporter. Peace and loving kindness be with him!

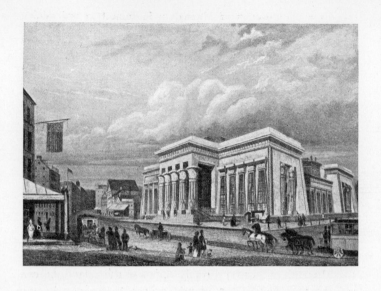

The old jail, popularly called "The Tombs,"
and the Criminal Court Building, joined by
the "Bridge of Sighs." Erected in 1838, of
stone brought from the Bridewell in City
Hall Park. The site is near the centre of
Collect Pond.

GETTING THE GRANITE FOR THE NEW COUNTY COURT HOUSE

OUR NEW CIVIC CENTRE STARTED AT LAST

A Visit to Deer Isle, Maine, Where the Stone Comes From

In Penobscot Bay, at high tide, there is an island for every day in the year. It was a New York skipper who struck the 366th one. "Didn't I keep tabs all right?" he asked his Yankee mate. And the mate growled back: "Yes, but this is Leap Year."

At low tide there is an island for every day in the year since Columbus discovered America. When the tide goes out in Penobscot Bay, it leaves you flat, mentally as well as physically. It seems to drift in expectantly, and go out with alacrity, wherein it resembles most of the persons who visit these Granite Islands for the first time.

This section of New England is very popular among a certain class, but I should say it was decidedly an acquired taste. In the dim and distant past these islands preserved their quaint and romantic names, derived from the Indians and reminiscent of French dominion in America. Isle Au Haute, Maniticus, Pamaquid, Grand Manan, petite Manan, Passamaquiddy, Deer Isle—are all of that charming period.

Now that "Summer people" have replaced the Indian and the trapper, we have such mellifluous nomenclature as Goose Rock, Mosquito Inlet, Black Horse, Turtle Back, Owl's Head, Chicken Ledge, Hog Point, etc., etc. By next year we shall probably have such startlingly original additions as Automobile Point, Movie Bay, Radio Rocks,

Magneto Landing, Gasoline Head, Film Island, Silver Screen Sound, etc., etc. The possibilities in this direction are limitless.

Stonington is the present-day improvement over the old-time name of Deer Isle. It contains the aforesaid granite for the aforesaid Court House. The *Governor Bodwell,* a diminutive half-portion of a real ferryboat, takes you from Rockland through the channels and around the islands that dot the way to Stonington. It is about 2½ hours sail, and should be most enjoyable; but like all these economical eastern steamboats, they never provide a chair with a back. You either have to sit on a child's size campstool or perch yourself on the wooden seat that encircles the rail, and twist yourself into a comfortable position—if you can. With the exception of the *James T. Morse,* from Rockland, I have yet to

find one of these Down East boats with the slightest appreciation of the torture that a passenger must endure, sitting on one of these wretched little things for half a day. The six-hour voyage from New Bedford to Martha's Vineyard and Nantucket is made under similar conditions, and should be brought to the attention of the S.P.C.A.

Real estate in Stonington is of two kinds—portable and permanent. I suppose somebody pays money for land on which to build a house on these islands, but it would not surprise me if the land were given away and the house thrown in as a bonus. The portable real estate, however, is a different matter. That is the granite. And when the City of New York needs some to build Riverside Drive, or Manhattan Bridge, or the Court House, this commodity becomes of real value. It is not a perishable commodity and it does not spoil, even if it some times waits a long time for a customer.

The granite which is being used in our Court House is of a most superior quality, both as to texture and color, and the sheets are found in such lengths and thicknesses that almost every desired requirement for the Court House can be met.

The location of the quarry is known as "The Settlement." In summer it is about three miles from the town itself, and in winter about three hundred. This, however, is overcome by blasting a bay that is frozen solid, using dynamite, and keeping two or three ice crushers busy all day, thus affording a channel for the *George A. Fuller,* a converted tugboat, which the company uses to provide comfortable transportation for its workers. In these days of unions and shortage of skilled labor a stonecutter must be coddled to an amazing degree. He is quite a pampered fellow; earns eight good American bucks a day, of which he puts $7.99 in the local bank, rain or shine. They are natives—natives of Genoa, Palermo, Mesopotamia and Quebec. The good old days when you heard the Yankee nasal twang have disappeared. A few of the Stonington people still drop their "g's" and slur their "r's"; but the average make a sort of cabalistic sign and mutter something about "No speaka da Eenglish."

I heard rumors to the effect that there was some garden truck raised on the few alleged farms on the island, but I cannot vouch for this statement. All the farms that I saw were busily engaged in raising more granite, or dodging what they had already raised. They had some modest little boulders sticking in the roadway, about the size of a church, and there were still others tucked away in the back yards. My conclusion is that anything grown to eat in Stonington comes out of the sea.

The only other live thing that is undoubtedly grown on this island is Angora cats. For some inexplicable reason the island is full of these peculiar members of the

THE OLD HARLEM RIVER BRIDGE AT THIRD AVENUE, 1861.

feline tribe. Some of them are of extraordinarily fine pedigree, and the fame of Stonington's Angora cats has spread far and wide. They bring fancy prices and are really worth them.

In this connection I was told of a remarkable occurrence, which I positively refused to believe until my own eyes were confronted with uncontrovertible evidence of its truth.

It appears that a lady, who was very fond of cats, passed from all earthly things and left her husband quite a lot of money, also minute instructions for the care and up-bringing of a raft of cats which alas, she was unable to take with her. It was perfectly natural, therefore, that his wife's pets were fairly killed with kindness. At all events, that is what happened. But imagine his horror a few weeks later to find on the tombstone of his dear departed the image of a black cat sitting on its haunches, gazing reproachfully at the panic-stricken husband! They tell me it was a flaw in the granite, and that flaws in granite frequently take eccentric and peculiar methods of expressing themselves. I refuse to accept this lame explanation, however. I know better. It is funny how the home instinct persists, even in this island. I asked my host Boniface Eaton, whose tavern "The Three Blue Pigeons" is the only survivor of Colonial days if he had ever been away from Stonington, and he told me, yes; he had been out in the West, where men are men: out in the open spaces, and all the rest of that bull that Bill Hart and Valentino spill in the movies every night. He had lived in Kansas for twelve years. Yet, when his old father wrote him that he was probably going home soon, and would he come back and take the old farm for his'n, the son dutifully bade farewell to Kansas drought and grass-hoppers and came back.

Undoubtedly this island inspires in its sons and daughters as pure and lofty an affection for home as can be imagined. Take another case—Daisy Miller, for instance. Daisy is not her name, neither is Miller, but never mind. Daisy was born on Deer Isle, and one of life's tragedies entered her life very early—mother and father separated, and Daisy was left to grow up among the neighbors. She must have been a nice sort of kid, even in those days. Even then she was of an imaginative temperament, for she used to carpet the stone steps leading from the high road to the Shore Road, with green moss, which to her childish fancy was the road down which some day Prince Charming would come, and she must have a covering fit for royalty.

In one of those inexplicable ways fortune gave to Daisy the blue of the sea for her eyes, the glorious coloring of the sunsets, for which the island is famous, for her cheeks, and for her hair the spun gold that the dancing waves reflected from the midday sun.

In course of time Daisy left the island home and went out into the world, and straight to perdition, in the opinion of her Puritanical neighbors, for she went on the stage! But Daisy played the game square. Her first task was to find her abandoned mother and make a home for her.

Last summer the *Governor Bodwell* among its passengers carried a very distinguished looking man and a strikingly handsome woman. They were strangers to the village, yet the woman seemed to find her way about as if she had lived there all her life. When they came to the sign of "The Three Blue Pigeons," the handsomely

Former site of New Court House. A view of Collect Pond, looking south, as it appeared in 1798. Columbia College, St. Paul's, etc., seen in the distance. From a contemporary sketch.

gowned woman did not at first enter, but sat in its solitary rocker and gazed wistfully and with tear dimmed eyes over the water that stretched before her. When the proprietor came out she asked a great many questions.

"Was the road over Tea Hill still open?"

"Yes, it was."

"Were the steps, leading down to the Shore Road, just the same?"

"They were."

"Was the Rich Man's Street still there?"

"It was."

Finally through the mist of years Mrs. Eaton recognized the Daisy Miller of her girlhood days. And the two old friends cried and hugged each other, to the utter bewilderment of the onlookers.

Presently Daisy left "The Three Blue Pigeons" and wended her way back in the island, to the section in which she had grown up as a girl. At the first little home the door was opened by a very old man, who was much abashed at the vision of beauty which confronted him. But at her first words: "Where is aunt Phoebe, uncle John?" the old man broke down, clasped his arms around her and said: "It's my little Daisy, come back again!"

For more than a week she stayed in the little village, tramped up and down the dusty roads to Tea Hill, gathered green moss and carpeted the steps, leading down to the Shore Road, just as she had done in her faroff girlhood days. Not a nook or corner that remained in her memory was left unvisited; not an old friend was left unremembered. Daisy had played the game square; was now the wife of a wealthy merchant, owned a beautiful home, in which the most important thing was the old mother, who was passing her declining days in peace and

Drawn by J. Smiley, from proposed
plans by Guy Lowell, architect of
the Court House.

The new County Court House as it will
appear in the proposed Civic Centre, now
building. The buildings at left are proposed
new Federal Court House and Post Office
to replace the old building now in City Hall
Park. At right is the proposed State Administration Building. The location is just
north of present Municipal Building, between Lafayette Street and City Hall Place.

comfort. So you see, the romance of Deer Isle is still a thing of reality, and the love of its sons and daughters for their sea girt home is a flame that knows no quenching.

Tea Hill, one of the prominent sections of the town, received its peculiar name from the fondness of the people in that neighborhood for that delectable beverage. It is related that upon one occasion a native came to the village with a pillow slip under his arm. He examined several chests of tea and finally decided upon one particular brand which caught his fancy. "Fill this up," he remarked to the astonished storekeeper, producing the pillow slip, "and if the sample pleases me I will be back for a regular supply."

There are quite a few automobiles, also schools, on the island, but hardly enough to justify the lavish outlay for signs, reading, "Drive slowly; school ahead." These signs are built so close they shut out the light. I saw some of the schools, but they were so small as to be hardly visible to the naked eye, that is, a New York eye. But they were clean and attractive. We struck rather a severe depression during a trip over this sign bedecked road, and I remarked on the depth of these island "thank ye mams." "That wasn't a 'thank ye mam,'" said the driver sarcastically, "that was a schoolhouse."

We wound up our visit delightful in every way with a fishing trip on the *Genesee*. We warned Captain Sellers in advance that we wanted no alibis. If the fish didn't bite, well and good. Only we wished to be spared the recital of the huge catches made "last week," or "yesterday" or any other time. We had never caught a fish and never expected to. It would be all right, provided no reference was made, as mentioned above. In

Southerly half of the new Civic Centre.
City Hall Park as it will appear when the
old Post Office is removed.

that event we told the Captain we would not be responsible for what happened.

We did not, of course, catch any fish. To make amends, the discomfited Captain asked permission to visit his lobster pots. They would be full of all kinds of fish. So we went. Two pots yielded one small illegal sized lobster and some one-inch starfish. The Captain quietly blew up.

But perhaps the most enjoyable feature, at least on our part, was the little talk we gave them the night before we left on the great City of New York. This was illustrated with many interesting and nicely colored slides. Dr. Tewksbury kindly placed his pretty little moving picture theatre at our disposal, put up a sign in his post office and a diminutive Town Crier went about, announcing the event.

This information having reached the ears of Captain Sellers, it inspired him with a sudden resolve to be avenged. Being an ex-bill poster he immediately placed a huge board on Main Street, reading as follows:

TONIGHT! TONIGHT! TONIGHT!
AT THE
TEWKSBURY THEATRE!
OLD CAPTAIN KIDD
AND
HIS TROUPE OF CELEBRATED TRAINED FISH
IN
YESTERDAY AND TODAY IN OLD NEW YORK
INCLUDING
LAST NIGHT, LAST WEEK, LAST MONTH, THIS
NIGHT, GOOD NIGHT!
MUSIC BY THE HORN-POUT BAND

Between the good doctor's efforts and the skipper of the *Genesee* public interest was aroused to fever heat and the hall was filled.

The first slide showed the great city in its infancy, the well-known "Hartger's View," taken about 1626-1628. Our great city was then about two years old, and the picture being the first view of New York ever shown to the world, naturally excited breathless interest. Even while they were looking at the little fort at the end of the island where the Custom House now stands, the scene faded out and in its place stood the dramatic contrast— the lower part of the gigantic modern city with all its tremendous towering skyscrapers, its trans-Atlantic shipping, its busy harbor and its crowded streets.

A skyline of these early days followed, showing the fort, a windmill and a few buildings, succeeded by a corresponding view from the North River, showing the Whitehall Building, Singer Building, Hudson Terminal, Woolworth Building, and others that now combine to make the skyline of today one of the wonders of the world. Next came a view of the old Dutch settlers, bowling on the green in front of Fort Amsterdam. Again the view faded out, and our imposing Custom House and Bowling Green appeared where the old fort stood and its merry villagers. A view of the little red brick dwellings that Old New Yorkers recall as Steamship Row was next thrown on the screen. The houses looked more like the ones they were accustomed to see in Stonington, but when they disappeared to give place to the new Steamship Row, comprising the immense block now occupied by the International Mercantile Marine, Bowling Green and Cunard Buildings, the enormous difference caused a gasp of astonishment and much applause. Then came pictures of the new Court House they were helping to build, etc., etc.

We entertained them in this way for about an hour. We are not exactly amateurs, for we all lectured last winter, and we rightly judged our Stonington friends would like it, and in this we were happily not disappointed. It was a great surprise and made us friends all over the island. It is a good idea, on jaunts like this, to try to give something to the people you visit. It invariably comes back in large measure, and this thought is worth remembering.

The old Hall of Records, in City Hall Park, built 1757, as "the New Gaol" and used as a prison during the Revolution. Removed some years ago, to the deep regret of all Old New Yorkers.

Close-up of Gracie Mansion.

BOYHOOD RECOLLECTIONS OF
GRACIE MANSION
By L. Standerman

The retreats of youth are devious and sometimes mysterious. The whisperings of the glen, the shadow of the mountain or the broken castle with its keep beneath the pavement of the yard, stir adolescent instincts to go to them or yearn for them. Among them, youthful companions sport, while once a week Troy falls and Hector is slain. I remember the last time his helmet spun about the gravel walk. It was on the Prim place, not far from the Gracie Mansion. There were no castles in Yorkville, but there were Colonial homes, in whose cellars more than once a Tory captive wept, or from whose attics the traitor's signal flashed to the enemies of our Revolutionary patriots.

And it behooved Hector to scale to the loft of Prim's ancient stable—the stable that had housed many a stately carriage on which the tax gatherer levied full heavily during Jefferson's administration. Upon his head, Hector had a skillet, and a boiler cover for a shield withstood Achilles' darts. The shield was his undoing, as, for reasons never explained, he volplaned from the ramparts of the stable into a barberry bush below. Oh! the uproar and the swooning females on the wisteria-vined porch of the historic mansion nearby. Six stitches in his scalp and an abrazed nose produced a bandaged hero, whose misadventure caused terror and retreat in Achilles' army. Now great Hector is a great manufacturer with works yonder on the palisades.

At Gracie's Point, there was an elm near two centuries old, beneath which I often browsed upon the history of New York in Oldboy's "Tours Around New York," in which Nicodemus, the philosophic author's cat, created much diversion. And, by the way, I am reminded of my pet deer, Mordecai, or, to be exact, it was a pre-empted pet, whose affections I had alienated from its master, and it wandered with me about Gracie's grounds.

I think the claw necklaces and earthen pot shards of Uganda and Matabili are better classified and preserved than the personal treasures and relics of tradition which were touched and lived amongst by our ancestors in New York. No history is more piquant or vivacious, no episodes more mirth-provoking, nor are any incidents more tragic than those of the time of Theodosia Burr. She charmed the assembly and led the fashion of the day. Her

Music on the Mall, Central Park, 1870.

wit and beauty deflected and the qualities of her character blunted the shafts of opprobrium which the political defection of her unscrupulous father brought upon her and himself. And in youth's bloom, she was engulfed in a raging Atlantic storm while voyaging coastwise from the South to meet her outlawed parent. A father, brilliant, resourceful and captivating, who bore the stain of Hamilton's blood ineradicably. Judge Pendleton, Hamilton's second in the historic duel; was a frequent visitor at the home of Archibald Gracie, and to the old mansion, indeed, the steps of all the men of affairs were often bent. Guests to the number of fifty, comprised of the first in commerce, literature and art, frequently enjoyed Gracie's hospitable board and genial company. Benumbed by grief, dejection and despair, Burr recalls to mind Balzac's hero of "The Magic Skin." His generosity begot disaster to those on whom it was lavished, and his engaging companionship devastated the honor of men who yielded to his schemes and enticements. Intellectually gifted, he was morally obtuse.

But, I have digressed unpardonably from my juvenile recollections of the Gracie country-seat in my unrequired eagerness to win favor for the romantic annals of New York. I once saw Charles Dana absorbed in the "Folk-lore of Iceland," and we all know the persistency with which news from Corea was thrust before our unwilling eyes by James Gordon Bennett. I often wondered, as I sat upon the Gracie homestead steps, why, if it were well to go so far afield to satisfy human curiosity, more notice was not first taken of the marvels of Manhattan Island. Among them, the huge round boulder, as big as a small cottage, that had been so gently set down and so perfectly poised on a smooth bald spot in the Bronx in the course of the fourth glacial drift, that a child's hand could sway it. It was not far from Lorillard's ancient snuff mill.

Along the edge of the East River, a trail led to Gracie's. It was a solitary walk, overhung by acacia and chestnuts. It ended at Hoern's or Rhinelander's Point, as it was sometimes called. There, years before, a pleasure house stood and thither Josiah Quincy came during his visit to Archibald Gracie while on his way as Massachusetts' chief spokesman in the House of Representatives at Washington in eighteen hundred and five. He viewed the prospect from the summer house with delight and strolled about the splendid gardens. Later, the impression given in a letter to a friend was that "the scene was beautiful beyond description."

The country-seat of Archibald Gracie was a rendezvous for the leaders in industry, philanthropy, the great writers and royalty from abroad. Louis Phillipe was often at his famous table. Louis' misfortunes were not unlinked with Gracie's successful career. Napoleon, the nemesis of the exiled Bourbons and the emigres, was also the author of the loss of a million or thereabouts to Gracie. The Berlin and Milan decrees subjected every American ship seeking entry to a European port to seizure. Many of Gracie's beautiful clippers had sailed before news of the decree reached our shores and some, indeed, embarked in defiance of them later. He had ships upon every sea. It was the heydey of the merchant marine, and, notwithstanding the Algerian pirates or the French and Spanish privateers, to whom were eagerly issued letters of marque by the Napoleonic ministry, the flag of the United States was carried to the remotest ports. On the seaboard, from Maine to Georgia, we prospered.

Archibald Gracie's private ensign of red and white floated above the fleetest and most gallant of our ships. The loss of a million did not cripple his fortune. This is evident by the record of the continuance of his philanthropy and his public-spirited enthusiasm. He was among the first to institute and sustain a free public school in New York for the education of those unable to attend the universities and who desired an education.

At a pitch from the walk along the river's edge, rocks lay covered with sea moss and kelp. They were in reality a deceptive ledge, hiding the precipitous descent into the deep and often turbulent channel which swept to Mill Rock or Hell Gate. Neither the marine creatures nor the flora and fauna of the spot had yet been asphyxiated by the gases from the furnaces of production, nor been driven off by the pollution incident to civilization. Curious species of varied colored shell fish sallied from the rocky clefts, the tom-cod, now extinct in those waters, invited the angler in winter, and the porgy abounded in spring, while bass were possible in the deep water off the picturesque point.

In the branches, there was sometimes an occasional oriole, and the chattering cat-bird inhabited the shrubs which were tangled and overgrown. An ancient owl was the star denizen. He was capable of making himself sensational at night; for this was a very lonely spot, and was it for no other purpose at all that Washington Irving wrote right here under the elms:

> No Will o' th' Wisp mislight thee,
> No snake or glowworm bite thee;
> But on thy way, not making a stay
> Since there are no ghosts to fright thee.

For timid folks, it was a comforting rhyme to repeat on awful dark nights about here. There was also the im-

Running to a fire. Almost the last days of the Volunteer Fire Department, which finally gave way to a paid force after much opposition. This was as late as 1868.

pertinent blue jay, and the rapacious robin abounded, as well as some red and a legion of gray squirrel. But it was only the owl that was a successful medium for the spiritual world.

In my boyhood, the Gracie Mansion was surrounded by high elms and some ancient walnuts. Nature endowed the spot generously. The althea, hibiscus, columbine, hollyhock and ragged sailor grew profusely and at their untrained will in sunny places. The violet nestled at the roots of the trees and demurely sought the seclusion of moss-covered stones; but the atavistic rose had flung modesty to the winds and had gone back to its wild state. The country-seat was often vacant, frequently totally neglected, but its walls were ever alive to reminiscence. Washington Irving came often to the fireside and consecrated it a shrine. His inspiration for "Astoria" and in part his labors upon that delightful book germinated and were pursued here and at Astor's mansion. And Tom Moore sat here briefly on his return from Bermuda to England. I loved the place and revered its memories. As a boy, I got as close to the spectres of Gracie's home as I could while the sun was up. What does Sir Oliver Lodge specify and vouch for in these matters?

My recollections would be incomplete if I neglected the little rustic farmhouse with its fences burdened by wild grape. It was behind the Gracie homestead. The road to it ascended a small, steep hill, on which perched the house and barnyard, and then descended as abruptly. It was the last bit of picturesque rusticity on the East River. It was the analogy and faithful expression of all that is seen in George Moreland's paintings.

MISS SPENCE

A Famous Educator and a Remarkable
Christian Character.

A most unusual personality passed away in the death of Miss Spence. The following tribute from one of her "old girls" is well worth preserving, but no pen, however eloquent, could do justice to so noble a conception of life and such lofty ideals as were the everyday privilege of the girls in this school.

Her pupils were the children of the very rich. It is no small compliment to them also that Miss Spence's School was preferred solely for its spiritual worth; and that no consideration of position or power ever weighed with this wonderful teacher where a question of principle was involved.

The death of Miss Spence of Miss Spence's School is such an overwhelming loss that the alumnae of her school, her "old girls," as she fondly called them, have been almost stunned. But with the passing days has come the need of expressing in words, inadequate as they may be, our gratitude for the inspiration of her life and our appreciation of her service to the world.

She was a truly great educator. Her high idealism, her sense of spiritual values, her standards of righteousness, which did not change with changing times, gave a loftiness to the meanest task, transformed the dreariest lesson, lent significance to all of life. It was only through this uplifting sense of the value of effort, the meaning of struggle, be it only a battle with arithmetic or history, the knowledge of progress toward an ultimate goal, that Miss Spence was able to maintain the high standards of scholarship for which the school is noted. Her girls were ever inspired to put forth fresh effort, to strive harder, knowing or gradually perceiving as they grew older that each lesson mastered, each duty honestly performed, was one more stone laid in the foundation of character. "Character is the greatest thing in life," she told us from first to last, and the building of character was her life work—such characters as would mark her girls as gentlewomen with culture and refinement, with trained minds and hearts tuned to the service of others. To this end, in spite of the size of the school, the classes were always limited to eight girls in order that each one might receive the individual attention she required and that her identity might never be lost in the mass.

Because of this every one of her "old girls" felt a personal loss, impossible to express. The daily contact with her at school but heightened the power of her vision, for as she taught us, so she lived. Her vivid personality, so full of vitality and the joy of living; her gayety of manner, her wit and keenness, the directness of her mental processes, her marvelous sympathy, her breadth of outlook, her courage and her faith, have given us an example never to be forgotten and humbly to be followed.

We feel sincerely that one of the great personalities of our day has passed. But the influence of a life so beautiful and so helpful will live on in her school and in the lives and hearts of Miss Spence's pupils, in their many activities inspired and guided by her, in the manifold interests, civic, national, and even international, that have been quickened by her spirit. So may we, her alumnae, truly prove that "not for school but for life we've learned."

President Thayer, of the American Telephone and Telegraph Company, at the historic moment when the telephone carried his voice to London, 1923.

Henry Clay Gets a *Manual*

The following letter, from no less a personage than Henry Clay the great Southern statesman, acknowledges a copy of the MANUAL from a well known New Yorker. It is singular, how true Mr. Clay's comment on the growth of the city is today, although his letter was written more than seventy years ago.

Washington, 25 Jan., 1850

My dear Sir:

I am under great obligations and owe many thanks for the copy of Mr. Valentine's "Manual," which you were good enough to send me. It seems, however, almost useless to attempt to keep pace with the growth of your great city. The "Manual" of today becomes old and obsolete tomorrow. Whilst one comes from the country to visit the city, the city is going to the country, which he came from, to establish itself there. When I first saw New York, less than half a mile up Broadway, from the Battery, would have included most of the wealth, position, and the elite of its population. Now Broadway has run, away many miles (I am sure I don't know how many) into what was then the country. And how much further it will stray nobody can tell, *if this Union is preserved*.

With great regard,

H. CLAY.

JAMES AUCHINCLOSS, ESQ.

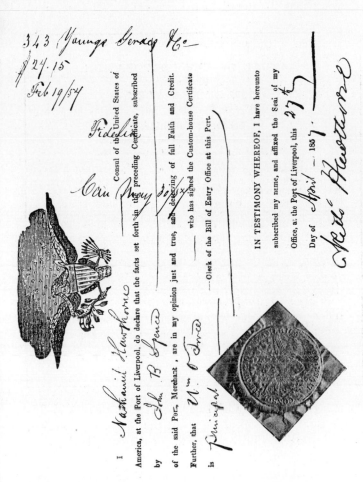

343 Youngs Terrace H Co
$24.15
Feb 19/54

Fidelia

I Nathaniel Hawthorne Consul of the United States of America, at the Port of Liverpool, do declare that the facts set forth in the preceding Certificate, subscribed by Jno. B Spence

of the said Port, Merchant, are in my opinion just and true, and deserving of full Faith and Credit.

Further, that Wm O'Since —— who has signed the Custom-house Certificate is Principal —— Clerk of the Bill of Entry Office at this Port.

IN TESTIMONY WHEREOF, I have hereunto subscribed my name, and affixed the Seal of my Office, a the Port of Liverpool, this 27th Day of April — 1857.

Nath Hawthorne

A clearance paper for the Black Ball packet *Fidelia*, signed by Hawthorne

Here is one of the old advertisements of the MANUAL showing that it catered to the general public just as we

---

MANUAL OF THE CORPORATION
of the
CITY OF NEW YORK,
For 1853.

By D. T. Valentine,
Clerk of the Common Council.
Published by Authority of the two Boards.

This illuminated Manual of the City and County of New York, from earliest incorporation to the present year, comprises five hundred pages of interesting statistics, embracing the entire period from 1653 to 1853, a term of two hundred years, having curious pictorial illustrations of many of its earliest as well as latest improvements.

All the civil, social and charitable institutions of the metropolis, with a full catalogue of their officers, are presented in this work, together with all the members of the City Government from the beginning, with a brief biography of each of the Mayors from Thomas Willet, in 1665, to Gideon Lee, in 1833, forty seven in number; since which time there have been thirteen other chief magistrates, making in all sixty, or an average of exactly one in each four years. Of this number, twelve have left no representatives for the Directory of 1853. Among them was WILLIAM PEARTREE, elected in 1703, who ruled honorably over the other trees of Gotham, for four years.

This work of Mr. Valentine's, comprises a vast amount of valuable statistics, published in excellent style, with many embellishments.

—Editor.

---

do today. Not many of these notices appeared and this one is a rarity. Everything about the MANUAL, however, is interesting and grows more so as the city develops.

P. T. BARNUM

Some Recollections of the Great Showman

Barnum is remembered by the present generation largely as a mountebank, with whose name the word "humbug" is usually associated. As a matter of fact, nothing is further from the truth. Mr. Barnum was an outstanding figure in his day and one of New York's most popular and respected citizens. He was a man whose every act was guided by the highest Christian ideals. He was against profanity and strong drink, when these frailties were almost universal. His reputation for honesty and probity were such that when he met with sudden misfortune, due entirely to the rascality of men in whom he trusted, public sympathy found expression in the tender of large sums of money, to re-establish himself financially. All of these offers were declined. At forty-one years of age, after giving up every dollar he possessed, and without even a home, he started over again. He speedily recouped himself and in a few years had amassed an even greater fortune than the one he had lost. His residence in New York was at 438 Fifth Avenue, and for a time he was President of the Crystal Palace.

His benefactions to his home town of Bridgeport were large and frequent, and the wonderful seaside park which that city owns today, and its beautiful cemetery, are both due to his foresight and generosity. Although he never denied that he loved to "humbug" the people, the fact still remained that no man or woman could truthfully say that they did not receive more than good value for every penny they spent in his shows. Those of us who can recall the closing years of his life and the annual advent of his circus in Madison Square Garden, can abundantly testify to the truth of this statement. And the greatest attraction of the circus was Mr. Barnum himself, who always personally appeared at the head of the cavalcade, when all hands made a circuit of the Garden. Some incidents—his famous sign—☞ THIS WAY TO THE EGRESS—and his celebrated encounter with the vestrymen of St. Paul's Church regarding the display of the American flag on Fourth of July, are worth repeating.

Barnum had succeeded in crowding his Museum with visitors, but they apparently hung around even after they had seen everything there was to see. Barnum tried to relieve the congestion. But let him tell the story in his own words. He had approached a family group whom he thought were seeking a way out.

"Step this way, madam," said I politely, "you will never be able to get into the street by the front door without crushing these dear children. We have opened a large egress here and you can pass by the rear stairs into Ann Street and thus avoid all danger."

"Sure," replied the woman indignantly, "an' I'm not going out at all, at all, nor the children aither, for we've brought our dinners and we are going to stay all day."

Further investigation showed that pretty much all of my visitors had brought their dinners with the evident intention of "making a day of it." No one expected to go home till night; the building was overcrowded, and meanwhile hundreds were awaiting at the front entrance to get in when they could. In despair I sauntered upon the stage behind the scenes, biting my lips with vexation, when I happened to see the scene-painter at work and a happy thought struck me: "Here," I exclaimed, "take a piece of canvas four feet square, and paint on it, as soon as you can, in large letters:

☞ TO THE EGRESS"

Seizing his brush he finished the sign in fifteen minutes, and I directed the carpenter to nail it over the door leading to the back stairs. He did so, and as the crowd, after making the entire tour of the establishment, came pouring down the main stairs from the third story, they stopped and looked at the new sign, while some of them read audibly: "To the Aigress."

"The Aigress," said others, "sure that's an animal we haven't seen," and the throng began to pour down the back stairs, only to find that the "Aigress" was the elephant, and that the elephant was all out o' doors, or so much of it as began at Ann Street. Meanwhile I began to accommodate those who had long been waiting with their money at the Broadway entrance.

His encounter with the vestrymen of St. Paul's was as follows:

I wanted to run out a string of American flags across the street on July Fourth, for I knew there would be thousands of people passing the Museum with leisure and pocketmoney, and I felt confident that an unusual display of national flags would arrest their patriotic attention, and bring many of them within my walls. Unfortunately for my purpose, St. Paul's Church stood directly opposite, and there was nothing to which I could attach my flag-rope, unless it might be one of the trees in the churchyard. I went to see the vestrymen for permission to attach my flag-rope on the Fourth of July, and they were indignant at what they called my "insulting proposition"; such a concession would be "sacrilege." I plied them with arguments, and appealed to their patriotism, but in vain.

Returning to the Museum I gave orders to have the string of flags made ready, with the directions at daylight on the Fourth of July to attach one end of the rope to one of the third story windows of the Museum, and the other end to a tree in St. Paul's churchyard. The great day arrived, and my orders were strictly followed. The flags attracted great attention, and before nine o'clock I have no doubt that hundreds of additional visitors were drawn by this display into the Museum. By half-past nine Broadway was thronged, and by that time two gentlemen in a high state of excitement rushed into my office announcing themselves as injured and insulted vestrymen of St. Paul's Church.

"Keep cool, gentlemen," said I; "I guess it is all right."

"Right!" indignantly exclaimed one of them, "do you think it is right to attach your Museum to our Church?

We will show you what is 'right' and what is law, if we live till to-morrow; those flags must come down instantly."

"Thank you," I said, "but let us not be in a hurry. I will go out with you and look at them, and I guess we can make it all right."

Going into the street I remarked: "Really, gentlemen, these flags look very beautiful; they do not injure your tree: I always stop my balcony music for your accommodation whenever you hold week-day services, and it is but fair that you should return the favor."

"We could indict your 'music,' as you call it, as a nuisance, if we chose," answered one vestryman, "and now I tell you that if these flags are not taken down in ten minutes, *I* will cut them down."

His indignation was at the boiling point. The crowd in the street was dense, and the angry gesticulation of the vestrymen attracted their attention. I saw there was no use in trying to parley with him or coax him, and so, assuming an angry air, I rolled up my sleeves, and exclaimed, in a loud tone—

"Well, Mister, I should just like to see you dare to cut down the American flag on the Fourth of July; you must be a 'Britisher' to make such a threat as that; but I'll show you a thousand pairs of Yankee hands in two minutes, if you dare to attempt to take down the Stars and Stripes on this great birthday of American freedom!"

"What's that John Bull a-saying," asked a brawny fellow, placing himself in front of the irate vestryman: "Look here, old fellow," he continued, "if you want to save a whole bone in your body, you had better slope, and never dare again to talk about hauling down the American flag in the City of New York."

Throngs of excited, exasperated men crowded around, and the vestryman, seeing the effect of my ruse, smiled faintly and said, "Oh, of course it is all right," and he and his companion quietly edged out of the crowd. The flags remained up all day and all night. The next morning I sought the vanquished vestrymen and obtained formal permission to make use of this tree on following holidays, in consideration of my willingness to arrest the doleful strains of my discordant balcony band whenever services were held on week days in the church.

Barnum was probably one of the great advertisers of all times. One day he hired a man who had applied to him for aid.

"Now," said I, "go lay a brick on the sidewalk at the corner of Broadway and Ann Street; another close by the

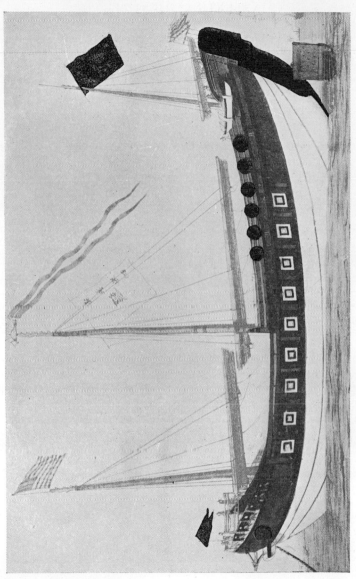

One of Barnum's great early attractions—The Chinese Junk *Keying*, which he brought from Canton, loaded with "Mandarins," lying in the Harbor of New York, 1847.

Museum; a third diagonally across the way at the corner of Broadway and Vesey Street, by the Astor House; put down the fourth on the sidewalk in front of St. Paul's Church, opposite; then, with the fifth brick in hand, take up a rapid march from one point to the other, making the circuit, exchanging your brick at every point, and say nothing to anyone."

"What is the object of this?" inquired the man.

"No matter," I replied: "All you need to know is that it brings you fifteen cents wages per hour. It is a bit of my fun, and to assist me properly you must seem to be as deaf as a post; wear a serious countenance; answer no questions; pay no attention to anyone; but attend faithfully to the work and at the end of every hour by St. Paul's clock, show this ticket at the Museum door; enter, walking solemnly through every hall in the building; pass out, and resume your work."

In a short time curiosity could no longer be resisted and finally one man, then another followed the bricklayer into the Museum to see what it was all about. The infection spread and soon the building was filled.

WINDMILLS

A Picturesque Feature of Early New York

Like most other Dutch villages of former times, the town of New Amsterdam exhibited to the traveler a striking feature in its windmills, which being generally situated on elevated points, towered above the humble edifices of the town, and spread their wings invitingly toward the vagrant breezes.

It must be remembered that windmills were very important machines in those days, when there was no water power convenient without going into the wildernesses of Westchester County and Jersey, and exposing Christian lives to the murderous savage; when steam was not thought of as a motor, and when the whole subject of economy of power was divided between the rival claims of horse power and wind power. There was a horse mill erected here almost as soon as the colonists settled the island (its locality being the present South William Street, near Broad Street), but upon the whole, as capital enlarged, it found its way into windmills in preference to the other method of wearing and tearing horse flesh; and indeed, upon the whole, it must be confessed that the greater popularity of this form of machine, was well deserved. Albeit its great unwieldy arms, its varying motion and the creaking of the sails, as they favored the course of the wind, were not exactly in accordance with the more scientific systems of machinery of modern days.

In the perspective view of the city, made by that accomplished merchant, Augustus Heermans, in 1656, the windmill adjoining the fort, and standing upon the present State Street, was the most prominent object in view of the traveler approaching the city; and no doubt it was a pleasing one to the weary wanderer from a far-off home of civilization. It recalled the scenes of the old country. It spoke of habits of industry, and the realization of ideas of bread, at least, in this new scene of future residence.

Another windmill occupied the eminence immediately north of Wall Street, the owner being Jan Vinje, at once farmer, brewer and miller. A curious sight it must have been to see the farmer's wagons laden with grain traversing the shore along the East River, winding up the romantic valley now called Maiden Lane, and depositing their loads at this edifice then standing in the midst of a clearing of forest trees of native growth. The snug little stone farm house, with its loop hole windows to keep out marauding savages, the low door way with its bull's-eye windows in the panels, the motley assemblage of domestic animals and slaves of all sorts and sizes, which then formed the great part of a domestic establishment, the waving grain of the adjoining fields, the newly planted orchard, all formed a picture which can hardly now be idealized in connection with that ancient and long populated part of the city.

Farther eastward on the heights along the East River shore was another windmill, opposite the ferry landing from Long Island. Here also was a brewery, and likewise a house of entertainment wherein the farmer solaced himself while waiting during the tedious intervals of the passage of the ferry boats. Some localities have their peculiar topics of conversation, and here it naturally turned to a discussion upon the changes of the tide, the probable duration of detention, the chances of the traveler reaching his home during the day, and kindred subjects. The "ferry" was as well known in those times as the City Hall is now.

Another windmill stood upon the south part of the present Park, then a desert spot, covered by stinted bushes and "hoop-pole" saplings, and offering no annoyance of forest trees to the free course of the winds above the underwood. It was here that the miller presented the attractions of his establishment to such of the farmers as cultivated the "vlachte" or flats of Harlem, then the agricultural garden of Manhattan Island, the rough road through the Commons bushes running directly past his door, which was in full view, though at a considerable distance from the city.

Then to attract the Jersey farmers, those venturesome men who had penetrated the wilderness and planted the fertile region of Hackgingsack, and those too along the Jersey shore, in sections called by the Indians Ahasimus, Hoboken hacking and Carnocuipa, there was another windmill erected on the North River shore, below the present St. Paul's Church.

These and several others, erected from time to time, on prominent points of the landscape, were distinguishing features of the Dutch city of New Amsterdam. The business of miller was one of the most profitable of that day, for this city was for a long period the staple port where all flour designed for exportation was bolted, and whence all flour was exported. It was said that this was the principal cause of its prosperity in early times; and that when the privilege was taken away the prosperity of the city was reduced one half.

OLD, OLD NEW YORK

Most histories are filled with accounts of wars, descriptions of contemporary rulers and political doings while the actual every-day lives of the people themselves are passed over practically in silence.

The little weekly papers like the "Gazette," "Post Boy" and "Museum" however seem to afford an intimate glimpse of the daily lives of the New Yorker, in a much more interesting way than is recorded from the Olympic Heights of history. Take, for instance, this little real estate advertisement of a stable in Wall Street, now the great financial street of the world—

Four of five stables in Wall Street to let, opposite Col. Wm. Livingston's, with stalls for from two to four horses, rooms for carriages, and large lofts for hay.

And the advertisement of Blackwell's Island—

Samuel and Josiah Blackwell offer for sale the well known farm of Jacob Blackwell, deceased, about six miles from New York, on the East River. It contains 160 acres and 25 acres of salt meadow.

And of a famous Tavern in the Bowery—

To be let, the "Dog and Duck" tavern, in the Bowery Lane, at the two mile stone; the house has eight rooms, with a large garden, and the best bed of asparagus on this island. Enquire of No. 44 Gold Street, opposite the Baptist Meeting-house.

It was almost the beginning of the century before a hotel was built in our city. Up to that time, travelers lodged in taverns or at the houses of friends, and the letters of travelers in that day are all filled with complaints concerning the overcrowded condition of the average tavern. The same condition seems to prevail today, as you probably know from bitter experience when arriving late in town, without having made a reservation. One enterprising tavern keeper formulated the following code to govern his establishment and posted the following rules on a sign which he hung outside his door.

Rules of This Tavern

Four pence a night for bed.
Six pence with supper.
No more than five to sleep in one bed.
No boots to be worn in bed.
Organ grinders to sleep in the wash house.
No dogs allowed upstairs.
No beer allowed in the kitchen.
No razor grinders or tinkers taken in.

The many opponents of the Volstead Act will doubtless approve of the verdict rendered in the following case which is spread on the records of 1786—

An Old Time Coroner's Verdict (1786)

"That the said Tatum's death was occasioned by the freezing of a large quantity of water in his body, that had been mixed with the rum he drank."

The little merchants of Old New York were just as energetic and enterprising as are their prototypes of to-

FAMOUS NEW YORKERS.

DeWitt Clinton. Marinus Willet. Portraits of the great-grandfather
and great-grandmother of Johannis De Peyster, the
first of this family in New York.

day. They advertised persistently, and were not unmindful of the value of publicity. It is interesting to note that many well-known names of today were equally well-known a hundred years ago, as may be seen from the following announcements, which appeared regularly every week.

Jacob Astor, No. 81 Queen Street, two doors from the Friends' Meeting House, has just imported from London, an elegant assortment of musical instruments.

Archibald Gracie has removed his Counting-Room from his dwelling house, No. 110 Broadway, to his new Fire Proof Store, No. 52 Pine St. where he has for sale a few chests of very fine Hyson.

Robert Lenox has for sale, remaining from the cargo of the ship Sansom, from Calcutta, an assortment of White Piece Goods.

A person lately from London, now stopping at 27 Little Dock St., has a composition for sale that will destroy the very troublesome vermin commonly called Bugs.

A fine lot of ground on the west side of Broadway, near the old Lutheran Church, is for sale. Enquire of Alexander Hamilton, in Wall Street, No. 58.

Here is an item that will recall the days when slavery was a New York institution. It may surprise a good many persons to know that it was fifty years after the Declaration of Independence when slavery finally became illegal in our city.

Augustus Van Horne, of No. 58 Smith Street, offers a Half Joe reward for the capture of his Negro slave. He is a very talkative saucy, impertinent fellow.

In those days as well as in our own it occasionally happened that the path of true love did not run smoothly, and so we observe in one of the papers the following announcement—

Benjamin Jacobs notifies the public that his wife Elizabeth has eloped from his bed and board, and that he will pay no debts of her contracting.

Elizabeth, however, did not suffer her husband's rebuke to pass in silence. She promptly appeared in print in the next issue with her side of the story, as follows:

Elizabeth Jacobs, who was advertised by her husband on the 5th inst., informs the public that she was compelled by his cruel treatment to leave him; that no person that knows him would trust him with a shilling; and she is happy that the law protects her from paying his debts.

Our heart goes out in sympathy to Col. William Smith, who has just moved to town from Red Mill, Dutchess County. He finds so many other Bill Smiths here even at this early date that he has added the letter M. between his first and last name to distinguish him presumably from the common herd of Bills. He ought to look at the telephone book today.

Notice.—Col. William Smith, late of Red Mill, Dutchess Co., informs his friends and the public that having moved into New York, and finding so many of his name, to distinguish himself from them, has added between his name the letter "M."

And so these old newspapers fill a niche in our records that is not found elsewhere. There is a human touch and a "close up" view of extraordinary interest. They are well worth a careful reading.

Broadway between Duane and Pearl Streets, 1806

CITY HALL PARK
AND ITS NEIGHBORHOOD

In view of the determined effort to remove the old Post Office from City Hall Park, a brief history of this section, easily the most historic on our Island, will be of interest to our readers. From the day the Dutch bought the Island from the Indians, this particular land has always been reserved for the benefit of all the people. Thousands of New Yorkers bitterly opposed the project to establish the Post Office there in 1868. Public interest in matters of this kind was not so keen in those days as now. We have grown older and realize as we never did before the obligation we are under to preserve what our forefathers created and which means so much in a spiritual sense to the patriotism and public spirit of the whole country.

Congress has already passed the necessary legislation for the return of this land in exchange for another suitable location for a new Post Office. The City has agreed to contribute an equally good site opposite the new County Court House, in the proposed new Civic Centre. The Commission appointed by the late President Harding consisted of three Cabinet officers, Messrs. Work, Daugherty and Mellon. The changes caused by the death of Mr. Harding need not necessarily delay this important work. It would be a splendid thing if this desirable improvement could be made so that on the Three Hundredth Anniversary of the Founding of New York, 1926, the work would be finished. It would be a fitting birthday gift from Uncle Sam to Father Knickerbocker.

The following sketch gives some early glimpses of the famous old Park or "Commons." The original boundaries of these city-owned lands extended north to the present line of Worth Street, including the famous Collect Pond, the site of which is soon to be occupied by our Civic Centre.

It was not until about 1812, when the present City Hall was formally opened to the public, that the immense importance of this little open space was realized. Gradually all the remaining buildings were removed and by 1830 there remained nothing but the City Hall itself and the old Hall of Records, used as a jail during the Revolution. This building should never have been destroyed and its disappearance is now keenly regretted.* It stood about in front of the present Bridge entrance. The City Court building and the County Court House now in the Park, in the rear of the City Hall, are the product of the Tweed era. When the new County Court House is finished the whole group should be cleared out, along with the old Post Office. Then the Park will resume its original, beautiful appearance.

The "Vlachte," or "Flat," "Second Plains," "Commons," "Fields," by which name the present Park has been known at different periods, was originally the common grazing place of the cattle belonging to the citizens of New Amsterdam. Following the plan of European villages, this place was left open to the public use, and is probably the first recognized public property on this island. Its jurisdiction and proprietorship thus tacitly fell to the people, and it has, in its subsequent history, been the scene of some of the most important political demonstrations ever witnessed. While the island was yet in the possession of the Indians, it has been surmised that their village was situated on this spot. There is no account, we believe, in our historical records, of the precise locality at which the tribe known as the Manhattans resided, but judging from what has been received as undoubted evidence of the establishment of an Indian village, namely the mixture of shells

* See page 206.

The City Hall and Park as it appeared about 1843, showing the first fountain with Croton water, presented by Mayor Havemeyer.

with the upland soil, this spot has been either the site of, or in the immediate vicinity of a large Indian village at some period more or less remote. When it came under the dominion of the Dutch, and its war paths were brought down to the more domestic purposes of cattle walks, it came under the general superintendence of a herdsman whose business was, for a certain stipend from each family, to perambulate the village of New Amsterdam and blow upon his horn a note of invitation at the garden gates of the inhabitants, whose cows being let out joined the common drove and were driven through the romantic valley road now called Maiden Lane, and having arrived at the common pasture were restrained from more distant perambulation by the watchful herdsman.

And in that manner, and to those uses was the "Vlachte" appropriated for many years. Afterward it became subject to less innocent and peaceful uses. It saw the warlike parade of the Dutch soldiery on training days. It witnessed the formation of a battle array under Captain Colve, destined to the capture of the city. It became the place of popular meetings for all sorts of purposes, among which were the holiday festivals of the English period, such as their Majesty's birthday, the anniversary of the discovery of the gunpowder plot, &c. It witnessed bonfires and illuminations, militia trainings, executions, burnings in effigy, and tumultuous meetings of Liberty Boys before the Revolution.

As an epitome of public acts relating to the Commons, the King's Farm and to the Fresh Water Pond, we present the following abstracts of resolutions and ordinances from the Common Council records:

No Holes to be dug in the Commons

1731.—It is enacted, that "if any person or persons whatsoever within this city or liberties thereof shall, at any time hereafter, dig any holes in the Commons of this city on the south side of the Fresh Water, or take or carry away any earth or mould, or shall cut, take, or carry away any sods or turf off any part of said Commons, he shall suffer a fine of forty shillings."

Law against taking Fish in Fresh Water Pond, in any other way except by Angling

1734.—Be it ordained, that "if any person or persons whatsoever do, from henceforth, presume to put, place or cast into the pond, commonly called Fresh Water Pond, belonging to this Corporation, any hoop-net, draw-net, purse-net, casting-net, cod-net, bley-net, or any other net or nets whatsoever, and shall take and catch any of the fish

The old *Staats Zeitung* Building, now site
of the Municipal Building, Chambers Street
and Park Row, 1870.

within the said pond therewith, or by any other engine,
machine, arts, ways or means whatsoever, other than by
angling with angle-rod, hook and line only, every person
so offending against the tenor of this law, shall, for every
offence forfeit and pay the sum of twenty shillings current
money."

Owners of Brick-kilns on the Commons in 1742

1742.—Joseph Paulding, Cornelius Cozine, Charles Dobbs
and Abraham Paulding, Jacobus Ryckman, William Wood.

Respecting the Tanners on the borders of Fresh Water Pond

1745.—*Ordered,* That the tanners who have, and shall
hereafter dig pits at the Fresh Water for the benefit of
water, may in future enjoy the benefit thereof, and no one
shall deprive them thereof.

The building of the Powder-house on the Island in the Fresh Water Pond

1747.—The Recorder acquainted the Board that it is the
opinion of the Governor and Council, and the Committee
of the Assembly, that the hollow near the poor-house is the
most proper place for building the magazine, and this
Board considering the same, agree to the magazine being
built there, provided the Corporation have the appointment
of the keeper, and the benefit of the storage of all the powder there belonging to private persons.

The Commons hired out for Brick-kilns

1751.—*Ordered.* A committee to inquire "what rents
are due from the brick-makers for brick kilns made on the
Commons of this city, and demand the same; and that
they also have power to treat with and agree for the
leasing of such parts of the said Commons for the making of brick kilns, as to them shall seem meet."

The Negro Burial-ground and Pot-house

1753.—Petition of John Teller, Jacobus Stoutenburg and
Mary Van Vlack, in behalf of themselves and others, praying that a grant of some lands belonging to this Corporation, in exchange for the negro burying ground; as also
for a small slip of land on which a pot-house, &c., are
built. Consideration deferred.

Removal of the Common Gallows from the lower end of the present Park to the present vicinity of the Five Points

1756.—A committee appointed to remove the gallows
from where it now stands to the place where the negroes

SOME EARLY MAYORS OF NEW YORK.

Richard Varick.   Edward Livingston.
Jacob Radcliffe.   James Duane.

were burnt some five years ago, at the foot of the hill called Catiemuts' Hill, near the Fresh Water.

Poor-house Burial-ground on site of present City Hall

1757.—A small piece of the ground "of the length of two boards," to the eastward of the work-house fence, ordered to be inclosed for a burial place for the poor of said work-house.

The building of the New Gaol (old Hall of Records)

1757.—Committee appointed to superintend and purchase materials for the new gaol, and to proceed with all speed in completing the same. (See page 206.)

The erection of Barracks in the time of the Old French War, along the present Chambers Street

1757.—The committee appointed to confer with carpenters respecting the building of barracks, report the following resolution, viz: That the said building be forthwith carried on under the direction and inspection of the abovementioned committee, who are hereby empowered to treat with such persons, and provide such materials for the carrying on and completing said work as they shall judge proper; and further ordered, that the said building contain twenty rooms on a floor, two stories high, to be twenty-one feet square, four hundred and twenty feet long, and twenty-one feet wide, to be built on some of the common lands of the Corporation to the southward of Fresh Water, between the new gaol-house and the house of Catiemuts.

Place of the Brick Yards along present Chatham Street, then the High Road to Boston

1759.—A committee appointed to "lay out in lots some ground belonging to this Corporation, which lie between the new gaol-house, and the house commonly called 'Catiemuts'" (present south-west corner of Pearl and Chatham Streets).

3d April, 1759. This being the day appointed for farming, by public outcry, several lots belonging to this Corporation, which lie between the gaol-house and the house of Thomas Brown, near the palisades; four of the same were let, three to Joseph Paulding, and one to William Copeland.*

The Land in Vicinity of the Negro Burial-ground

1760.—Henry Van Vleck, merchant, attending the Board in behalf of his sisters Sarah and Eve Van Vleck, and pro-

* For brick yards.

A famous old-time Theatre—Harry Miner's on Eighth Avenue.

posed the leasing of three lots of ground contiguous and adjoining to the Negroes' Burying-place,† on part of which said lots their father built a pot-house, pot-oven, and sunk a well, supposing at that time the said lands were his property, whereupon this Board, having taken the same into their consideration, resolved to lease the same to said Sarah and Eve Van Vleck, and for nineteen years and six months, at forty shillings rent for each lot of twenty-five by one hundred feet.

Extension of Broadway through the Commons

1760.—Mr. Marschalk, one of the City Surveyors, produced to this Board the draft or plan of a road which he hath lately laid out by direction of this Corporation, viz: Beginning from the Spring Garden house,‡ where the street now is of the breadth of eighty-two feet six inches, and extending from thence north thirty-seven degrees, east thirty minutes, until it comes to the ground of the late widow Rutgers, leaving the street thereof fifty feet in breadth, which is approved of by this Board, and ordered that the same be recorded in such manner accordingly.

The King's Farm

1761.—Trinity Church released their claim to several streets in their land commonly called the "King's Farm," lying north of the present St. Paul's Church.

Place for Pitch, etc., on Commons

1762.—A certain place appropriated near to the house of Elias De Grusha near the Negroes' Burial-place, for the reception of pitch, tar, turpentine, and shingles, and ordered that no such articles be kept in any other place south of Fresh Water.

Whipping Post, Stocks, Cage and Pillory

1764.—Ordered that the Committee of the new gaol have power to cause to be erected opposite the said new gaol, a public whipping post, stocks, cage and pillory, in such manner as they shall think proper.

---

† The Negroes' Burial-ground, was situated near Stewart's marble store on Broadway.
‡ Present site of Astor House.

COUNTRY RESIDENCE OF DAVID PROVOOST, FIFTY-SEVENTH STREET AND EAST RIVER, 1858.

The old carriage entrance at Wanamaker's.
Fleischman's Bakery opposite, since removed
to enlarge the grounds surrounding Grace
Church. About 1890.

The proposed Dutch Reformed Burial-ground on present Pearl, William and Rose Streets

1766.—Petition of the Ministers, Elders and Deacons of the Reformed Protestant Dutch Church of the city of New York, was preferred to this Board, setting forth that their predecessors have, for near a century past, made use of the cemetery church-yard adjoining to the old Dutch Church for the burying their dead, which, from the length of time and the contracted limits of the ground, is now so full of dead bodies that it is hardly possible to open the ground for a grave without digging up some of the corpses there interred, a circumstance very disagreeable and indecent; and therefore praying that this Board would be pleased to grant unto them and their successors forever, a certain piece of ground in the Commons, contiguous to Mr. Cuyler's Sugar-house, the east end of which fronts the main road that leads to Fresh Water, upon which it is ordered that this Board will grant to the petitioners the aforesaid piece of ground, containing twenty-eight lots, ten of which front northerly to Queen Street,* eight others easterly and southerly upon Thomas Street,† and ten others fronting westerly upon George Street,‡ some larger and some smaller, and that such grant be to the petitioners and their successors forever, under the rent of £70, to be paid annually.

The City Hospital in Contemplation

1771.—The institution of a public infirmary or hospital within this city, being not only a laudable but useful undertaking, this Board being willing to encourage the same, have agreed to grant all the right and interest they have in and to the westermost half of the lot formerly belonging to John Harris, deceased, but now to this Corporation, containing in breadth in front on the Commons 124 feet, and in length 248 for the purpose of building the said hospital.

1772.—The Governors of the New York Hospital, having purchased a more suitable site for their building than that offered them by the Corporation, petition for a grant of money in lieu of the land proposed to be given; whereupon £1,000 is voted.

Chatham Street Named

1774.—Ordered that the street, beginning at the house of Andrew Hopper, nearly opposite St. Paul's Church, and leading to Fresh Water, be called Chatham Street.

* Present Pearl Street.
† Present William Street.
‡ Present Rose Street.

The Manhattan Company selecting a Site for their Reservoir

1799.—The Manhattan Company addressed the Corporation the following queries: 1st. Whether they were willing to sell the property formerly occupied by Mr. Collis for a well and reservoir; or 2d. If the Corporation preferred leasing it forever; or 3d. If the Corporation would permit the Company to occupy the grounds aforesaid until it could be ascertained whether the waters were pure and wholesome and adequate to supply the city. The city, on the first two points reserved an answer, but granted the permission asked for in the third proposition.

1799.—A letter from the Manhattan Company stated that they would require a part of the inclosed ground in front of the Bridewell (the present Park in front of the City Hall), to raise a reservoir for supplying the city with water. A committee was thereupon appointed to confer with the company.

Part of the Negroes' Burial-ground, south of Chambers Street (in the present Park), Question, as to ceding to the City

1796.—The Board determined that if the proprietors of the land called the Negroes' Burial-ground, north of the Alms-house and Bridewell, would, on or before the first day of May, 1797, surrender to the Corporation all their ground south of Chambers Street, the Corporation would release to them certain lots in Augustus Street (City Hall Place) and the vicinity.

The Records of the City for several years about this period, have been abstracted. The index is, however, preserved, from which we find as follows:

The stable and barn at the Alms-house in the Park were ordered to be pulled down.

A report was made on opening a canal from Broadway to Hudson River.

An order was made for opening the same immediately.

The erection of the present City Hall was resolved upon, and the building commenced.

It is resolved to fill in the Collect, and the work continued during several years, the dirt having been taken from the neighboring hills.

The Manhattan Company applied to purchase the Collect Pond.

Lispenard's Meadows were regulated.

Duryea House, on Newtown Creek, Bushwick.

OLD BROOKLYN
THE EASTERN DISTRICT IN THE 70's

Around the old Union Baseball Grounds still linger some of the pleasantest memories of my boyhood. The adjoining land was passing through that period where the farms were rapidly changing into building lots. A fairly good sized stream ran west of Marcy Avenue, and a pond of respectable depth and dimensions still did duty as an "old swimming hole." The neighborhood, however, was fast building up, and the spectacle of unclad boys seen from the near distance provoked frequent complaints to the police. In addition there was the traditional enmity between the boys on the Harrison Avenue side, known as the "Rocks," and the Marcy Avenue boys who called themselves the "Roosters." If a kind Providence enabled the

"Rocks" to descend suddenly and unexpectedly on the "Roosters" while the latter were disporting themselves in the pellucid waters of the "Dumb-bell," as the pond was known, the garments of the latter were promptly seized as spoils of war, and the unluckly owners driven by their enemies into the thickly settled portion of the neighborhood. Consequences of an embarrassing nature naturally followed, removed shortly, however, by the appearance of the police who generally compelled the victors to relinquish their ill-gotten spoils and restored the threatened collapse of decency to a distracted neighborhood.

I look back on these street fights with mingled feelings

Bergen House, on Bergen Island, Flatbush.

Bushwick Church, View 1820.

of dismay and thankfulness. During the progress of a battle, large groups of boys would unknowingly become wedged in between scattered buildings, presenting almost inescapable targets for the shower of stones and missiles that filled the air from the opposing groups. I was in many of these fights, but rarely was a boy seriously injured. I do not now recall any that required a surgeon's care, but the damage was very real and escape from almost fatal consequences seems to me to have been nothing short of Divine interposition mercifully displayed toward a lot of heedless and careless youngsters. With the advent of new buildings and the gradual filling up of the vacant land, these belligerents disappeared, or became assimilated in a friendly relation. None of us grew up to be criminals, nor was there any particular opprobrium attached to being a member of this or that "gang." In fact, we rather prided ourselves on our membership, and such of us as aspired to leadership were looked up to with considerable awe by the younger boys of our neighborhood.

This peculiar spirit of scrappiness was not confined to any one part of Brooklyn, but seemed to be common all over the city. New villages were constantly being absorbed by the city's growth, and as soon as we reached say Bushwick, we had to have a fight with the Bushwickers. The Flushing Avenue gang, the Greenpoint gang, the Kent Avenue gang, the Dock Rats, and a dozen others figured in these amateur battles. And feuds between certain public schools were always in evidence. Even in the older and quite thickly settled portions of the city, such as "The Heights," the same custom prevailed. Capt. Charley Low in his "Recollections" tells us of the many fierce encounters between the Classical

South Third Street Presbyterian Church,
Williamsburgh. (Dr. Wells'.)

School which he attended and the Hegeman Street school nearby. The Classical School being usually victorious, the Hegeman boys combined with the next Public School on Henry Street. Many were the contests which followed with varying fortunes. The practice seems to have been general and must have caused the neighborhood much annoyance. There were, of course, serious results at times, but nothing in my judgment to what I think the law of average would indicate.

A Mr. Cammeyer then owned the land embraced in the Union Grounds. It is now occupied by a State Armory. Mr. Cammeyer's son seemed to me to be the most favored individual who ever lived or ever would live. Not only had he "carte blanche" as to the number of boy friends whom he might invite to see such classic games as a match between the Mutuals and Athletics, but he actually had a nine of his own which he called the "Young Mutuals." They had real uniforms, too, just like a regular nine, and sported a dozen bats or more. There was also a rival team, of which I think the Captain was Joe Knapp, son of the founder of the Metropolitan Life Insurance Company. All of us attended "Pop Dunkley's" School, formally known as Public School No. 16, Wilson Street. Dan Wilson, afterwards the well-known carriage builder (A. S. Flandreau & Co.), Maurice Grey, are among some of the names that I recall.

In winter the grounds were flooded and turned into a Skating Rink. Skating at that time was a wonderfully popular sport in Old Brooklyn. The Capitoline Grounds in the Bedford section was another popular resort. Washington Park in South Brooklyn was, however, probably the best known and most popular of them all. There is in existence a very large lithograph, showing a Carnival

Mr. Charles Pratt. Founder of the Pratt Institute, Brooklyn, a famous vocational educational college.

held here in the winter of 1868. As all the guests were in costume, and as this picture was a very expensive undertaking for those days, it is fair to assume that public interest in the sport must have existed to an extent that we can hardly realize today. In later years Prospect Park became the chief resort of the skaters, and the excellent ice, the greater beauty of the surroundings, contributed in no small degree to the continued popularity of the pastime.

Another winter sport very popular among the younger set was sleigh rides on the old Hamilton stages. These huge caravansaries carried as many as a hundred passengers and were drawn by eight or ten horses gaily capari-

Thomas Kirk's Printing Office, Adams Street; where the Brooklyn Sunday School Union was organized.

Barney Williams' Country Seat, Bath, View 1860.

soned and loaded with tuneful sleighbells. On a moonlight night the drive out to Prospect Park through Bedford Avenue—at that time scarcely built up beyond Hewes
Street—was a delight long to be remembered. The
musical cadence of the bells, the nodding of the brilliant
colored plumes, and the laughter and singing of the
young people in the sleigh, brings back to my mind a
fascinating picture. And the expense of such an outing,
compared with today's prices was so reasonable as to be
laughable by comparison. There was no lack of enjoyment among the boys and girls of Old Brooklyn.

Dancing was, of course, a popular diversion, but not
to the same extent as today. We were all more or less
influenced by the attitude of our churches, and the
Methodists were certainly opposed to the practice. It

Delmonico's farmhouse, on Delmonico Place. Known for years as the "Haunted House."

must be remembered that Brooklyn was peculiar in the matter of churches. We all belonged to one or another, as a perfectly natural thing. And there were several kinds of Methodists. Most of the young people, however, decided the matter for themselves and the great majority were in favor of moderate indulgence. In this I feel that they were right. Most of the dancing was done among ourselves in private homes. Occasionally there would be a ball at the Armory, or some extraordinary occurrence which would take us to some public assemblage like the Academy of Music, but these occasions were largely the exception. A more liberal spirit began to manifest itself later among the Methodists; for one thing they had ceased to discipline their members for infractions of this rule, and there was a very decided feeling that it was one of those questions that were better left undisturbed. The Annual Conference, however, continued to froth at the mouth and imply all sorts of evil as directly resulting from this pernicious practice; but in time I think they took a more liberal view, but could never bring themselves wholly to approve of the practice.

In another respect we were equally narrow-minded. I do not now recall any minister in good standing admitting that he ever attended a theatre, or approving of the institution. The Rev. John Hyatt Smith might possibly have proved an exception. He was at one time quite a popular preacher, but developed a liberal tendency that certainly brought him into disfavor. His own church on Lee Avenue itself became a theatre, and in it Mrs. Langtry appeared for the first time in Brooklyn. What the innermost feelings of the clergy actually were on this interesting question, I never knew. If they secretly attended a performance, it was wholly unknown to their congregations. I doubt if the best of them could have retained his position had he been guilty of this indiscretion.

So on these two points the young people of the Eastern District had to decide for themselves. Knowing them as I do, I am quite sure that a little of their enjoyment was possibly spoiled because their church affiliations did not wholly approve of their sinful practices. They were very deeply attached to the church, as a great part of their social life was bound up in it. And so it was only natural that a little conscience pricking would be felt now and then under these circumstances.

The present-day dances were then unknown. The Waltz, Polka, Polka Mazurka, Lanciers and Quadrille,

Howard House, Atlantic and Alabama Avenues.

were about the extent of the list. The "square" dances were often acceptable to young ladies who drew the line at waltzes. In fact, the vials of wrath were generally poured upon the latter, frequently to the entire exclusion of the former. I have seen some of our otherwise intelligent and well educated ministers, lash themselves into a perfect fury over the alleged iniquity of the waltz. And for a time they even influenced me. The peculiar relation between the laity and the church was something not readily understood by the reader of today. In another chapter I will endeavor to describe the unusual posi-

THE BEEKMAN HOUSE, FIFTIETH STREET AND EAST RIVER, IN 1860. ROOM IN WHICH MAJOR ANDRE
RECEIVED HIS FINAL INSTRUCTIONS FOR HIS MEETING WITH BENEDICT ARNOLD.

tion occupied by the Church in Brooklyn in its relation to the home and the social life of its people. No such counterpart existed in any other part of the country.

The views in this article are from *Old Brooklyn,* by Eugene L. Armbruster, a work now in course of preparation. The author has been for forty years a close student of the history of Brooklyn and Long Island, and has assembled an extensive collection of views and documents relating to these sections. We have asked Mr. Armbruster to give us a little more data concerning these various pictures to which he kindly consented. His remarks follow:

"Originally the City of Brooklyn embraced the former town of the same name. The City of Williamsburg and the town of Bushwick were consolidated with Brooklyn on January 1, 1855, and gradually the other country towns were annexed, New Lots being the first in 1886. During the 90's the others followed suit, until the entire County of Kings formed the City of Brooklyn, now the Borough of Brooklyn.

"While it is today a matter of, at the utmost, an hour's ride in the subway, to reach any one of these places, a visit to the former town, in the olden days, was quite an excursion. About the middle of the last century they could all be reached by the stages, often advertised as 'flying machines'; but much time was required and when the place of destination was finally reached, one needed some more time to get into a fit condition to be able to survive the trip back to little Old New York.

"The next step toward rapid transit was the horse car. The body of the stage coach was set upon a platform, which had two low wheels on either side. In the center of this platform was an iron bolt standing upright. An opening in the bottom of the stage made it possible to bolt the latter in its place. A king-pin on the front part prevented the movement of the stage body to either side. When the terminus of the line was reached, the pin was released, and the horse, turning in the opposite direction, moved the upper part around, while the platform remained stationary. After the pin was put back into its place, the horse car was ready for its return trip. Seymour L. Husted had been one of the principal stage coach operators and became the head of the new transit company. His later residence at Myrtle and Clinton Avenues is represented among the views.

"The Duryea farmhouse on Newtown Creek, where the Penny Bridge runs across from the foot of Meeker Avenue, was erected about 1681. It was a veritable fort; its stout stone walls were provided with portholes for a cannon, as well as for guns, and a center wall with similar portholes formed a second line of defense. A supply of powder was kept in a room which had no window openings, and in another room a big iron ring was fastened to the wall, to which prisoners, such as unruly slaves, could be secured. The family burial place back of the house was removed in 1890, and the house was torn down in 1921.

"Houston Street Ferry House, at foot of Grand Street, Williamsburg, as it appeared in 1853, when the Waterbury, Withers and Winant families were the owners.

"The Bergen House on Bergen Island, in the former town of Flatlands. Elbert Elbertse Stoothoff purchased this island in 1665 and he erected the original portion of the house. In 1791, the island came into possession of Tunis Bergen. Bergen added, in 1801, the easterly wing and enlarged the main building in 1819. His son, Cornelius,

Brooklyn. Interior view of the New England Kitchen, at the great Sanitary Fair in aid of the soldiers during the Civil War, 1865.

added the westerly wing. John C. Bergen, the son of Cornelius, sold the property in 1893, to a group of men who established Bergen Beach.

"The Presbyterian Church of Williamsburgh, at South Third Street and Driggs Avenue, was dedicated in 1846. The church is now known as the South Third Street Presbyterian Church and best known as Dr. Wells' Church.

"Thomas Kirk's Printing Office, on Adams Street, between Sands and High Streets. Here the first district school was established on May 6, 1816, of which Judge John Dikeman was the teacher. In this room also the first session of the Sunday School in Brooklyn was held in the following year.

"Delmonico Stone House on the Delmonico farm, South of the Newtown Road, stood at Delmonico Place, between Ellery Street and Park Avenue. The frame house, which was occupied by Longi, the manager of Delmonico's in New York, built on a portion of the farm, is still standing.

"The Union Ferryboat *Wyandank,* on war duty on the Potomac River in 1862, removing guns from the Confederate batteries at Cock Pit Point.

"The second Howard House, at Atlantic and Alabama Avenues, East New York, was erected in 1853, by Philip Howard Reid. This was the lineal successor of the Howard Halfway House which became famous in the Revolutionary War, and which stood at the junction of Broadway, Jamaica Avenue and Fulton Street. The second Howard House served as a railroad station and was long a landmark.

"View of the original Bushwick Church on Metropolitan Avenue and the Woodpoint Road in 1820. The second edifice was erected nine years later on the same place.

Brooklyn.   The old Wyckoff Homestead on Canarsie Lane, part of which is still standing.

"Pieter Claessen Wyckoff farmhouse on Canarsie Lane, west of Ralph Avenue, Flatlands, was built in 1664. The brick stones used for the chimney fireplace, etc., were imported from Holland, as were the white cedar shingles, some of which may still be seen on the south side of the old structure. In 1819, the overhang of the roof, on the north side, was shortened, which extended far out and within a few feet of the ground. The north and east sides were at that time re-shingled and a few rooms were plastered for the first time. The oak beams on the ceiling of the dining room have assumed the color of walnut. The shingled roof was overlaid with a tin roof."

Old Blacksmith Shop of S. Wortman

OLD-TIME FERRY BOATS TO BROOKLYN

Quaint and Curious Customs Before the Days of Bridges and Tunnels

By James Blaine Walker
Sec'y Public Service Commission

The ferry to Long Island was the first municipally-owned ferry in New York. It was established prior to 1664, the year in which the Dutch rule ended, for the first English Governor confirmed to the city government the right to maintain such a ferry as had already existed under Dutch rule.

Both Dutch and English, however, were content with municipal ownership of the ferries and only attempted municipal operation when a proper tenant or lessee could not be found to operate them, and such occasions were rare, even in the early days before increasing travel made them very valuable as a business enterprise. Their value to the city, however, was always keenly appreciated, so much so that the English rulers of the municipal government frequently mortgaged the receipts of the ferry to raise money. Some of these purposes, considered legitimate and proper two hundred years ago, provoke smiles now from the American unused to the customs of royal subjects. For instance, in 1693 the "mayor, aldermen and commonalty" of New York felt it incumbent on them to give a loving cup to the new Governor, but the municipal treasury was empty and the cup cost "106 pounds."

But the Mayor of New York knew how to "raise the wind" and at once bethought himself of the one and only revenue producer, the Long Island ferry. It had been leased to John Arsen for 140 pounds a year, and what was easier than to borrow 106 pounds on a revenue of 140 pounds. The Mayor at the time was A. DePeyster, Esq. He was authorized to devise means to purchase the loving cup, and he reported a plan to mortgage the ferry receipts.

The aldermen of those days were just as willing to spend borrowed money as those of today, and in formal session on July 20, 1693, they adopted resolutions accordingly.

Mortgaging the ferry receipts proved to be such an easy way to raise money that the city fathers soon had recourse to it again. Early in 1694 they decided that the city needed a battery for its defence. Accordingly they resolved to place a platform and battery at the "point of rocks," probably the point now known as the Battery. But it took money to buy cannon, and to get it they again turned to the ferry. Notwithstanding that the mortgage for the loving cup had not been satisfied, the Council resolved to mortgage ferry receipts three years in advance to raise the funds. Here an entry telling of the transaction, dated April 13, 1694, is in the minutes of the Council.

In due course of time Alderman Merrett became Mayor, and profiting by the financiering of Mayor DePeyster, pursued a liberal policy of public improvement which he financed by again mortgaging the ferry. At a meeting of the Council on June 26, 1696, it was decided to build a new city hall and a powder house, presumably to store the ammunition for the battery built out of the first ferry mortgage. After deciding on these improvements the following action was taken, as shown by the minutes:

Coney Island in the days of Norton & Murray (1873).

> "Mem.—Itt is proposed that ye Easiest and best way for the building a City Hall, Powder House, etc., is to mortgage the rent of ye Ferry for fifteen years."

It therefore appears that municipal ownership of a public utility enabled the New Yorkers of two hundred years ago to buy a gold loving cup to keep the Governor in good humor, to erect a battery of guns for the city's defence and to provide means for building the first city hall.

After the Dutch had been driven out by the English, one of the first petitions made by the citizens to their new rulers included a prayer for the grant of the ferry privilege to the city. It was conceded by King George II. in the first English charter of the City of New York.

This was granted to Governor Thomas Dongan in 1686. It is known as the Dongan Charter, and the original document, a parchment wrinkled and yellow with age, is still preserved in the archives of the city. With other early charters it may be seen in its case in the Public Library. The writing is still legible.

The request for the ferry grant was made three years earlier. It was noted in the minutes of the aldermen as follows:

> "Att a Councell helde in New Yorke ye 6th day of Decemb. 1683; present The Governor, Capt. Anthony Brockholls, Mr. Fred Phillips, Mr. Steph. Courtland, Mr. Lucas Sancton:
> "The petition of ye Mayor and aldermen being read, the governor in Councell gaue answer thereto in ye ffolowing Resolutions and Reposalls:
> "Their ffirst request concerning ye Charters is already Granted, and a Recorder according to their fformer desires. The Ferrys Granted with a prouiso that two boates for passengers be kept on each side of ye Riuer and one boate for Cattle on each side of ye Riuer also."

The next allusion to the ferry is in the minutes of the meeting of the mayor and aldermen on February 23, 1688, and at that meeting it was thereupon unanimously

Ordered that

> "Mr. Alderman Inian, Mr. Alderman Pinhorne, Mr. Nicholas Demyer or any two of them ordered and apoynted as a Committee to Examine the Orders and Regulacion Relating to the Ferry to Long Island and to draw up Suteable Order for the future Management and accommodation thereof. And the Rates and Prizes. And to Lett the same for Terme of Years by the Advice and Consent of the Mayor. Reserving a Rent to be annually Payd by Quarterly payments for the Publique use of this Citty."

The committee tried to lease the ferry by private negotiation, but the largest offer made was for 100 pounds a year. This was not deemed sufficient, so the aldermen decided to put up the ferry privilege at auction, or as it was then called "Public Outcry." This auction was held November, 1691, and is reported as follows in the minutes:

> "Pursuant to a former Order of Common Council this day the FFerrey was ffarmed out att Publick Outcry to John Arietsen for Seauen Yeares Commencing the fiue and Twentieth day of March next att the rate of one hundred fforty and Seauen pounds per annum to be paid Quarterly."

It would seem that the former keeper of the ferry had made some improvements in the property for which he expected remuneration from the city, for before the lease just recorded took effect a commission was appointed to appraise the value of the ferry house. This is recorded in the following entry under date of March 30, 1692:

> "The Mayor, Recorder, Aldermen and Assistants did nominate Coll. Stephanus Cortlandt and Coll. Nicholas Bayard on Be halfe of the Citty And William Morris, late keeper of the fferry, did nominate James Graham, Esq. and William Nicholls, Esq. on his behalfe to view and appraise the house and barn belonging to the fferry, and both parties consent that in case the said four gentlemen cannot agree in their appraisement they shall haue liberty and Power of themselves to make choice of and Nominate an Vmpire at their Discretion who Shall haue power to determine the value of the said house and barn in difference."

That the appraisement was made and approved seems

evident from the next entry relating to the ferry, which appears under date of June 13, 1692, as follows:

> "The Houses and Barns at the fferry are lett together with the little house on this Side to John Arientsen the whole time that he shall hold the fferry and pay his Rent according to his lease at the rate of nine pounds per annum, he to keep them in good and sufficient repairs his condition for the House commencing the 25th of this Instant June."

"John Arientsen" becomes "John Arsen" in the next allusion to the ferry, and John appears to have been aware of the value of a monopoly. Having agreed to pay the city 147 pounds per annum as rent for the ferry, he was of the opinion that he leased an exclusive franchise. Evidently the fares pocketed by John the ferryman were coveted by other boatmen, doing business on their own account, who interfered with his trade as official ferryman to such an extent that he had to appeal to the authorities to protect him in the enjoyment of his privileges. That he did not appeal in vain is shown by the following entry of August 8, 1692:

> "That whereas the citty hath lett to ffarme the fferry to John Arsen for seuerall yeares to come and the Said John Arsen hath applyed himselfe to the Mayor and Commonalty of this Citty complaining of Derrick Janzen, Cornelius Seabrook and others that they make a dayly practice of bringing ouer passengers and corn from Long Island to this citty greatly to the prejudice of the Said ffarmer.
>
> "Ordered that no person besides the fferryman shall bring any passengers or Corne or any other produce of the Island from any place between the red hook and the Wall about but shall forfeit for eury such offence the Sume of twenty Shillings, one halfe to the Vse of the fferryman and the other to such officier of this Citty or others that shall informe of the breach of this order."

This entry shows the antiquity of the designations "Red Hook" and "Wallabout," which are still recognized terms in Brooklyn topography. The bounds of the ferry thus set and in which poaching was forbidden were practically from the present Navy Yard to the Erie Basin.

At the auction in 1700 Dirck Benson was the highest bidder and secured the ferry privilege, agreeing to pay therefor 145 pounds per annum for seven years. He was required to sign a contract pledging himself to abide by certain conditions, and this he did. Among the conditions was that he maintain a schedule of ferry charges established by the city. In view of the present charges for ferry service, this schedule of over two hundred years ago will be of interest. It was as follows:

"That the said Farmer Shall not Impose or take any Other Rates or Prices for ferriage than what are hereafter mentioned, viz.

Evry Single person to pay for going Over Eight Stivers in Wampum or a Silver two pence.

Each person in Company four Stivers in Wampum or a Silver penny; if after Sunsett Double ferriage.

Each horse or Beast Single One Shilling; in Company nine Pence.

Each Colt or Calfe, three pence.

Each hog, Eight stivers in Wampum or a Silver two pence.

Each Sheep, four Stivers Wampum or A Silver penny.

Each Barrell of Rum, Sugar, Molasses, Oyle, Porke etc. three pence.

Each Empty Barrell, four Stivers Wampum or A Silver penny.

A Beast's hide the like.

A Firkin or Tub of Butter two Stivers Wampum.

Every Three Bushells of Corne A Silver penny or four Stivers Wampum

A Pale of Butter two Stivers.

Every Bushell of Salt two Stivers.

Every Hogshead of Tobacco Nine pence.

The before mentioned Rates to be paid by all Passengers att their going into the ferry Boate, and for all Cattle, horses and Other goods or things when the ferry man Receives the same into his Boate, in silver or Wampum."

A "Stiver" was a coin of the Netherlands worth about two cents in present United States coinage, so that the ferry patron of 1700, propelled by oars across the East River, had to pay for the privilege the equivalent of sixteen cents in our money.

In the latter part of the 18th century these were succeeded by horse boats; that is, boats propelled by paddle wheels which were made to revolve by two horses walking around a shaft in the middle of the boat.

Steam was applied to the North River ferries in 1811-12 by Robert Fulton, and soon after to those on the East River. In 1813 the lease for the Long Island ferry expired, and a new lease, providing for steamboats, was given to Robert Fulton and William Cutting at No. 34 Nassau Street. Mr. R. Fulton Cutting, who is a grandson of William Cutting, rescued it from oblivion in a second-hand bookstore and had it placed in a frame. The Cutting family sold their ferry property to the city a few years ago.

Union Ferryboat *Wyandank,* on war duty, 1862.

EARLY DAYS OF SCHOOLS AND SCHOOLMASTERS IN OLD NEW YORK

By Marion T. Eltonhead

When the Dutch established the Colonies of New Netherlands in America the attitude in Holland regarding education was entirely dissimilar to the English idea then prevailing. Holland was far in advance of every state in Europe. May writes in "Democracy in Europe," Vol. II, pp. 67-72, "The whole population was educated, the higher classes singularly accomplished, the University of Leyden founded for the learned education of the rich and *free schools* were established for the general education."

This attitude the directors of the W. I. Company took to the new Colonie; schools must be established, and the youths gathered together for instruction in not only "Worldly matters, but religious affairs as well."

The first *official* Schoolmaster, Adam Roelantsen Groen, was his full name, though he preferred using only the two first names, came over in the ship, the South-berg (Salt Mountain) in 1633, in company with Van Twiller, Cornelius Van Tienhoven, "the bookkeeper of Wageo," and Dominie Everard Bogardus. He was a native of Dockum, Friesland, North Holland, about eight miles from the North Sea. Born about 1606, he came to the colony as a young emigrant for he is recorded 1633.

There was probably a small school in the Fort previous to 1633, as a pre-nuptial contract of the mother of Jan Vinje, contracted to "send the children to school." Roelantsen had a home with a good sized garden, fifty feet on the north by one hundred on Stone Street.

Roelantsen was not an agreeable character, he drank and gossiped and was a busy body. In 1638 he was sued for slander; he set up his school in his home, there being no provision for a public building, though the people petitioned for one as a necessity. The salary he received was inadequate to his needs, he established a private laundry to help him out, for there is a court record in which he appears as defendant to recover a bill for services rendered in 1638.

He married Lyntie Marten and hired a new home east of the old one on the north side Stone Street in 1642. He sailed for Holland in 1646; during his absence his wife died, leaving several little children, the youngest only four and two years old, "the sad case of these infants" was brought to the notice of the Council and four neighbors: Philip Geraerdy, Hans Kiersted, Jan Stevensen, the schoolmaster and Stevenson Van Cortlandt were appointed guardians "until the arrival of the father or some news about him." Roelantsen returned July, 1646 in the ship, *St. Jacob*.

He was hailed into court for an offense 17th Dec., 1646. Sentence pronounced and the order entered, but in "Consideration that the aforesaid defendant has four small children without a mother and a cold winter is approaching the actual banishment of the above sentence is delayed by the Director-general and Council until a more favorable opportunity, when the defendant may leave the country."

Roelantsen did not leave and was in the Colony three years later "on parole."

In 1647 he was appointed jailer and was in New Amsterdam in 1649. Again we hear of him in 1653 in the employ of the W. I. Company as a packer in their ware-

From the rare contemporary view by Peter Schenck.

A VIEW OF THE LOWER PART OF THE CITY. EAST SIDE FROM THE END OF THE ISLAND TO WALL STREET, 1667.

house on Pearl Street, and quite as contumacious as in the early records.

The school which he taught was a free school, supported by the W. I. Company in Amsterdam, Holland, and under the supervision of the Classis and this little school was the foundation of the present "School of the Collegiate Reformed Church in New York City."

Jan Stevensen succeeded him and taught school in his own house, "The W. I. Company was not bound to erect school houses, churches nor orphan asylums," though, we read in the "proposed" Articles for Colonization and Trade in New Netherlands, dated August 30, 1638, "That each householder and inhabitant shall be taxed for Schoolmasters, &c."

There is a record of one Arien Jansen Van Tipendam who opened a private school during this period, which continued in favor some ten years, the terms of tuition being, "two beaver skins per annum."

The official successor to Roelantsen was Petersen, dating in the Register of New Amsterdam from 1643. He continued the school in his dwelling house and it seemed to have been inadequate to the needs.

In 1647 public education was suspended owing to lack of suitable accommodations. In 1649, the *New York Colonial Mss., Vol. 1, p. 317*, records: "There ought to be also a Public School provided with at least two good teachers, so that the youth in so wild a country where there are so many dissolute people, may first of all, be instructed and indoctrinated, not only in reading, writing but in the fear of the Lord. Now the school is kept very irregularly . . . . . according to his fancy as long as he thinks proper."

No school building could have materialized: (The

Holland Documents contain p. 423, Secretary Van Tienhoven's answer to the remonstrance from New Netherlands, the original Mss. is in the Royal Archives, the Hague, and bear date Nov. 29, 1650.)

"Although the new school house toward which the community contributes something, has not yet been built, it is not the Director, but the Church Wardens, who have charge of the funds. The Director is busy providing a place for a school, of which Jan Cornelissen has charge. The other teachers keep school in hired houses, so that the youth are not in want of schools to the extent of the circumstances of the country. 'Tis true there is no *Latin School* nor Academy; if the community require such they can apply for it and furnish the necessary funds."

This letter appears to have been an answer to one dated Oct., 1649, also among the Royal Archives at the Hague, the title of which is:

"Of the reasons and cause of the great decay of New Netherlands," p. 30, Vol. 1, Holland Mans.

"The plate has been a long time passed around for a common school, which has been built with words, for as yet, the first stone is not laid, some materials also have only been provided. However the money given for the purpose hath disappeared and it is mostly spent, so that it falls somewhat short and nothing has as yet been affected for the purpose."

Jan Stevensen was teaching in 1648, for he had a petition in court to receive "certain moneys from the W. I. Company."

Director's letter to Stuyvesant, April 20, 1650. "The schoolmaster (William Veretims taught school in New Amsterdam till 1655 when he returned to Holland) for whom you asked goes out with this ship; God grant that

Entrance to the College of the City of New York, successor of the old Free Academy which stood at the corner of Lexington Avenue and Twenty-third Street. Largest college maintained by any city in the world for free higher education.

he may confirm the good character which he has borne here and continue for a long time in the edification of the youths."

Letter from Director in Holland to Stuyvesant, 28th Jan., 1649: "At your request we have engaged a schoolmaster, who is also to serve as comforter of the sick. He is considered as an honest and pious man and will come over by the first chance."

William Vestrus was next sent from Holland and kept school in a room of his own. Jan Cornlissen had succeeded Stevensen in 1649; he is said to have come down from Albany or near there, but was very unreliable and too fond of drinking, "hot and rebellious liquors." It was during this time that the directors became conscious of the importance of regular and systematic rules of education and for that there must be a permanent school building.

Bluff Governor Stuyvesant with his wooden leg banded with silver, wrote: "Nothing is of greater importance than the early instruction of youth," and said Dominie Megapolensis, sent by the Amsterdam Classis in 1642. "A lack of schoolmasters means a ruined youth and bewilderment of mind."

A license was necessary to teach and the term "schoolmaster" embraced several duties in the early days.

William Vestrus applied to Council for leave to return to Holland. In the minutes dated Jan. 26, 1655, we see him cited as "Schoolmaster and Christen." And sometime this was combined with sexton and bell ringer.

In a letter from the director in Holland to Governor Stuyvesant, April 4, 1652, they write: "We agree with your proposition to establish there a public school and believe a beginning might be made with a schoolmaster

(Typodistasculum) who could be engaged at a yearly salary of 200 to 250 guilders. We recommend for the position Jan de la Montagne, whom we have provisionally appointed to it and you may use the building of the City Tavern if you find it suitable."

The City Tavern was built under the auspices of the W. I. Company in 1640, near the shore of the East River, the road behind being the Coogh Strict, where in 1634 it became the Tavern Hall or Stadt Huys, the narrow lane in the east side was Coenties Alley.

The strict Burgomasters could not give up the meeting place where schnaps and gossip both circulated, for when Hermanus Van Hobooclen came in 1656 he petitions the Burgomasters in Amsterdam "to grant him the hall and side room for the use of the school and as a dwelling, inasmuch as he, the petitioner, does not know how to manage for the proper accommodation of the children during winter, for they much require a place adaptable for fire, and to be warmed for which the present tenement is wholly unfit."

New Amsterdam was now quite a busy village, more than a hundred houses and a population of a thousand or more souls, there was need of a second school. Jacob Van Vorlear applied for a license to start one in his home, but objection was made and he was compelled to close it.

In 1650 in the draft of Conditions offered by the City of Amsterdam to New Colonists, Article 8, says: "The City shall erect a home for a school which can likewise be used and occupied by the person who will hereafter be *Sexton, Psalmsetter* and *Schoolmaster*."

Religion and Education were closely allied during this period in New Amsterdam. Director Stuyvesant in 1647 in the Council meetings asked, "What provision is to be made for a school as there is none in New Amsterdam, and the youth are running wild?" And also asked the *Nine Men* as to the best mode to provide a *school house,* repair the fort and complete the church."

There seems to be no record of a permanent building. There was a school at Onckenay, kept by a Mr. Wyles, who furnished information relating to how New England felt toward the Dutch.

A letter from the directors in Holland to the Governor, April, 1652, reads rather quaintly: "There comes on board the ship Remeyn, as super-cargo, a person by name Fred Alken, who has been schoolmaster at Hoorn. He writes a good hand. If his habits are as good as his penmanship and a schoolmaster is wanted, you might consider him, but let him be thoroughly tested, for we have noticed that the climate over there does not improve people's character."

In 1652 Dominie Samuel Drisius, accomplished in Dutch, French and English, came as colleague to Dr. Megapolensis and had a salary of 1,450 guildern. In the documents, relating to early colonial settlements. Vol. XIV, p. 419, dated May 20, 1658, is the extract: "Dominie Drisius has repeatedly expressed to us his opinion that he thought it advisable to establish there a Latin School for the instruction and education of the young, offering thereto his own services.

"You must not fail to inform us how such an institution can be managed to the best advantage of the community and kept up with least expense to the company. To encourage the said Dr. Drisius in the performance of his duties we have increased his board money from 250 to 300 florins."

A letter of 13th February, 1659, from the director to

The Elevated at 110th Street curve, showing surroundings in 1880.

Stuyvesant, states: "The argument brought forward, why for the establishment of a Latin School there, it is necessary to send from here a fit and honest man to instruct the children in the elements and foundation of the language, have induced us to decide that such a teacher shall be inquired for, care being taken that he writes a good hand, to teach the children also calligraphy, you may expect him by the ship sailing from here during the spring."

Pp. 436, April 25, 1659, we read: "How much trouble we have taken to find a Latin Schoolmaster is shown by the fact that now one *Alexander Carolus Cureins,* late Professor in Lithuania, goes over, whom we engaged as such at a yearly salary of 500ff., board money included; we give him also a present of 100ffs in merchandise to be used by him upon his arrival there, as you may learn by the enclosed extract from our resolution, or by the contract made with him."

Later Governor Stuyvesant heard:

"The books required by the Schoolmaster, now coming over for the instruction of the young people in Latin, could not be procured in the short time, before the sailing of the ship; they will be sent by the next opportunity."

By order of the Lord Director

A. B. DE DECKER, JR.

The board granted Dr. Drisius a piece of land for a garden or orchard, and he was privileged to give private lessons "if without prejudice to the duties for which he is engaged."

He arrived safely and the Governor notified Holland, adding: "We hope and trust that the community shall reap the desired fruits through their children, to which God may give his blessing."

Later the schoolmaster found his salary too small for

Fine view of City Hall Park as it appeared before the Post Office was built. Prospects for removal of the latter are encouraging. The old Park Bank Building, Knox and *Herald* are shown at right, 1869.

his needs in the colony and as the director had no discretion as to the finances, letters were dispatched to Holland, saying: "As to his services and diligence we must truly testify that his industry is astonishing and the progress of the young people remarkable."

In 1661 Algidus Luyck, a young man though of much reputation, came and his school soon drew pupils from the then distant provinces of the Carolinas and Virginia. He remained in the colony after English rule, for there is a petition signed by him with two others to Governor Andros in 1675, "that they be released of the obligation of taking the oath of allegiance to the English and bearing arms against the Dutch."

Evert Pietersen was the last schoolmaster appointed before 1664, Curtius resigned in 1661. There is a mention of one Jan Galurt, "schoolmaster and overseer of the goats," rather a peculiar combination, for as late as 1655.

Pietersen had also several duties. Dunshee, Hut of the Dutch schools, p. 44, relates he was comforter of the sick, schoolmaster and precentor. There is a letter from him among those in the Stadt Huys, Amsterdam, dated August 10, 1657, Fort New Amstel on the South Run, in N. N. and ending "I already begin to keep school and have 25 children, etc."

There is a record of a set of instructions sent him from Amsterdam Council:

1. He shall take good care that the children, coming to his school, do so at the usual hour, namely, at eight in the morning and one in the afternoon.

2. He must keep good discipline among his pupils.

3. He shall teach the children and pupils in the Christian prayer, commandments, baptism, Lord's Supper, the

Corner of Wall and South Streets in 1850. From a sketch made at the time. It vividly recalls the Clipper Ship era.

Old East River Boat that plied to Glen Island and other Sound points in the 80's—the *Pomona*.

questions with answers of the Catechism, which are taught here every Sunday afternoon in the church.

4. Before school closes he shall let the pupils say some verses and a psalm.

5. Beside his yearly salary he shall be allowed to demand and receive for every pupil quarterly as follows: For each child whom he teaches A, B, C, and reading, 30s; for teaching to read and write, 50s; for teaching to read, write and cipher, 60s; for those who come in the evening and between times pro rata, a fair sum. The poor and needy who ask to be taught for God's sake, he shall teach for nothing.

6. He shall be allowed to demand and take reward from everybody who makes arrangements, etc., etc.
Minutes of the Orphan Masters, Vol. II, pp. 115-6.

In 1664 when New Netherlands became a colony of Great Britain, the little city on Manhattan Island had a population of some 1,500, while the Dutch rule ceased, the influence remained in force, the English laws had no provisions regarding schools. Pietersen remained in charge under the supervision of the deacon while the consistory contributed the funds.

Smith, the historian, writes that "Our schools are in the lowest order, the instructors want instruction." And it was in 1731, with a population of 50,289, the instructor could not make enough to get bread for himself.

An act was passed 1732 to encourage:

"A public school in the City of New York; it was inactive for years, yet was the beginning of the broad system of the public school of the present."

The act passed in 1702:

"To encourage a public school in the City of New York" that went no further.

Broadway at St. Paul's Chapel, showing old
Western Union Building, where now stands
its successor, the American Telephone and
Telegraph Building. 1880. Barnum's Museum was opposite.

Governor De Witt Clinton was first principal of the Public School Society, founded in 1805.

The Dutch laid the foundation of the schools, the English established the college.

The first schoolmaster in Breuckelen came July 4, 1661. Next a petition was sent to Amsterdam, saying they had accepted the suitable person, one Carel van Beanvois, to whom they appropriated the sum of 150 florin and a fine dwelling.

The first school was in the little church, near the intersection of Fulton and Bridge Streets. The second public school in the country was in Bushwick, the Dutch "Boswhyck," the House in the Wood, and the first schoolmaster Bondwyn Manot, December 28, 1662.

The third school was in Bedfirs, at the Cross Roads, center of village, began in 1663 and became Public School No. 3. (History of the City of Brooklyn, Ostrander, Vol. III, p. 96-105).

BIBLIOGRAPHY

American Commonwealth Series..........*Roberts,* New York

History of the Province of New York, Vol. I........*Smith*

Documents, Relating to Colonial New
York..*E. B. O'Callaghan*

Calendar New York Historical Manuscripts, Dutch,
1630-64.

The Planting and Growth of the Empire
State, Vol. I, p. 43; Vol. III, 262..............*E. H. Roberts*

The Story of New York................................*E. S. Brooks*

Schoolmasters—New Amsterdam

1633—Adam Roelantsen, resigned in 1639.

1643—Jan Stevensen, resigned in 1648.

1647—No school for these months on account of no proper
place, Aryam Jansen, David Provost.

1648—Peter van du Linde, Jan Cornelissen, Adrian Van
Itpudan.

1652—Jan de la Montagne.

1655—William Verstius, Herman Van Hoboocken.

1658—Jacobin Van Corlear.

2 Papers from 1664 to 1800—Sketch Kings (Columbia
College).

OPENING OF THE AMERICAN ACADEMY OF ARTS AND LETTERS

An important event in the cultural life of New York began when the American Academy of Arts and Letters entered into possession of its new home in the beautiful Audubon Quadrangle at Broadway, 155th-156th Streets, on February 22, 1922.

ORDER OF EXERCISES

Opening Address, *William Milligan Sloane, President of the Academy* ....

Address to the American Academy of Arts and Letters, *Sir Frederic Kenyon, former President of the British Academy with greeting from Lord Balfour, actual President*....................................

Response, *Brander Matthews, Chancellor of the Academy* ....

Presentation of the Gold Medal to Mrs. Schuyler Van Rensselaer, *The President*....................................

"The Youngest Academy," *Poem by Henry van Dyke, Read by Augustus Thomas* ....

Greetings from Absent Members, *Read by Robert Underwood Johnson, Secretary of the Academy.*

WOODROW WILSON.
BASIL LANNEAU GILDERSLEEVE.
BRAND WHITLOCK.

[298]

The old Hopper House, Second Avenue and Eighty-third Street, East River.

ROBERT GRANT (*Also President of the National Institute of Arts and Letters*).

And from:

The Académie Française, JEAN RICHEPIN, *Directeur.*

The Académie des Beaux-Arts.

The France-Amerique Committee,
GABRIEL HANOTAUX, *President.*

The Royal Society of Literature.

The opening address was delivered by William Milligan Sloane, President of the Academy, and in part is as follows:

In the cornerstone of this building are the names of two persons, neither name announced to the public because both givers desire that their left hand should not know what their right hand doeth. They intend that this should be a temple, dedicated to the service of truth, and as Cervantes said, "Where truth is there is God." It is committed in perpetuity to the care and use of the American Academy, because the givers believe that the history of Literature and the Fine Arts in any land is the truest record of the spirit and aspiration of those who dwell in that land, the one they both love best. For those of us therefore, who have seen the birth and watched the nurture of the Academy, its formal entry in possession of a home is alike a solemn and a joyous occasion. We are a company seeking the ideal. We aim at nothing less than the preservation of the great inheritance in beauty and substance, which has come down from the fountains of Hebraism and Hellenism, blended in Christianity, through the ages; to discipline a folk-federation compounded of peoples from the ends of the earth.

Every year the Academy and the Institute hold public sessions, at which papers are read by members on the subjects with which they are concerned. These meetings are attended by audiences of some hundreds, the most select and intelligent of the community; and not only the metropolitan community, for we have organized similar meetings at various centers far and near, all gladly welcomed and well, even enthusiastically, attended. Naturally, too, we honor our pre-eminent dead. The Memorial Meetings for Clemens, Howells, Saint-Gaudens, Burroughs and others have attracted large and sympathetic audiences. The members of the Academy and of the Institute are greatly heartened in the performance of their tasks by the good will of similar companies in Great Britain, France, Belgium, Italy, Spain and Brazil, a goodwill already shown by many acts. To-day they are especially cheered by having as their guest of honor, a distinguished scion in a race of scholars and statesmen, himself a soldier at the front throughout the World War, Sir Frederic Kenyon, ex-President of the British Academy, Director of the British Museum and preëminent as an apostle of the humanities in his own land, in our own mother country. We bid him welcome in each of these capacities and are happy to hail him as the first ambassador guest amid our new surroundings.

It is most important that the American spirit should in some measure be personified, elusive as it is, and however temporary its shadowy form. Already in our history, at least three states of society have succeeded each other. The sovereign people renews itself by natural generation or immigration about once in each half-generation. Yet the national soul propagates itself with an almost biological persistence. Even as colonists we had

Rare view of Broad Street, from the Morgan corner almost to Exchange Court, as it appeared in 1865. Sites of present Morgan and Mills Buildings.

an inchoate literature and art, faintly distinguishable from that of Europe. Under the stress of public life in our early independence, we opened a further advance, and now in certain artistic achievements we may claim to be the peers of our coëvals. The American world is full of beautiful things and the men who think it no shame to take their own from the past and present, for the delight of their own people, are largely assembled in the Academy and in its mother society, the National Institute. That fact alone is an achievement of enormous import: we exist as an element of national life.

Furthermore the great medal of the Academy has been once bestowed for supremacy in English style, an American Order of Merit; that of the Institute annually year after year for similar excellence in architecture, painting, sculpture, the drama, history and poetry. We mark distinction along the line of tradition. And just now we have received a noble foundation for two practical purposes—first, to aid any American commonwealth with advice in founding or developing a museum of the fine arts; and, second, to stimulate good diction on the stage. The methods of administering this fund is already the subject of careful study, and will later be made public.

This list of our activities might be extended somewhat; for instance, we have held, tentatively, one exhibition which in the field of "black-and-white" was a pronounced success. But this brief account of our stewardship must suffice: it is a retrospect which may well encourage us to believe our path rightly chosen and our cautious but courageous advance assured, as we know ourselves and our people better, and as the nation understands more clearly our purposes.

The old Hazard House, a famous roadhouse n the days of the trotter, at Third Avenue and Eighty-fourth Street, then the Boston Post Road, 1835.

ADDRESS TO THE AMERICAN ACADEMY
OF ARTS AND LETTERS
By Sir Frederic Kenyon

It is a great privilege for me to be allowed to address the American Academy of Arts and Letters as the representative of the kindred institution in England, the British Academy. You will not accuse me of affectation or false modesty when I say that I could wish that our Academy were represented on this occasion by either my predecessor or my successor in the Presidential chair; for I was preceded by Lord Bryce and succeeded by Lord Balfour. I think you will bear me out when I express my belief that no two recent British statesmen stand higher in the respect of Americans. It is unnecessary for me to dwell upon their merits. Lord Bryce you have probably all known and heard; at once the much-travelled Ulysses, with knowledge and wisdom drawn from a thousand sources, and the Nestor of our time, who had known three generations of men and was a king among the fourth; who combined the wisdom of age with the alertness of youth, and who was always ready to place his great gifts at the service of any good cause. Lord Balfour you have seen less, but you know his great record; and it was no surprise to us to hear, when he visited America in the service of his country, that you recognized his gifts of character and intellect, and welcomed in him a representative of British statesmanship at its very best. His courage in action, his independence and distinction in thought, give him a position unrivalled by that of any other statesman of our time; and you will readily believe how proud we are to have him as our President.

I wish indeed that either of them could have been here to speak to you. You know what interest Lord Bryce would have taken in this new stage of progress in American Scholarship; how heartily he would have sympathized with any movement which aimed at co-ordinating and strengthening the organization of Art and Letters in the country to whose welfare he was so warmly devoted. Of Lord Balfour it is not necessary for me to conjecture what he might have said; for I am charged by him with a message to you. When he heard that I had been invited to be present on this occasion, he authorized me to speak in the name of the British Academy, and he wrote this letter which he asked me to read to you.

"My dear Sir Frederic,

I am delighted to hear that you are going to be present at the opening ceremony of the new building of the American Academy of Arts and Letters, and that you will on that occasion represent the British Academy. Nobody could fill that position more worthily than yourself.

The ceremony, I understand, is to take place on the anniversary of George Washington's birth, and I reflect on the fact with peculiar pleasure. For unless I entirely misread the tastes and character of that great statesman, there is nothing to which he would have attached more value than the establishment on both sides of the Atlantic of institutions which would foster the vigorous life of that great literary tradition, which is the common property of all branches of the English-speaking peoples."

If, therefore, I may come before you between these two powerful sponsors, and you will allow me to regard myself as the hyphen connecting two names which bespeak your sympathy and respect, I shall be emboldened to perform the duty which I am here to discharge, namely to convey to you the heartiest good wishes of the British Academy on this auspicious occasion. Perhaps I may con-

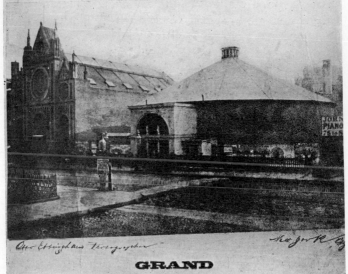

THE HIPPOTHEATRON,

AND

NEW YORK CIRQUE,

FOURTEENTH STREET, OPPOSITE ACADEMY OF MUSIC.

GRAND
EQUESTRIAN & GYMNASTIC
PERFORMANCES.

Courtesy Mr. E. H. Sauer

An unusually rare view of Fourteenth Street opposite the old Academy of Music when it was the Grand Opera House. The Hippotheatron was a favorite place of amusement. From an old photograph.

fess to a twinge of envy when I reflect what the occasion is. You are already inaugurating a spacious and sumptuous building of your own, while we,—unsupported by the state as yet unassisted by any Maecenas, such as the soil of America appears to produce so plentifully—have no roof over our head, and are dependent on the hospitality of our elder and very distinguished sister, the Royal Society. But I am not here to lay our grievances before you. I am here to rejoice wholeheartedly that the American Academy is entering on life so vigorously, so prosperously, and with such an assured future of enlightened service to mankind.

It is not for me to dwell on the service which your Academy will render to Art, Letters and Learning in your own country. You know best what your needs and your aspirations are.

In one important respect your Academy differs from ours. You are an Academy of Arts and Letters, while we are an Academy of History, Philosophy and Philology. You are representative of genius in all the great arts, we claim only to be representative of learning. You are akin, in scope and object, to the Académie Française; we are of the same class as the Académie des Inscription et Belles-Lettres and the Académie des Sciences Morales et Politiques, and as the Academies of Germany, Italy, Austria and most other European countries. This is a great difference in principle, and it would be possible to say much as to the nature and utility of Academies of either class. But I prefer to dwell on the points which we have in common.

The object of our Academies, whether they be Academies of the Arts or of Learning, is the service of civilization in our respective countries, and, through our coun-

tries, of mankind. Each is an organization of the aristocracy of mind in certain of its provinces, just as an Academy of Science is an organization of the aristocracy of
mind in certain other provinces.

One is rather afraid to use the word aristocracy in
America; but this is an aristocracy that is entirely com-
patible with democracy. Aristocracy in its literal sense,
the rule of the best, is what we all desire and aim at.
Democracy implies that everyone, in whatever station he
may be born or placed, shall have the opportunity of
proving himself to be one of the best. That is the sort
of aristocracy that we have in mind; an aristocracy with
open doors, to which all may have access who prove themselves fit. But an aristocracy there must be. Even if all
men are born equal,—and as your Declaration of Independence says they are, I presume they are,—they do not
remain equal. In every department of life, in politics,
in law, in science, in literature, in learning, the best thinking is done by a few men. Democracy,—the open opportunity, the expression of the popular judgment—is the
machinery for bringing these few best men to the top,—
the Washingtons and Lincolns in politics, the Shakespeares
and Miltons in literature.

But what one needs is that this aristocracy of intellect
should be in touch with the mind of the nation, that its
work may be known, that its influence may be felt, and
that it may speak, if need arise, in the name of the nation in intellectual matters. For this purpose, in these
days, organization is needed; and here is the function of
Academies. A National Academy has two main duties;
to promote learning and culture in its own country, in
the particular departments of thought with which it deals,

and to be, in those departments, the official organ and representative of its country.

It is here, in spite of the differences in principle underlying the organization of our Academies, that I think there is scope for common action. And I trust it is not indelicate to dwell upon such common action between England and America in these matters. It has been my privilege in recent years to be associated in friendly co-operation with the representatives of other nations, and particularly with those of France and Belgium, in matters of international relationship. I greatly prize that co-operation and that friendship. But it is no derogation from it to say that special opportunities and special responsibilities arise out of the kinship in blood and in traditions of England and America.

It is my earnest wish that their co-operation may be developed in every quarter. Co-operation between two persons or two countries does not imply hostility to others; and particularly is this the case in the spheres of action of which I am thinking. "With malice toward none, with charity for all," England and America can co-operate in the service of our common civilization.

One of the objects, or at any rate, one of the consequences, of the formation of Academies is that they become the natural medium of intercommunication with the bodies which represent learning and letters in other countries. There are at the present day problems of international intercommunication which are not free from difficulty, and in which America and England can, in my opinion, usefully co-operate. The subject is one of some delicacy, as those who have taken part in these international gatherings will realize; and I wish to hurt no susceptibilities. But with a world still so unsettled after the convulsions of the war, it is inevitable that there should be some reactions from its unrestfulness even in the cloistered seclusion of scholarship. One of the services that men of culture,—men, that is, who have been trained to study human nature, to take large views, to profit from the teachings of philosophy and history—can render to their generations is to try to heal the wounds that war has caused. This involves no abandonment of the ideals with which we entered on and carried through the war. I am not in the least one of those, who, when a great struggle is over, are at once prepared to plume themselves on taking a detached and impartial view, to say that no doubt everyone was equally to blame, and that the best thing is to forget all about it and to act as though nothing had happened. But breaches, however deep and however righteously made, must be filled up if civilization is not to be wrecked; and it is for the men of the widest education to try to seek out the better spirits on the other side of the chasm, and gradually to renew relations of intellectual intercourse.

Old time street cries in New York—"Hot Corn"—(City Hall
Park at Warren Street).

The old Henry Coster House, Thirtieth Street and First Avenue, bought by Anson G. Phelps in 1835.

EARLY STEAMBOAT DAYS ON THE HUDSON RIVER

Some time ago, we announced a series of articles on the North River, that mighty stream to which New York owes much of its affluence. While it belongs to New York primarily, its beauties, and its honors are the possession of the whole world.

As early as 1825, the most ambitious publication from a business point of view, was undertaken on behalf of this noble river. It consisted of a series of plates, twenty-two in number, reproduced by the aquatint process, each plate measuring about 24 x 20, including the margin. It was known as the *Hudson River Portfolio*. The last copy, which appeared at an auction sale brought eleven hundred dollars.

There is no publication describing any part of our country, old or new, the appreciation of which is so emphatically expressed in dollars and cents as this tribute to the North River, published so many years ago. That such a work could have been undertaken on such an elaborate scale, is another evidence of the great interest which this beautiful river excited the world over, as most of these books would naturally find their customers in Europe.

In the preparation of these papers it was our great good fortune to have had the co-operation and supervision of our good friend, the late Mr. Stuyvesant Fish. To our inexpressible regret, our dear friend was removed from us last winter, and the series must of necessity suffer a diminution in both historical value and quantity, in consequence. We have, however, felt impelled to publish as much as is completed.

We who see the palatial steamers of the Day Line and all the multitudinous river craft of one description and another can scarcely realize that it is all the product of less than a century—a mere moment in the history of mankind. Fulton's great invention produced the most intense excitement the world over. He was granted an exclusive patent by the State of New York to operate boats driven by steam on all the waters, rivers and bays of the entire country. This was bad for the new invention. Endless litigation ensued, as the other States refused to be bound by the patents of New York. As a result, the industry languished. While Fulton and Livingston were still spending fruitless and priceless years in the courts, European nations, free from this entanglement, made wonderful progress in developing and improving this new method of transportation. It was Daniel Webster who finally destroyed Fulton's monopoly. And, strange to relate, the man who backed Webster financially in the fight and made it possible for him to win was no other than that old-time friend of the people, Commodore Vanderbilt. Vanderbilt did not appear personally. He used one of his captains—Thomas Gibbons. The case is known as "Gibbons against Ogden" and is widely celebrated. The decision of the Supreme Court in this litigation forms the basis for much of the procedure now followed by the Interstate Commerce Commission, and the recently organized Port Authority.

The waters of all the States being now open to free navigation, tremendous progress ensued. Stage coaches on land and sloops in the river had been practically the only means of travel. A sloop would sometimes take

Courtesy of Mr. John Jay Chapman

The Hudson River. Scene at Barrytown, showing landing as it appeared in 1845. Contemporary sketch.

nine days for the up-river trip. When the *Chancellor Livingston* made the run in nineteen and a half hours, the people thought it a miracle and called her the "Skimmer of the River."

The trip by stage was always rough and very fatiguing. The heavy spring rains caused accidents. The cold in winter was intense. In summer the heat was stifling. The fare was $8.00 and it never took less than two days and one night.

Yet the sloops were also inconvenient and even dangerous. Squalls on the Hudson appear without warning from behind the headlands. When the boom of one of these old packet sloops started to "jibe," it swept everything before it. Occasionally a passenger would be knocked overboard by the ponderous stick and drown. For this, and for greater speed, the sloop was finally abandoned in favor of steam, and the sloop became a freight carrier exclusively.

Yonkers, being the first stopping point on the trip to Albany by stage and the last before reaching New York, was naturally keenly interested in any changes affecting transportation. The growing popularity of steamboat travel therefore, should have been of immediate concern. Instead, the new-found means of communication with the outside world was sadly neglected. For many years passengers desiring to go from Yonkers by boat, must first cross the river to Alpine and there connect with the steamer. Passengers for this village also debarked there and were brought over by ferry. A little later this service was improved by an arrangement with the steamers whereby they "slowed up" to receive passengers, who put out in rowboats. This was some improvement, but not much. There was a sloop landing quite a little distance

The Riker Mansion, foot of Seventy-third Street, East River, 1866.

Early train on Hudson River, about 1850.

from the river on the Saw Mill, just below where War-
burton Avenue runs into Main Street, and this little
place became in time quite an important part of the village steamboat life.

A regular dock was soon built here, and on this dock
was erected a hotel, general store, post office and a row of
dwellings. A garden adjoined the hotel. It was kept
by John Bashford, and for many years was an attractive
little spot. It afforded something in the way of neighborhood sociability. It kept the people in touch with the outside
world. In addition to its transient visitors, it was also
the meeting place of local politicians, public gatherings
and such like. For a number of years Bashford's Hotel
and his Sloop Landing played a very popular part in the
everyday life of the little village. Mr. Bashford himself was evidently a citizen of some parts, as he was one
of the original directors of the present First National
Bank, along with Lemuel W. Wells, Robert P. Getty,

"Queen of the Hudson"—*Mary Powell.*

William C. Waring, Ethan Flagg, William G. Ackerman, and other prominent men of that day. A portrait of his daughter, Miss Joanna Bashford, adorned the bills of the bank till it became a national institution. One of these old bills is a treasured possession of the First National to the present day.

The increasing traffic on the river finally induced Mr. Lemuel Wells to construct another wharf an eighth of a mile long.

When the new wharf was completed, all the steamboats made it a regular stopping place. The *Orange* and *Rockland* from Peekskill had the honor of being first. There was now fierce competition among the various boats on the river. Speed seemed to be the great objective—everything had to be sacrificed to the passion of haste. It got so bad that captains finally ceased to make complete stops. All they would do was to slow down. Passengers had to hop ashore as best they could, their baggage being thrown after them. Incoming passengers were treated in the same way. The result was numerous accidents. The practice finally became so dangerous that the Legislature stepped in with a law compelling all captains to come to a full stop and so remain till the receipt and discharge of passengers had been accomplished in an orderly manner. Deprived of this means of saving time, the rival boats entered into a series of racing contests that were even more hazardous. The night boats were particularly reckless. This practice led to one of the most disastrous calamities ever witnessed on the Hudson—the destruction by fire of the *Henry Clay* and the loss of over eighty lives. The boat was on fire as she neared New York on an early July morning and was beached in front of Edwin Forest's home at Mount St. Vincent. He and others were among those to render first aid to the unfortunate victims. A monument in St. John's Cemetery marked the spot where many were buried.

The danger from fire, and especially from boiler explosion, was very great in those early steamboat days. The steamboat in the early stages of its development had a very unpleasant habit of bursting its boiler, with often fatal consequences. To avoid too close proximity to such occurrences, a separate boat was built which was towed behind the steamboat, called a barge.

These barges were rather pretentious and were most comfortable. They were nicely furnished, with staterooms and a dining room. Quite a little style was observed at meal time, the captain taking his place at the head of the table, just as if he were on a regular ocean liner. Canvas awnings provided shade on the deck and much attention was paid to the comfort of ladies and children. It was certainly an ideal mode of travel. This improvement, however, was gained at the sacrifice of speed and was never popular. New ideas in the marine boiler were meantime constantly perfected, and presently a device for controlling the steam pressure proved successful and a new type of steamboat was the result. It combined the roominess and comfort of the barge, while at the same time permitting the requisite speed and safety so necessary if the steamboat was to hold its own against the rapidly growing power of the railroad.

This was accomplished by the invention of what is known as the "hog frame" method of construction—a new principle whereby the front and rear sections of a boat are held together by a superstructure built amidships on the port and starboard sides so that the dead weight of the engines and boilers would no longer "break the vessel's back," as it were. With this great improvement successfully achieved, the length of a boat had practically no limit. Handsome cabins, tastefully furnished, individual rooms, lounging decks and other comforts and conveniences were now possible and were speedily introduced. River travel therefore became a delight, and the business of the new boats increased by leaps and bounds.

The barges, however, remained as useful vessels for the transportation of hay and other bulky produce from the river farms to the city. Even that business had eventually to give way before the advancing power of steam, and the last days of these fine old barges were spent in the service of churches, clubs, etc., for picnics to various points up the river, when Alpine and Dudley's Grove were popular among the Sunday schools of New York and Brooklyn.

Names like "Albany," "De Witt Clinton," "Clermont," etc., have been frequently duplicated as successive ships have borne them. Here are some of the popular boats of this period.

Champlain	*Isaak Newton*
Highlander	*Thomas Powell*
Rochester	*Albany*
Chancellor Livingston	*Armenia*
Henry Clay	*Alida*
Rip Van Winkle	*New World*
Francis Skiddy	

Aside from the larger craft, a number of local lines between New York and Peekskill ran regularly, making Yonkers one of their stops. Many of my readers will doubtless recall the old *Chrystenah*. Before her were the *Antelope, Riverdale, Shady Side* and *Rockland*. These boats made frequent trips each day to New York and enjoyed a lucrative patronage till well into the 80's. They went as far north as Peekskill.

No mention of that glorious era of fast river sailing would be complete without generous reference to that most lovable of all the old craft that plied her waters the *Mary Powell,* "Queen of the Hudson."

And Queen she was. For more than forty years this superb steamer remained the unbeaten champion in her class. She ran with the precision of a watch and slipped into her dock exactly on the minute. She was a prodigious favorite with people, and hardly a wedding was celebrated fifty years ago but included a trip up the river on the

Mary Powell. Her run was between Kingston and New York. She rarely went to Albany. No matter what the wind or tide, fog alone excepted, the *Mary Powell* would poke her nose around Kingston Point promptly on time every night and tie up exactly at the same minute day in and day out. She was sailed by her owner, Captain Anderson, and despite the growing competition of newer and more luxurious boats, the old *Mary Powell* maintained her popularity to the end. As she sailed past New York on her last trip there was many an eye that was strangely dim to think that never again would they tread the deck of the fine old steamer. It was endeared to them by association with some of their pleasantest and dearest memories. Both Captain Anderson and his son, who succeeded him, have also passed away, which seems a fitting and appropriate happening now that the *Mary Powell* herself is no more.

OLD TIME FISHING ON THE
NORTH RIVER

We no longer go fishing, nor is the bathing so attractive as it was when a pebbly stretch of beach along our shore front was a constant invitation to plunge into the cooling depths. Movies and motor cars seem to occupy the first claim on our affections, despite the fact that John Reid, a Yonkers man, introduced the game of golf in this country, thereby giving a great stimulus to the love of outdoor sports the country over.

During the administration of Governor Hughes, which is not so far off as to be real history yet, a delegation of river boatmen called upon him to protest against the vast number of nets which the shad fishermen had spread all along the shores opposite Yonkers, and which they claimed interfered with navigation. In those days one could row out to where the fishermen were hauling in their nets and get all the most delicious roe shad he wanted for a quarter.

That is only a few years ago, but already a shad seems about as extinct as the dodo. It is morally certain that shad have virtually disappeared from the sludge-infested waters of the Hudson. While factories are more or less unavoidable, the reckless and wanton pollution of the waters of the Hudson is an insult to our intelligence as a people. It is utterly unnecessary, and this wonderful source of cheap and delicious food is still within our reach had we but the sense to apply the remedy.

"Tom Cods" or Lafayettes were plentiful at the first appearance of frost and all the shore front of our city provided excellent vantage points from which to make a catch. They too have gone. Whitefish and bass also abounded, but not so plentifully. They are rarely caught nowadays. And the seven and eight-foot sturgeon exist only in the mythical tales of a Baron Munchausen, although more than one man has seen them and assisted in their capture.

While one rarely hears of any considerable fishing nowadays off the docks or in the immediate vicinity, there still gather quite a few enthusiasts who form a fringe around the string piece at Riverdale and Greystone. The solitary figures that once dotted the shore line all the way up, beginning at Spuyten Duyvil, are gradually disappearing. When the season opened this miniature Izaak Walton was never missed. In rainy days or clear it was all the same. Occasionally he would be hidden behind a huge umbrella when it stormed, but as a rule he was content with the protection of a slicker.

Young Morisini who lived at Riverdale was a most enthusiastic fisherman. Down in old Dutwill's bait shop in Forty-second Street can be seen a fine picture of Giovanni holding in his hand a magnificent bass measuring thirty-six inches and weighing over seventeen and a half pounds. We wrote Mr. Morisini for a copy, and he very kindly brought it to our office himself and spent a delightful half hour recalling the fine old fishing grounds between Yonkers and Riverdale. The fish in his picture was captured right between the two places, and was only one of many that fell to his skill as a fisherman. For some peculiar reason there was a little section just where the Harlem joins the Hudson that was a favorite feeding ground for bass. Half a dozen boats were usually anchored there, more or less, all through the summer.

The old tree that stood opposite the Franklin Mansion, occupied by Washington as his residence while President, corner Cherry Street and Franklin Square, 1789.

Like many other old attractions, fishing has gone to join the Indians.

There also seemed to be more activity along the water front thirty or forty years ago than there is today. The Corinthian, the Palisade and the Yonkers Yacht Clubs were flourishing organizations and some of the boats owned by members enjoyed more than a local reputation. I recall the *Henry Ward Beecher,* sailed by Jack Warren, and owned by Charley Bevers and Wardy Tompkins of Hastings. The *Beecher* was probably the fastest sloop on the river at the time and for many years won nearly every contest in which she entered.

Old time North River Ferryboat.

A PLACE UP THE HUDSON

In the good old days (which as usual were sandwiched in with the bad ones) there was a phrase "A place up the Hudson," and blessed was the creature who owned such a spot for his summer days.

In the Fifties, Sixties and Seventies, Rocky Glen was one of these—a lovely, ample, old-fashioned estate with the lordly Hudson for its next-door neighbor. It was the summer home of William M. Peck, opposite New Hamburg. Mr. Peck was one of old New York's ship owners in the days of the canvas-clouded clipper, before the arrival of the funnels with their soot, stokers and storage. One of his ships—the *Rocky Glen*—carried the name of his estate across the seven seas, and mayhap signalled a distant vessel only to find that it was the *William M. Peck* or the *Wallace Peck* of New York.

Almost lapping the foundations of the old mansion lay the Hudson with its twelve-mile stretch of river view to be seen from the piazza, while at the back of the house stretched a long hill, covered with a wondrous growth of *Arbor Vitae* (white cedar) sufficiently noteworthy to receive honorable mention in the works of Downing, America's pioneer landscape gardener. Nature has this trick of especially adapting a certain restricted spot to a given vegetation, and then bidding the latter to revel in its own particular promised land. This she has done in specially selected localities all over the world.

In the era of *Rocky Glen* the Hudson was a never-ending panorama, with its day and night boats, and its frequent tows chaperoned by such towboats as the *Norwich, Alida, Belle, McDonald, Ontario, Anna, Oswego, Vanderbilt, Connecticut,* and other picturesque ex-passenger steamers, with their huge olden time hog frames. Each steamboat made its own distinctive sound in progress, so that the native could tell which one was coming, when the boat was still some distance away. Each boat developed its own characteristics, its own atmosphere. The boys around Rocky Glen used to delay their swim until evening so as to get the comber swell of the *Thomas Cornell* when she came "up." Not another swell like it on the river! Finally, there was another thing to be watched at all times—something which has vanished from the later river—fleets of sailing vessels, including that craft peculiar to these waters, the Hudson River Sloop. The trim Sloop, that had once been a passenger carrier, in competition with the lumbering stagecoach, and the uneventful canal boat.

And when, upon "the Fourth," complete sets of ship's bunting (including the various code signal flags used at sea) floated from Rocky Glen's huge flagpole (every Hudson River place must have its prominent flagpole!) its

Courtesy E. Gottschall

Old time street cries in New York—the little Flower Girl at lower entrance of City Hall Park, about 1840.

private boat house, and other points along the place, the diminutive Day Line boats of those times—the *Chauncey Vibbard* and *Daniel Drew*—in passing, gave their passengers the sight of a long line of brilliant banners, framed amid the dark, deep-green foliage of the hillside *Arbor Vitae,* and upon that day of days (as our gran'thers truly considered it!) there was a Punch Bowl set out upon the lawn—and it wasn't empty! (Lemonade. Honest, it was!)

One recollection of the old place is that of the Boys in Blue cheering these flags as they sailed down the river in their progress "On to Richmond." Another recollection is that of a considerable body of torchlight paraders, coming up the river in barges from Newburg, landing at the private dock of Rocky Glen, and marching at night through the place, with torches flaring and bands playing, *en route* to Marlboro to attend a *Republican Grand Rally for Grant and Colfax.* The country fun, the country good cheer, the country beauty were not alone to be found in the old Virginia estates!

Owing to the fact that the river channel ran close to the house, these Day Boats passed so near that friends on board were often recognized from the porch of the mansion. The river was an intimate highway in the good old days. The county line ran through the middle of the house, so that one could strop his razor (old-fashioned blade, please) in Orange, and shave in Ulster County.

The one physical feature of "Rocky Glen," which made it known to river and tourist folk, was its huge stone wall facing the water, so high, long and broad that people mistook it for a fort. This wall was originally built to afford a more commanding site for another dwelling projected by the owner.

"Rocky Glen" was situated in a land of plenty, and a water of plenty! Directly in front drifted the nets which gathered the three really great fish crops of those days, successively shad, herring and sturgeon. A glorious roe shad, right out of the water cost 15 cents. The herring were salted by the barrel for winter use. And last of all came the sturgeon. Each morning the forward deck of the *Eagle* or *Martin* was filled with this "Albany beef," shipped to the State Capital, where these huge sturgeon brought the fishermen $5.00 each, caviar included! The boys used to consider the sturgeon fisherman as a hardier, brawnier breed than the mere shad and herring catcher— a sort of a fresh water whaler, as it were. And hadn't real salt water whalers gone forth from Poughkeepsie, only nine miles above?

And here was the south end of the great Central Hudson raspberry belt, a tract so sharply defined along the west shore that two lines of night boats used to load berry crates to their gunwales at Milton and Marlboro, while at the very next landing there would not be a berry to take aboard! Nature again at her tricks. The legend of the raspberry, or "Antwerp," was that back in the Forties some stranger left a few strange plants in a Poughkeepsie drug store. The druggist, out of curiosity, planted them and these were the start of the great berry industry, which sprang up in that locality. The growers had difficulty at first in finding a market—the people actually had to be "educated" up to these luscious berries! "Rocky Glen" nightly shipped to New York its 3,000 baskets to tickle Father Knickerbocker's palate next morning. Did you ever get in the scented wake of a Hudson River night boat, going south with a load of freshly-picked Milton-Marlboro raspberries? Such an aroma cannot be found within a French perfumery bottle.

The end came when the West Shore Railroad was built. "Rocky Glen," at least the river shore part of it, disappeared from the map.

BLACKWELL'S ISLAND
Why Change Its Name?
By Alexander J. Wall
Librarian New York Historical Society

This island, the name of which is so familiar to all New Yorkers, has recently (April, 1921) been changed to "Welfare Island" by action of the Board of Aldermen. Without a public hearing or advance notice this change was effected and the historic associations which the name Blackwell has held for the interested inquirer are at once dimmed and in time our local history is in this way destroyed. For it is often the interest of people to know how and why a street or locality received its name which leads them to learn more of our local history and of the individuals who helped to make it, inspiring them to seek the pleasure of recalling the delightfulness of the past. In this instance the name of Blackwell has been associated with that island for 245 years and a sketch of its history is here related:

It was known to the Indians as "Minnahanock," meaning on or "at the Island," and was purchased from them July 16, 1637, by Governor Wouter Van Twiller for his estate. The Dutch named it "Varchen" Island, meaning Hog. As early as August 30, 1642, a report of referees as to improvements on Varchen Island made by Jan Claessen Alteras shows that he had spent three hundred gilders in the construction of a house, goat-pen, sowed garden, and fences, which Governor William Kieft was to pay on account of the West India Company to Jan Claessen Alteras. This is the earliest record of an inhabitant on the Island after its purchase from the Indians.

In July, 1652, the Indian sale to Van Twiller was declared void by Governor Stuyvesant and the same year granted the Island to Captain Francis Fyn by order of the West India Company, who on May 10, 1652, wrote to Governor Stuyvesant enclosing a copy of their resolution granting the Island to Captain Fyn and stating that they had since been informed that the Island "would be particularly useful for the Company in the imminent or any future differences with the English being adapted for fortifications to be built thereon to defend our places" and trusts he will "have an eye upon the interests of the Company and the shareholders and inform us of your opinion."

The Resolution of the Amsterdam Chamber of the West India Company, dated May 2, 1652, reads as follows:

"At the request of Hendrick Fredrick Monsvelt, father-in-law of Francoys Fyn, it was approved to write to the Director and Councillors of New Netherland, that if the Company cannot be considerably injured or prejudiced by the cession of Varchen Island, that Francoys Fyn shall be accommodated with the same. And in case the said Varchen Island, for above stated reasons, must be retained, then he shall be shown and granted other fit lands there for cultivation."

Fyn apparently leased the Island and that there was some dispute in reference to it is shown by an entry in the register of Solomon La Chair, viz:

"Petition regarding judgment pronounced March 7, 1662, concerning the lease of Varchen Island, etc. Answer of Pieter Lamberts, defendant, to Matheus De Vos, attorney of Francoys Fyn, complainant."

Under the terms of the capitulation of the Dutch to the English and by the decree of October 10, 1665, this

Present site of the Mills Building, in Broad Street, as it looked
in 1865, as the office of Schafer Bros., Brokers.

Island was confiscated and on February 3, 1668, was granted to Captain John Manning, who had been appointed Sheriff of New York.

It thereafter bore the name of Manning's Island. Captain Manning was a mariner and appears in the records of the General Court at New Haven, Conn., on April 26, 1654, where he was charged with trading with the enemy, the Dutch, the previous winter and supplying them with provisions. Upon instructions from the Governor he was examined at Milford, Conn., April 19, 1654, in reference to his trade with "Munnadoes" (Manhattan) and "Vergenia." His answers not being satisfactory, he was brought to New Haven before the Governor and the General Court who found him guilty and confiscated his vessel and all his goods.

On July 24, 1667, Captain John Manning was appointed Sheriff of New York and enjoyed the confidence of Governor Lovelace in whose absence he was in command of Fort James, and it was while he was thus in charge that on August 9, 1673, he surrendered the City of New York to the Dutch for which he was court martialed on February 2, 1675, and accused of treachery and cowardice. While his life was spared he was publicly disgraced, after which he retired to his Island, where he continued to live and entertain friends. The Rev. Charles Wooley, in his journal kept while in New York, 1678-1680, speaks of Captain Manning being condemned to exile "to a small Island, from his name called Manning's Island, where I have been several times with the said Captain, whose entertainment was commonly a Bowl of Rum-Punch."

Previously on August 1, 1668, there had been a settlement of the Island in a deed of trust to Matthias Nicoll for use of said Manning during life and after his death, for use of his wife and then to Mary Manningham (said to be a daughter of Mrs. Manning by a former husband) and in default of her heirs to her brother Henry Manningham.

Mrs. Manning died in 1673, while on a voyage to England with the Captain after the surrender of New York, where he went to see the King and explain his actions in surrendering the city.

On April 26, 1676, Mary Manningham and Robert Blackwell were granted a marriage license, and from this time the name Blackwell is associated with the Island.

How long after Captain Manning lived is not known, but on March 25, 1685, Mary Manningham, alias Blackwell, entered a caveat that the patent of Manning's Island may not be granted to John Manning longer than "durante vitâ," till the same be decided before the Governor.

The last mention of him is in the will of Matthew Taylor, of New York, dated February 20, 1687-8, in which John Manning, of Manning's Island, received 20 shillings to buy a ring and is acquitted of any claims due the testator which according to an inventory of the Taylor estate was a "mortgage of John Manning, his Island."

Robert Blackwell is mentioned as one of the early settlers of Elizabeth, New Jersey, from the fact that a deed mentions him as "late of Elizabeth-town, in New Jersey, merchant." He died about 1717, leaving a son Jacob, who married Mary Hallett. In the will of his son Jacob, proved December 19, 1744, no mention of the Island is made, but his son, Jacob, born November 20, 1717, and died October 24, 1780, leaves a will dated August 29, 1779, in which he leaves to his sons James and Jacob "my Island known by the name of Blackwell's Island."

During the Revolutionary War, after the retreat of the American Army from Long Island, the British extended themselves a considerable length on the shore bordering the Sound and a large number of them landed on Blackwell's Island "about three miles from the city," but the shot from the batteries soon made them recross the river. In 1782, a contemporary newspaper states "that Sir Guy Carleton has visited all the prison ships at New York, minutely examined into the situation of the prisoners and expressed his intentions of having them better provided for: That they were to be landed on Blackwell's Island, in New York harbour in the day time, during the hot season."

Two years later after the peace, we find the first advertisement offering for sale Blackwell's Island. It was offered by James Blackwell, to whom, with his brother Jacob, it was bequeathed in 1780. This charming advertisement is so descriptive of the Island that it is here printed in full:

For Sale, that pleasant agreeably situated Island,
known by the name of
BLACKWELL'S ISLAND,
On the East River, about four miles from this city.

"It is without exception one of the most healthy situations in this state. It is remarkable for the number of fish and fowl that is caught there in the different seasons. There is on the premises, two small dwelling houses, a Barn, Bake and Fowl House, Cyder Mill; a large Orchard, containing 450 of the best grafted fruit trees, such as Newton & golden pippins, spitsinburghs, peirmans, bow apples, pears, peaches, plumbs, cherries, &c. There is a number of the best stone quarries, ready cleared to begin

ROBBINS REEF AND LIGHTHOUSE IN THE LOWER HARBOR OF NEW YORK.

breaking immediately; and the subscriber has a complete set of quarry tools, with all his farming utensils and stock to dispose of at the same time. The Island abounds with running springs of most excellent water. The above contains 107 acres, eight of which are salt meadow, and the whole has been considerably improved with manure, and in good fence.

Any person inclining to purchase the whole or half of the said Island, may be further informed by enquiring at Mr. Joseph Hallet's, No. 204, Water Street, New York, or on the premises of James Blackwell."

But apparently nothing came of this offer to sell the Island, and the reason for offering it may be judged from a subsequent notice in the newspapers of 1785, which states that James Blackwell is an insolvent debtor and all his estate was assigned to James Hallett and Joseph Stringham as assignees, who requested all creditors to produce their accounts before September 1, 1785, on which date a settlement would be made and that on April 20, 1785, the Southwest part of Blackwell's Island with two small houses, "barn, bake house and cyder mill," an orchard, stock and farming utensils, household and kitchen furniture would be sold at public vendue. On the same day Jacob Blackwell offered the northeast part of the Island for sale, both parts completing the whole Island.

In spite of these circumstances and offers of sale, the Island remained in the hands of the Blackwell family, for on January 22, 1794, half of it was again advertised for sale and for particulars to inquire of Joseph Hallett, 204 Water Street or of the subscriber, Josiah Blackwell, at Newtown, L. I.

On April 9, 1823, James Blackwell and wife Elizabeth deeded the Island in consideration of $30,000 to James L. Bell. Bell died at his residence on Blackwell's Island on January 12, 1825, and by a foreclosure the Island again became the property of James Blackwell, who, on July 19, 1828, conveyed it to the Corporation of the City of New York for $32,500.

A claim set up by Magdalena Bell, widow of James L. Bell, contested the title in this transfer which was settled on September 11, 1844, by the payment of $20,000 by the city to Mrs. Bell.

Mrs. Elizabeth (Hallett) Blackwell, wife of James, died at Blackwell's Island, April 17, 1823. He died November 25, 1831, aged eighty years.

The city purchased Blackwell's Island as a site for a penitentiary, the corner-stone of which was laid July 10, 1828, and the address delivered by the Rev. John Stanford. The Comptroller's Report of the City of New York, for 1829, states the building cost $16,569.88.

On July 22, 1858, the corner-stone of the new hospital on Blackwell's Island was laid, the building of which is on the site of the old one and the cost estimated at $150,000, the old hospital having burned on February 13, 1858.

The Island, since its acquisition by the city has become the home for its hospitals, asylum and corrective institutions. During its long tenure by the Blackwell's, it was the scene of many entertainments of that family whose records show numerous marriage ceremonies were performed there and these associations are foundation stones or our local history. Why then should a name of such long association be substituted for one which conveys nothing of all that has gone before. In 1911, an effort

The Eden Musee, a famous Wax Works Show, on site of the Schermerhorn residence, 57 W. 23rd Street. Over thirteen million persons visited this attraction in its day.

was made to change the name of this Island to "Hospital Island," but protests successfully prevented it. Without notice "Welfare Island" is now a reality and the name Blackwell erased.

A Plea for Its Restoration as a Public Park

The foregoing gives a complete history of this delightful retreat in the midst of a beautiful river. At the time it was selected as an abode for derelicts it was far removed from town and judging by the means of transportation was many miles further away than its present location indicates.

It is now in the heart of our great city, adjacent to one of the most densely populated sections of New York. It should be turned into a public park, and all the East River Islands as well. The Museum of the City of New York would like to see this change effected as early as possible.

[EDITOR.]

THE TOMB OF DAVID PROVOOST, JONES' WOODS, NEW YORK, 1857.

View looking north, from Gracie Mansion, showing New Haven Bridge connecting Long Island with the Bronx. Gracie Mansion at lower right hand corner above the star.

CONCERNING BACK ISSUES OF THE "MANUAL." ORDER MISSING NUMBERS NOW

A number of persons may this year receive a copy of the MANUAL for the first time. Elsewhere in these pages we have given a short sketch of the origin of this book and of the important part it has played in recording the annals of New York in the past.

To those who are interested in the growth and development of our city, these old records are of absorbing interest. The quaint, simple pictures, contrasting as they do with the splendor of the present, are a never-failing source of interest. About six hundred of these rare old views have now appeared in the pages of this journal, each number containing about a hundred, many of them beautifully reproduced in their original colors.

Each issue of the MANUAL is complete in itself, both as to pictures and text. The entire set now consists of eight

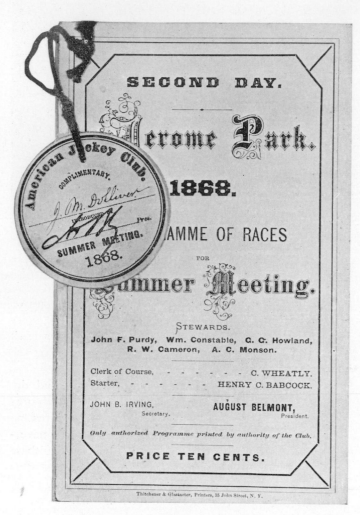

SECOND DAY.

Jerome Park.

1868.

PROGRAMME OF RACES

FOR

Summer Meeting.

STEWARDS.

**John F. Purdy,   Wm. Constable,   G. G. Howland,
R. W. Cameron,   A. C. Monson.**

Clerk of Course, - - - - - - - C. WHEATLY.
Starter, - - - - - - - HENRY C. BABCOCK.

JOHN B. IRVING,
Secretary.

AUGUST BELMONT,
President.

Only authorized Programme printed by authority of the Club.

PRICE TEN CENTS.

Thitchener & Glastaeter, Printers, 35 John Street, N. Y.

JEROME PARK

New York's most fashionable old race track now
covered by the Jerome Park Reservoir.

numbers. No. 1 was published in 1917; No. 2 in 1918, etc. No. 8, the present one, is dated 1924.

There are still a few of each of the back numbers available. No. 3, however, lacks the supplement and there are only a few copies left. The others are complete, but No. 4 is almost exhausted. There will be no advance in price while they last. They will not be reprinted. Many of the engravings being on stone, have long since been destroyed.

Like the old MANUALS, the present set will constantly increase in price as the demand, though slow, is constant and persistent. If you desire to obtain a full set, order at once. The following are the prices for the different styles of binding:

	Per Number
Cloth	$ 5.00
Half Morocco	10.00
Full Morocco	15.00

When a full set is ordered at one time we allow a special discount to old readers of ten per cent.

Other books that we also publish, of special interest to New Yorkers, are: *New York Yesterday and Today,* a superb volume of generous size, 9 x 12 inches, on heavy art paper showing over a hundred contrasting views of well-known sites. Thirty-two of these pictures are in full color, and it is a splendid book to give to an absent friend or send abroad. Everybody is interested in New York, and all can appreciate the significance of these wonderful pictures. We sell a lot of them for souvenirs of the city. Price $5.00, in handsome decorated binding.

Then there is Mrs. Lamb's monumental *History of the City of New York,* in three superb volumes bound in half morocco. It is *the* standard work, beautifully written. It is part of the original edition profusely illustrated by old time wood cuts. The pictures were drawn by Edwin A. Abbey, Winslow Homer, Charles Rhinehart and a host of other artists, who have since achieved fame. Price for the three volumes, $35.00. A wonderful gift book.

Miss Kate Haven's *Diary of a Little Girl in Old New York* (her own experiences), should also be mentioned. No more delightful volume can be imagined. One of the funniest, quaintest little books ever printed and a wonderful glimpse of a girl's life eighty years ago. Now in its second printing. Price $2.00, bound in cloth.

A Miniature History of the City of New York, for advertising purposes, bound in limp leather, is also worth while. It has 224 pages, but can go in your hand bag. Size 2¾ x 3½. Price 50 cents. Discounts in quantities.

JOHN CALVIN COOLIDGE,
NOTARY PUBLIC

No event in recent history has so touched the hearts of the American people as the simple story of that night in his father's modest farmhouse when Calvin Coolidge took the oath of office as the thirtieth President of the United States. A finer example of what American Democracy really is has seldom occurred. It seemed to us wise to preserve this wonderful story in a more permanent form than the fugitive pages of a daily paper where we found it. It is from the columns of the New York *Herald*.

If Main Street has ceased its homely reign in the White House the Old Homestead is to move in. Fuller details of the inauguration of Calvin Coolidge as President of the United States were supplied by members of the new President's party as they rolled into New York yesterday afternoon. Mr. Coolidge himself refused to talk. Those about him strove vigorously to save him from further interviews. He "was feeling fine" and had "had plenty of sleep last night."

Coolidge talks through one side of his mouth like one long accustomed to hold a contemplative wisp of straw in the other side. From that shrewdly distorted orifice flows what has come to be known the world round as the "Yankee twang."

The oath, long associated with the great east portico of the Capitol at Washington, saluting troops, massed bands, robed justices and the carven head of the first President of the United States rising above a sea of faces, was tendered to this red-headed son by an aged father, a notary public, a dirt farmer, in the middle of a New

England parlor, or as near the middle as the great central wood-burning stove with its vent through the ceiling would permit, and with framed newspaper photographs and cartoons of the President and his family pasted to the bookcases and the walls.

It was seventeen minutes before three o'clock in the morning. In that farmhouse there was no electric light. Kerosene lamps were the only illumination, and even they were weak. A few moments before the oath had been administered Mrs. Coolidge, hanging on the words of her spouse, heard him complain about an insufficiency of light.

"Wait a minute, Cal," said she, "I'll get the lamp from the bedroom."

That was the nearest thing to a spotlight upon the inauguration of the thirtieth President of the United States. Even the reporters were not there. They had hurried off to telephone. It was only thirty minutes after he became President, that telephone linemen, working through the woods and over the Vermont hills, succeeded in installing in this temporary White House the first telephone it has known in all its long years.

And it will be many more long years before Plymouth, Vt., forgets the night between the 2nd and the 3rd of August, 1923. They still go to bed early in Plymouth and thereabouts. This neighborhood knows not the rattle of the flivver, the flicker of the movie or the dingle of the telephone. Like all the rest of the world, it had been reassured by Thursday's earlier bulletins on President Harding's recovery. By 9 o'clock Thursday night the Coolidge household was abed, lights were out and, country fashion, folks were sleeping against the call for early morning chores.

The day before.

How early the call was to come and what the chore was to be they little imagined.

Newspaper reporters were lodged at the Ludlow Tavern in Ludlow, twelve miles from Plymouth. At 11:20—really the middle of the night in New England, where they don't keep daylight saving time—they were aroused by the first messages announcing President Harding's sudden passing. There was a wild scurry for taxicabs and motor cars. Within a few moments the road between Ludlow and Plymouth was seething as it had never seethed in the days of Ethan Allen and his Green Mountain Boys.

But the newspaper men were beaten. Eight miles on the other side of Plymouth lies Bridgewater, and there were lodged E. W. Geisser, Mr. Coolidge's assistant secretary, and a young man who will go down to fame as the new President's first chauffeur, one Joseph McInerney, who, as may be judged from his name, is not a Yank.

George Christian, President Harding's secretary, knew they were at Bridgewater and it was thither he sent his message. It arrived twenty minutes after the newspaper bulletins had reached Ludlow. But McInerney drove his eight miles twenty-eight minutes faster than the newspaper men could drive their twelve. He was eight minutes ahead of them at the Coolidge door.

At that hour of the morning it was a dark and forbidding door. Geisser rapped and rang, however, and in a moment a gaunt figure peered anxiously into the night. It was the seventy-eight-year-old proprietor of the farm, clad in trousers pulled over his nightshirt, but startled into life by the whisper Geisser gave him. He went straight to the guest room, where Mr. and Mrs. Coolidge were asleep and there in the light of a flickering lamp with

JOHN CALVIN COOLIDGE, NOTARY PUBLIC

The bible on the table is the one used by Pres. Coolidge on taking the oath of office.

the souvenirs of all the hardships and all the rewards of the hard work of a New England farm about him, this simple father gave his simple son the news than which no American can ever hope to hear greater. "Cal,"—the old Colonel's "Cal"—was President of the United States.

What passed between the two remains unknown. Their talk was broken into by the bellowing of the horns of the arriving newspaper men. Father Coolidge, ever hospitable, hustled down to open the door. His son, the new President of the United States, waited until he could get into the nearest approach to formal garb that lay to hand.

Mrs. Coolidge came with him downstairs, she in a hurriedly donned gown of summer black and white, and he in a dark blue formally cut sack suit and a black tie with a stiff collar. She was weeping. Throughout the long night when she tried to play host to everybody and to take care of Cal, her eyes were always near to the brim with tears and ever and anon she would exclaim:

"Poor Mrs. Harding! Her own illness—and then this!"

He was plainly under the spell of this thing that had for the moment descended upon his shoulders in the middle of peaceful sleep. He spoke to the reporters, each of whom gravely congratulated him and then he withdrew to the dining room to frame a telegram to Mrs. Harding and the brief statement announcing his continuation of Mr. Harding's policies and personnel in the Government.

Meanwhile all New England began to stir like a pot coming to the boil. From the outskirts of this rural community reporters, officials, secret service men began to gravitate at stellar speed toward this new center of American affairs far off in the Vermont hills. As they moved they roused the countryside, and by dawn half the population was gathered about the Coolidge home.

But before they could reach their destination, the first act of the little drama had been played. Communication had been established with Washington and word had been received that the aged father was capable of administering the greatest American oath to his son. Attorney General Daugherty had urged from San Francisco that the ceremony be carried out at once. In the meantime Representative Dale of the second Vermont district had arrived with two secret service men. They, Mrs. Coolidge, Secretary Geisser and Joe McInerney were the only witnesses to the taking of that oath.

It's a simple room. It belongs to the era of New England farmhouses just after the "parlor" ceased to be closed, except for weddings and funerals. The Coolidge family used it as a living room. In addition to the big wood-burning stove that dominates it from the center there is one large and one small table, a couple of rocking chairs, a couple of armchairs and two or three straight chairs. There is a goodly supply of books on the shelves. There are no stuffed birds, antimacassars or horsehair upholstery. But the family Bible recounting the births, deaths, and marriages of the Coolidge family for generations lies on the larger table.

It was across this that father and son presently faced one another. Mrs. Coolidge stood beside her husband. A framed photograph of Mr. Coolidge at the time he was elected Governor of Massachusetts hung above his father's head. A card bearing the great seal of the State of Massachusetts was stuck in the corner of the frame and across the card was written, "From His Excellency, the Governor."

Father and son each raised a right hand. Witnesses do not seem to remember whether or not the President placed his hand on the Testament. There can be no doubt of the deeply religious feeling with which he took the oath, however. Pausing a moment after its formal words were over he added fervently:

"So help me God!"

After this persons say Mr. and Mrs. Coolidge both went back to bed and both slept for three hours or three hours and a half. They were not seen again until nearly 7:30. In the meanwhile the world had more than begun to wear a path to the Coolidge door.

From both ends of New England; from Boston, from Springfield, from Troy, great motor cars were rushing people into the little hill hamlet. Newspaper men will long remember the dash some of them made. One Boston newspaper man beat his colleagues to the spot because, as he admitted, he was an hour nearer Vermont across Boston's interminable suburbs than they were.

From Springfield, Chester and Woodstock, Vt., came others, roaring in motor cars, and from hamlets and houses nearer by, neighbors, aroused by this unwonted traffic, did not hesitate to hitch up the old sidebar buggy and a "democrat" wagon or two to go call on the Colonel's Cal.

The Colonel never went back to bed again. Deputy United States Marshall Harvey from Chester, Vt., was the first thing resembling an official bodyguard on the scene and he and the President's father paced the porch, answering the questions of visitors and tried to prevent unnecessary noise.

A. L. McCormick, of the secret service probably made the record trip. From the Washington headquarters of

Father of the President, on the right

the President's bodyguard came orders to him, on his vacation in Boston to go. And he went.

In a big Packard car he started out at sixty miles an hour over the Boston streets. He hardly slacked through Massachusetts and across the corner of New Hampshire, though he was soon off the metalled highway and careening from side to side of the dirt roads. He had telegraphed the President that he was coming and the Presidential departure had been timed to let him arrive. He started from Boston after 2:30 in the morning and he was within reach of Plymouth when a tire blew out.

A party of Boston newspaper men, making only a little less speed than he, found him a few minutes later cursing like a maniac in the middle of the road. They took him in and they caught the Presidential caravan just before it pulled into Rutland, nearly 9 o'clock.

But others had meanwhile arrived at the peaceful Plymouth farmhouse. Neighbors who had licked the President of the United States for stealing their apples, strolled in at daylight. They didn't ask for the President of the United States. With the dignity that attaches to the New England farmer on his native heath, they sauntered up to the agitated old man on the front porch.

"Mornin', Colonel," they greeted.

"Mornin', Will," or Henry or Zeke as the case might be, just as if it were any other morning in the farmer's round.

"Where's Cal?" they would ask.

"In the kitchen eatin' breakfast," the proud father would answer with a toss of a thumb over his shoulder and one by one these neighbors tramped around to the back door, the friendly way to enter a New England farmhouse, and stumped in to greet Cal with a handshake and a "good luck and God bless ye."

There are only forty souls all told in the little hamlet of Plymouth. Yet by 7 o'clock there were more than a hundred farmer folk gathered on the little lawn and in the short lane from the Coolidge front door to the high road. It was too many for a breakfast handshake, so the new President was called out to see them altogether.

He was dressed in a blue sack suit that in the morning's light plainly showed the wear of other days. His shoes were almost run down at heel. He wore a soft collar and he had substituted a dark green for the black tie of the early morning meeting with the newspaper men.

He chatted with those he knew, quietly, bravely, almost fearfully, it seems, and then the photographers came and he posed for picture after picture. One picture he himself insisted should be taken. He took by the hand his youngest relative present, James Wilcox, aged 2, son of Judge James Wilcox, of Plymouth, a cousin of the President.

"Look at the President," the photographers called to the youngster. But he was far more interested in such things as cameras. The man who held him by the hand was an old story for him. Then a photographer got an inspiration.

"Hey, kid," he yelled. "Look at the funny face Uncle Cal's making."

The result was an excellent photograph, with a youngster gazing in rapt wonderment for the fraction of a second at his great relative. But that youngster's faith in photographers is probably shattered forever. Uncle Cal was making no funny face. He probably couldn't, if his life depended on it.

Meantime the new telephone had been buzzing. Strange echoes it must have awakened in that peaceful home, echoes never, perhaps, to be stilled again. The outside world had entered in. The twentieth century had conquered another last stronghold of the more peaceful, ruggeder, perhaps happier, nineteenth. Secret service men were asking where they could meet the President. Great railroads were offering him their every facility. He was denying all but a private car. He refused to accept a special train from Rutland to Troy.

At 7:40 in the morning the President left his retreat. Every effort to induce his father to accompany him to Washington failed. In northern Vermont the harvest is not yet in, and there is some suspicion that the old gentleman was still in nothing but nightshirt and trousers, poor gear for the Willard at Washington.

Here, too, Joe McInerney rose once more to glory. Leading the procession with the President, he could not have been more careful had his load been eggs. Over the steep, winding mountain roads, Joe led the way at a safe crawl. At every grade crossing he came to a full stop and looked and listened as no chauffeur in history ever did before. He nearly fell out of his seat when a raucous roar came from behind him and a great car shot by. It was only McCormick, the Boston secret service agent, however, and McCormick insisted on a pilot car ahead. Thereafter the procession made better time.

Up through the Vermont hills people did not yet know that President Harding was dead. They gazed in wonderment at the whirling procession of great cars. It was only when they came to the outskirts of Rutland that President Coolidge came in contact with that world of adulation which will be his share from now on whenever he moves about.

People ran to the street corners and held up waving children as the car passed. Two thousand people were gathered about the railway station in Rutland, among them Governor Redfield Proctor and Earl S. Kingsley, Republican National Committeeman from Vermont. As at all the other stations along the line the greeting was more respectful than enthusiastic. People were obviously still laboring under the shock of the tragedy they had just read in their morning papers.

At North Bennington a large crowd was also gathered. There Mr. Coolidge insisted the train be held until Michael Hennessey, dean of the Boston newspaper reporters, could board the train. Here too, the President got his first greeting from young America. Bernard Sinay, eight years old, barefooted, in shirt and overalls, one of the real tough kind that hang around the station, edged his way through the crowd and stuck forth a grimy paw. The President shook it and it will go tough with any boy of his own age in North Bennington, who attempts, in the future, to call Mr. Sinay by his old name of "Punky."

MUSEUM OF THE CITY OF NEW YORK
Election of Officers

At a regular meeting held at the office of Cadwalader, Wickersham & Taft, 40 Wall Street, counsel to the Museum, on Tuesday afternoon, October 16, 1923, the following officers were elected:

President	*Secretary*
MR. PHOENIX INGRAHAM	MR. ROBERT LE ROY
Vice-President	*Treasurer*
HON. VICTOR J. DOWLING	MR. HENRY RICHMOND TAYLOR

Assistant Treasurer
MR. GUY EMERSON

The following gentlemen have accepted membership on the Board of Directors to date (October 31, 1923):

MR. ARCHER M. HUNTINGTON	MR. MICHAEL FRIEDSAM
MR. JAMES SPEYER	MR. GEORGE A. ZABRISKIE
MR. HENRY W. TAFT	MR. JAMES MORTIMER MONTGOMERY
MR. WILLIAM RHINELANDER STEWART	MR. LEWIS GOUVERNEUR MORRIS

Invitations to become directors have also been extended to Mr. Edward de Puyster Livingston, Mr. Arthur Curtiss James, Mr. J. P. Morgan, Mr. T. J. Oakley Rhinelander, Mr. T. Coleman du Pont, Mr. Edward S. Harkness, Mr. V. Everitt Macey, Mr. Payne Whitney, Mr. W. H. Nichols, Mr. Edward Robinson, Mr. Clarence Dillon, Mr. H. Fairfield Osborne, Mr. John D. Rockefeller, Jr., Mr. John McE. Bowman and Mr. E. H. Gary. Temporary absence from the city and other circumstances may operate to deprive the Museum of the valuable services of some of these gentlemen. The necessity of going to press before their replies can be received prevents our announcement of the full board at this time, but a complete list will appear in all the newspapers as soon as available. —EDITOR.

INDEX

A

Hawthorne, Nathaniel, 219.
Hayes, Rutherford B., 113, 163.
Hazard House, 305.
Herrmans, Augustus, 227.
Hegeman Street, 256.
Hell Gate, 23, 60, 73, 212.
Hell Gate Ferry, 43.
Helle-Gat, 59.
"Henry Clay, The," 187, 325.
Henry, Gen., 117.
Henry Street, Brooklyn, 256.
"Henry Ward Beecher, The," 332.
"Herald," The, 28.
Herald Building, 291.
Her Majesty's Opera Co., 114.
"Herring, The," 74.
"Het Vosje, The," 73.
Hewes St., Brooklyn, 259.
Heye Foundation, 122.
High Bridge, 10.
"Highlander, The," 327.
High Street, 268.
Hildreth, ——, 157.
"Hippotheatron, The," 309.
Hispanic Society, 122.
Hitchcock, Darling & Co., 86.
Hoboken, 141, 228.
Hoern's Point, 211.
Hoffman House, 92, 93, 98, 162, 163.
Hoffman, Samuel Verplanck, 181.
Holland, 47, 48, 71, 72, 73, 74, 75,
    76, 109, 135, 270, 279, 280, 283,
    284, 286, 290, 292.
Holland Documents, 284.
Holly, Willis, 123.
Homer, Winslow, 23, 358.
Hoorn, Holland, 288.
Hoorn, Reindert Jansen, 76.
"Hope, The," 74, 76.
Hopper, Andrew, 248.
Hopper House, 299.
Horen (Horn's) Hook, 58.
Hosmer's Studio, Miss, 29.
"Hospital" Island, 352.
House of Representatives, 211.
Houston Street Ferry, 251.
Houston Street Ferry House, 266.
Houttuynd (Woodyard), The, 75.
Howard, Frank, 42.
Howard, Joe, 114.
Howard House, 262, 268.
Howard Halfway House, 268.
Howells, ——, 302.
Hubbard, Samuel T., 181, 187.
Hubert Street, 51.
Hudson, Hendrick, 47, 72, 78, 140.
Hudson River, 71, 73, 78, 84, 141,
    145, 146, 189, 248, 317, 319, 320,
    321, 324, 325, 326, 329, 330, 333,
    334, 338.
Hudson River Day Boats, 334.
Hudson River Night Boats, 338.
Hudson Terminal, 205.
Hughes, Chas. E., 329.
Huntington, Archer M., 180, 181,
    187.
Husted, Seymour L., 266.
Hylan, Mayor John F., 181, 182.

I

Indian Manners and Customs, 59 to
    62.
Indian Museum, 122.
Indian Settlements, 140.
Indians, The, 341.
Ingoldsby, Richard, 43.
Ingraham, Phœnix, 182.
Indian, Alderman, 275.
International Mercantile Marine, 205.
Interstate Commerce Commission, 318.
Irving, Washington, 104, 176.
"Isaack Newton, The," 327.
Isle au Haute, 191.
Italy, 302, 310.

J

Jacobs, Benjamin, 233.
Jacobs, Elizabeth, 233.
James, Arthur Curtiss, 181, 187.
James, Thos. Lemuel, 113, 104, 115.
"James T. Morse, The," 192.
Jansen, Aryan, 297.
Janzen, Derrick, 276.
Jefferson's Administration, 208.
Jerome, Larry, 100.
Jerome Park, 356.
Jerome Park Reservoir, 356.
Jewell, Marshall, 114.
Johnson, Robt. Underwood, 298.
Jones, Frank, 40.
Jones Residence, 70.
Jones Woods, 36, 70, 354.
Jordan, Julian, 32.
Joris, Adrian, 73.

K

Kansas, 197, 198.
Katchhook (Lime Shell) Point, 143.
Kelby, Wm., 186, 187.
Kellogg, Clara Louise, 158.
Kelly, John, 98.
Kelly, J. W., 44
Kent Ave., Brooklyn, 254.
Kensington Museum, 175.
Kenyon, Sir Frederick, 298, 302,
    367.
Kerr, Lawrence, 159.
Kerrs, The, 155.
Kidd, Capt., 54, 150, 152.
Kieft, Wm., 47, 48, 75, 341.
Kiersted, Hans, 280.
King Charles, 109.
King Edward VII, 166.
King Francis, 78.
King George II, 274.
King George III, Statue of, 58.
King James, 109, 110.
King of Portugal, 78.
King Street, 55.
"King Solomon, The," 76.

N

O

Old Dominion, 120.
Old Dutch Church, 248.
Old New York, 2, 180, 182, 186, 205, 206, 229, 230, 265.
Old New York Costumes, 19 to 46.
Old New York Customs, 17 to 46.
Old New York Free Academy, 285.
Old New York Schools, 279, 296.
Old Slip, 53.
Old South Church, 113.
Old Tea Water Pump, 146.
Old Time Cherry Tree, 331.
Old Time Fishing, 329.
Old Time Ordinances, 238 to 259.
Old Time Ships, 71 to 77.
Old Time Songs, 12, 42, 44.
Old Time Tow Boats, 334.
Olyphant, Robert, 117.
Omaha, 100.
Onckenay School, 288.
One Hundred Fifty-fifth St., 122, 298.
One Hundred Fifty-sixth St., 122, 298.
One Hundred Tenth St., 36, 289.
One Hundred Twenty-seventh St., 36.
Ontario, The, 334.
Orange County, 336.
"Orange, The," 324.
"Orange Mountain, The," 96.
"Orange Tree, The," 75.
Orient, The, 8.
Orphan Master, 294.
O'Ryan, Maj. Gen. John F., 181.
Osborn, Prof. Hy. Fairfield, 182.
Osgood, Samuel, 113.

P

Pabst Hotel, 169.
Pacific, The, 74.
Palisade Yacht Club, 332.
Parade, The, 58.
Park Avenue, 2.
Park Avenue, Brooklyn, 268.
Park Row, 113, 172, 239.
Park Theatre, 162.
Parson, Hubert T., 182.
Pastor, Tony, 44.
Paulding, Abraham, 240.
Paulding, Jos., 240, 242.
Peabody, Geo. Foster, 182.
Pear Tree, Old, 76.
Pearl Street, 53, 248, 283.
Peck Slip, 10.
Peck, Wallace, 293.
Peck, William M., 333.
Peeck, Jan., 76.
Peekskill, 76, 324, 327.
Pegram, M. J. Sanford, 187.
Pennsylvania, R. R., 2.
Penobscot Bay, 191.
Peters, Wm. F., 187.
Petersen, J., 283.
Phelps, Anson G., 316.
Philadelphia "Times," 134.
Phillipse, Fredk., 274.

Phœnix, Daniel, 135.
Pier 3, 41.
Pietersen, Evert, 292, 294.
Pietersen, R., 76.
Pine Street, 3, 41.
Players' Club, 85.
Platt, Thos., 92, 101, 124.
Plon Plon, 89.
Plymouth, 74, 362, 367, 368.
Plymouth, Vt., 360.
Police Band, 119.
Polk, James, 181.
"Pomona, The," 293.
Poorhouse Burial Ground, 242.
"Pop Dunkeley's" School, 256.
Port Authority, 318.
Post Office, New, 201, 235.
Post Office, Old, 113, 115, 203, 235, 236, 291.
Post Road, 57.
Potomac River, 268.
Potters Field, 57.
Poughkeepsie, 337.
Pratt, Chas., 257.
Pratt Institute, 257.
Presbyterian Church, Williamsburgh, 268.
"Princess, The," 75.
"Prince Maurice, The," 75.
Prince of Wales, 28, 29, 86, 89, 166.
Proctor, Gov. Redfields, 371.
Prospect Park, Bklyn., 22, 258, 259.
Providence, 171.
Provoost David, 297.
Provoost Tomb, 149, 354.
Public Library, 112, 274.
Public School Society, 296.
Pulitzer, Jos., 172.
Purdy, Lawson, 182.
Putnam, Geo. Haven, 104.
Putnam's Sons, G. P., 104.

Q

Quarterly Review, 136.
Queen Street, 54, 232, 248.
Quincy, Josiah, 211.

R

Radcliffe, Jacob, 241.
Ralph Avenue, Brooklyn, 268, 270.
Rankin, McKee, 40.
Rapid Transit, 2, 14, 17.
Raymond, Henry W., 98.
Rebellion, The, 90.
Rebellion of 1688, 110.
Red Cloud, 45.
Redcoats, The, 126.
Red Cross Line, The, 9.
Red Hook, Bklyn., 276.
"Red Jacket," The, 9.
Red Mill, The, 233.

St. Denis Hotel, 157.
St. Germain Hotel, 154, 159.
"St. Jacob, The," 280.
St. James Hotel, 163.
St. John's Cemetery, 325.
St. Nicholas Church, 119.
St. Nicholas Hotel, 156.
Staats-Zeitung, 239.
Stadt Huys, The, 92, 287.
Stafford House, 175.
Stanford, Rev. John, 350.
Stanton, Edwin McMasters, 91.
Stars and Stripes, 224.
State Capitol, 337.
State Building, 201.
State Street, 148, 227.
Steamer "Emily," 10, 12.
Steamship Row, 205.
Steenwyck, Cornelius, 76.
Stern, Benjamin, 102.
Stern, Bernhard, 102.
Stern Bros., 102, 103.
Stern, Isaac, 102, 103.
Stern, Louis, 102.
Stephenson, ——, 116.
Stetsons, The, 155.
Stevens, Paran, 86.
Stevenson, Jan, 3, 4, 6, 280, 297.
Stewart, A. T., 31, 182, 244.
Stewart, Wm. Rhinelander, 181.
Stewart's Cafe, 118.
Stirling, Lord, 150.
Stokes, Edward, 162.
Stone, Melville, 114, 181.
Stonington, 4, 7, 192, 205, 206.
Stringham, Jos., 349.
Sturtevant Hotel, 164.
Stuyvesant, Gov., 342.
Stuyvesant Garden, 137.
Stuyvesant, Peter, 7, 8, 57, 74, 284.
Suffering Exiles, 126.
Sullivan, Mike, 42.
Sulzer's Harlem River Park, 36.
Supreme Court, 318.
Swamp, The, 81.
"Sylvan Dell, The," 4.
"Sylvan Glen, The," 2.
"Sylvan Grove, The," 10.
"Sylvan Shore, The," 10.
"Sylvan Stream, The," 2.

T

Tammany Hall, 111.
Tammany Society, 98, 119, 123, 124, 125, 126, 129.
Tappaanes, 59.
Tavern Hall, 287.

Taylor, Matthew, 345.
Tea Water Spring, 142.
Teller, John, 240.
Tenth Street, 10, 103.
Tewksbury, Dr., 204.
Thatcher, Primrose & West, 42.
Thayer, H. B., 181, 217.
Third Avenue, 2, 7, 8, 10, 40, 96, 171, 305.
Third Avenue Cars, 10.
Thirtieth St., 40, 164, 316.
Thirty-first St., 162, 164.
Thirty-fourth St., 164.
"Thomas Cornell, The," 334.
"Thomas Powell, The," 327.
Thomas Street, 248.
Thompson, Corporal, 82.
Thompson's Road House, 80.
"Three Blue Pigeons, The," 197, 198, 200.
Three Hundredth Anniversary, 180, 235.
"Three Kings, The," 75.
Tilden, Samuel J., 98.
"Times, The," 96, 100.
"Times" Building, 169.
"Tombs," The, 190.
Tompkins Square, 114.
Tompkins, Wardy, 332.
Tory Captives, 208.
Tory Occupation, 126.
Train, Geo. Francis, 100.
Transatlantic Shipping, 205.
Travers, Billy, 100.
Trinity Church, 54, 244, 340.
Trinkle, Gov. Lee, 117, 118, 120.
Troy, 366.
Twain, Mark, 101.
Twentieth St., 86, 95.
Twenty-fifth St., 58.
Twenty-fourth St., 71, 101.
Twenty-ninth St., 6, 164.
Twenty-second St., 103.
Twenty-sixth St., 153, 165.
Twenty-third St., 81, 82, 83, 84, 86, 90, 92, 96, 101, 102, 351.
Turtle Bay, 49.

U

Ulster County, 336.
Uncle Sam, 235.
Union, The, 74.
Union Club, 80, 89, 100.
Union Ferry Boat, 278.
Union Grounds, 256.
Union Place, 157.
Union Square, 15, 157, 159, 160, 161.

[385]

Y

Z